NAPOLEONIC BATTLES

JONATHAN SUTHERLAND

Airlife

Copyright © The Crowood Press Ltd 2003

Text written by Jonathan Sutherland
Maps drawn by Peter Harper

First published in the UK in 2003
by Airlife Publishing, an imprint of The Crowood Press Ltd

British Library Cataloguing-in-Publication Data
A catalogue record for this book
is available from the British Library

ISBN 1 84037 423 3

Printed in China

*Contact us for a free catalogue that describes the complete
range of Vital Guides and other Airlife books.*

Airlife

A division of The Crowood Press, Ramsbury,
Wiltshire SN8 2HR
E-mail: enquiries@crowood.com
Website: **www.crowood.com**

Contents

Introduction

With the possible exception of the Second World War, more books, articles and material have been written about the Napoleonic period than any other conflict. Napoleon's strategies, tactics, campaigns and battles have been studied by literally millions of students since at least 1817 (when a course was instituted at the US Military Academy), yet few truly factual descriptions of the battles exist. It is impossible to unravel the truth from the fiction, for indeed the Napoleonic period is not like other conflicts as it is shrouded in half-truths and propaganda.

Reading accounts of the battles, from the perspective of the different nations, one would be excused for believing that one is being told very different stories of radically different engagements. The Russian accounts of Borodino or Austerlitz read like French defeats. Even Tolstoy's classic *War and Peace* cannot be taken at face value.

Alongside Alexander, Hannibal, Caesar, Gustavus Adolphus, Frederick the Great, Lee and Grant, Napoleon was a master of warfare. In his time, he met few that could counter him, perhaps a handful of men with luck, terrain and solid troops in their favour. Notably, Wellington (constantly named as such in this book despite the fact that for much of the period he was known as Wellesley) beat both Napoleon and all of his ablest commanders at one stage or another. There were other reverses, other examples of over-confidence or contempt of the enemy that proved his undoing, but for the most part, Napoleon strode like a colossus through Europe, sweeping all before him.

He was a consummate leader and competent at the art of warfare. As General Wavell wrote: 'If you discover how Bonaparte inspired a ragged, mutinous, half-starved army and made it fight as it did, how he dominated and controlled generals older and more experienced than himself, then you will have learnt something.' For this reason alone, the study of the Napoleonic battles remains fascinating and imperative to all with an interest in military matters.

Men would willingly die for him; he shared their dangers and their hardships as a good general should, but he was harsh and vengeful when necessary.

At sea, the reputation and supremacy of the Royal Navy was cemented by heavy defeats for the French and the Spanish at the hands of audacious British naval commanders. The Napoleonic period is not just the time of Napoleon and Wellington; a part quite rightly belongs to one of the greatest seamen of all time – Horatio Nelson.

The enduring interest in this relatively short period of history encompasses all of the major conflicts between the Europeans over little more than twenty years. Contemporary with the period, but outside the remit of this book, is the American Revolution and the War of 1812 – both conflicts very much 'Napoleonic' in nature. The colour, the dash and the intrigue of the period have been brought to life by fictional characters, notably Forester's Hornblower and Cornwallis Sharpe, but in truth they were no bigger characters than those who found themselves leaders of men during the period.

This book encompasses the rise, the fall, the second rise and the final end of Napoleon's ambitions for a French-dominated world. The battlefields spread from Buenos Aires to Cairo and from Paris to Moscow in what was undoubtedly a series of true world wars in which all European powers found themselves embroiled; many at times pro-French and at others their implacable enemies.

In terms of military strategy, many of the fundamental manoeuvres of warfare were created or refined during this period: envelopment, feints, refused flanks and fronts and battles of attrition. The experts on the field wielded vast armies, sometimes of dubious quality, in vast sweeping manoeuvres over immense distances. For many, the Napoleonic period remains the archetypal mix of neatly uniformed soldiers coupled with dash and heroism against a massive canvas of total warfare.

Acknowledgements

I am indebted to two major sources of photographs to illustrate this book, having taken the decision not to choose the stereotypical art images of the period. My thanks go to Mario Tomasone, a very talented and active Italian Napoleonic enthusiast. His Napoleonic re-enactment information and photographs can be accessed at http://www.mclink.it/personal/MC7831/home.html. Much is in Italian, but Mario is gradually adding translated pages in English. I am also very grateful to Lynn and Jon Holmes, creators of the 2nd Queen's Royal Regiment of Foot web pages at http://www.jaholmes.demon.co.uk/secndft/index.html. Lynn's photography has greatly enhanced the book and I am grateful to her, Jon and the Napoleonic Association and Ondrej Tupy, The Club of Military History, Novy Jicin, Czech Republic for their permission to use their images.

Chronology of Napoleonic Battles

Year	Date	Conflict
1792	20 September	Battle of Valmy
	6 November	Battle of Jemappes
1793	18 March	Battle of Neerwinden
	28 June	Battle of Valenciennes
	August–September	Siege of Toulon
	15–16 October	Battle of Wattignies
	28–30 November	Battle of Kaiserslautern
	22 December	Battle of Fröschwiller
	23 December	Battle of Savernay
	26 December	Battle of Geisberg
1794	24 April	Battle of Villers-en-Cauches
	18 May	Battle of Tourcoing
	28 May–1 June	Battle of Ushant
	26 June	Battle of Fleurus
1795	23 June	Battle of Lorient
	16–20 July	Battle of Quiberon
	22 July–16 August	Battle of the Cape of Good Hope
	24 November	Battle of Loano
1796	12 April	Battle of Montenotte
	13 April	Battle of Millesimo
	14–15 April	Battle of Dego
	21 April	Battle of Mondovi
	10 May	Battle of Lodi
	4 June	First siege of Montua
	16 June	Battle of Wetzlar
	9 July	Battle of Malsch
	3 August	Battle of Lönato
	5 August	Battle of Castiglione
	24 August	Battle of Amberg
		Battle of Friedberg
	3 September	Battle of Würzburg
	5 September	Battle of Caliano
	8 September	Battle of Bassano
	12 November	Battle of Caldiero
	15–17 November	Battle of Arcola

Year	Date	Conflict
1797	14–15 January	Battle of Rivoli
	14 February	Battle of Cape St Vincent
	23 March	Battle of Malborghetto
	18 April	Battle of Lahn
	11 October	Battle of Camperdown
1798		Irish Rebellion
	21 June	Battle of Vinegar Hill
	21 July	Battle of the Pyramids
	1 August	Battle of Aboukir Bay
	22 August	Battle of Killala Bay
	25 August	Battle of Castlebar
1799	19 March–May	Siege of St Jean d'Acre
	25 March	Battle of Stockach
	5 April	Battle of Magnano
	17 April	Battle of Mount Tabor
	27 April	Battle of Cassano
	4–7 June	First Battle of Zurich
	17–19 July	Battle of Trebbia
	25 July	First Battle of Aboukir
	15 August	Battle of Novi
	16 September–2 October	First Battle of Bergen-op-Zoom
	25 September	Second Battle of Zurich
	6 October	Battle of Castricum
1800	20 March	Battle of Heliopolis
	20 April–4 June	Siege of Genoa
	3 May	Battle of Stockach
	5 May	Battle of Möskirch
	16 May	First Battle of Ulm
	9 June	Battle of Montebello
	14 June	Battle of Marengo
	19 June	Battle of Hochstadt
	3 December	Battle of Hohenlinden

Year	Date	Conflict
1801	21 March	Second Battle of Aboukir (Alexandria)
	2 April	Battle of Copenhagen
	6–12 July	Battle of Algeciras
1805	8–21 October	Second Battle of Ulm
	21 October	Battle of Trafalgar
	30 October	Battle of Caldiero
	16 November	Battle of Oberhollabrunn
	2 December	Battle of Austerlitz
1806	25 June	First Battle of Buenos Aires
	4 July	Battle of Maida
	10 October	Battle of Saalfeld
	14 October	Battle of Jena and Auerstadt
	7 November	Battle of Lübeck
	26 December	Battle of Pultusk
1807	8 February	Battle of Eylau
	18 March–27 May	Siege of Danzig
	10 June	Battle of Heilsberg
	13–14 June	Battle of Friedland
	5 July	Second Battle of Buenos Aires
	16 August–20 October	Siege of Copenhagen
1808	19 July	Battle of Baylen
	17 August	Battle of Rolica
	21 August	Battle of Vimeiro
	21 December	Battle of Sahagun
	26 December	Battle of Benevente
1809	16 January	Battle of Corunna
	28 March	Battle of Medellin
	11–12 April	Battle of Basque Roads
	16 April	Battle of Sacile
	20 April	Battle of Abensberg
	21 April	Battle of Landshut
	22 April	Battle of Eckmühl
	12 May	The Battle of Douro (Oporto)
	21–22 May	Battle of Aspern-Essling
	14 June	Battle of Raab
	5–6 July	Battle of Wagram
	27–28 July	Battle of Talavera
	19 November	Battle of Ocana

Year	Date	Conflict
1810	5 February	Siege of Cadiz
	9 July	First Battle of Ciudad Rodrigo
	27 September	Battle of Busaco
1811	5 March	Battle of Barrosa
	11 March	First Battle of Badajoz
	3 April	Battle of Sabugal
	3–5 May	Battle of Fuentes de Oñoro
	16 May	Battle of Albuera
	28 October	Battle of Arroyo dos Molinos
1812	9 January	Battle of Valencia
	8–19 January	Second Battle of Ciudad Rodrigo
	16 March–6 April	Second Battle of Badajoz
	19 May	Battle of Almaraz
	22 July	Battle of Salamanca
	23 July	Battle of Mogilev
	17–19 August	Battle of Smolensk
	19 August	Battle of Valutino Gora
	7 September	Battle of Borodino
	19 September–22 October	Siege of Burgos
	24–25 October	Battle of Maloyaroslavets
	16–17 November	Battle of Krasnyi
	26–28 November	Battle of Berezina
1813	2 May	Battle of Lützen
	20–21 May	Battle of Bautzen
	21 June	Battle of Vittoria
	26 July–1 August	Battle of Sorauren
	23 August	Battle of Grossbeeren
	26 August	Battle of Katzbach
	26–27 August	Battle of Dresden
	30 August	Battle of Kulm-Priesten
	28 June–31 August	Siege of San Sebastian
	6 September	Battle of Dennewitz
	3 October	Battle of Wartenberg
	16–19 October	Battle of Leipzig
	30 October	Battle of Hanau
	10 November	Battle of Nivelle
	9–13 December	Battle of Nive

Year	Date	Conflict
1814	29 January	Battle of Brienne
	1 February	Battle of La Rothière
	10 February	Battle of Champaubert
	11 February	Battle of Montmirail
	12 February	Battle of Château-Thierry
	14 February	Battle of Vauchamps
	18 February	Battle of Montereau
	27 February	Battle of Orthes
		Battle of Bar-sur-Aube
	7 March	Battle of Craonne

Year	Date	Conflict
1814 Cont.	8 March	Second Battle of Bergen-op-Zoom
	9–10 March	Battle of Lâon
	13 March	Battle of Rheims
	20–21 March	Battle of Arcis-sur-Aube
	25 March	Battle of La Fère-Champenoise
	30 March	Battle of Montmartre
	10 April	Battle of Toulouse
1815	2 May	Battle of Tolentino
	16 June	Battle of Quatre Bras
		Battle of Ligny
	18 June	Battle of Waterloo
		Battle of Wavre

The Battle of Ushant (1794)

Battle Name	Dates	Campaign
Ushant (Quessant)	28 May–1 June 17	
		'Glorious 1 June'
Troops Involved		
France	30 ships	
	6,500 losses	Commanded by Villaret-Joyeuse
Britain	26 ships	
	1,098 losses	Commanded by Howe
Outcome:		
British victory		

This naval engagement took place west of the island of Ushant; the French were escorting a large convoy of merchant ships carrying grain from America, bound for Brest.

At 0600 on 28 May, the French fleet was spotted and both sides prepared to manoeuvre for action. By around 1000 it seemed that a battle was imminent, but suddenly when they were only a few miles apart, the French turned and ran. Towards the end of the day an epic struggle between Pashley's *Belleorphon* and the French 120-gun *La Revolutionnaire* was fought out. With the aid of the *Audacious*, the French ship was badly damaged and headed off.

The pursuit continued into the next day, with a further indecisive action being fought. Fog now hid the French until 1 June, just after daybreak. At 0715 Howe signalled to attack, with instructions that each ship should choose an individual target and engage to stop the enemy from getting away. The battle got underway at 0930 when the leading French ships opened fire. The *Defence* was the first to break through the French line between the *Mucius Scaevola* and the *Tourville*. The latter made off, but the former engaged with the *Marlborough*.

The *Queen Charlotte* headed for the *Montagne*, but was beset by the *Vengeur*, the *Achille* and the *Jacobin*. Elsewhere, the *Royal George* and the Brunswick had also pushed through the French line. The *Brunswick* now took on the *Achille* and the *Vengeur*, but the *Ramillies* arrived to save her. The *Bellerophon* tailed the *Ecole* whilst the *Royal Sovereign* attacked the *Terrible*. After inflicting heavy damage on the *Terrible*, the *Montagne* and the *Jacobin* tried to stop the *Royal Sovereign*, also badly damaged, but were forced off.

The *Impregnable* roughly handled the *Le Juste* and when the French vessel came under fire from the *Queen Charlotte*, she struck her colours. The *Defence* was still chasing the *Mucius Scaevola* but she strayed too close to the *Marlborough*, which was now fighting the *Montagne*. The *Marlborough* remained in grave danger until the *Aquilon* came to her aid.

By now, any integrity for either fleet had been lost. The French, however, sensing that a British victory was imminent, headed off as best they could. Six of the ten vessels underway were captured by the British; most of which were littered with French dead and wounded. Howe had won, but the merchant ships had slipped away and Joyeuse could claim a moral victory.

The Battle of Montenotte (1796)

Battle Name	Dates	Campaign
Montenotte	12 April 1796	1st Italian Campaign
Troops Involved		
France	9,000	
	880 losses	Commanded by Napoleon
Austria	6,000	
	2,500 losses (including prisoners)	Commanded by Argenteau
Outcome:		
French victory		

The Austrian and Piedmontese allies were distrustful of one another; Beaulieu commanded the Austrian army and Colli the Piedmontese. They maintained separate lines of communication back to Mantua (the Austrian administration centre) and to Turin (the Piedmontese capital). Whilst the allies were thus divided, the French could take advantage of the situation and launch an offensive against one of them.

The blow fell at Montenotte on 12 April 1796. La Harpe's 9,000 troops advanced through thick fog in the early hours of the morning to close with Argenteau's 6,000 troops positioned at Montenotte.

The most significant aspect of this whole operation, of which Montenotte was the first engagement, is that it was Napoleon's first independent command. He had assumed control of the Army of Italy on 27 March, inheriting a disjointed and ragged force which he would mould into an efficient and proud force.

La Harpe's troops split into two columns, with La Harpe heading straight for Mount Pra and Rampon, some way to the south-east. They would converge on the main Austrian position whilst a brigade of Meynier's cavalry, under Massena, would work around the Austrian right flank having passed through the Col di Cadibona.

Argenteau knew nothing of this until the fog lifted and he found himself confronted and outflanked. He immediately ordered a withdrawal to Montenotte Superior, but was beaten back by Massena's men. The garrison holding the Bric Castlas, at the centre of the Austrian position, was overwhelmed and Argenteau lost control of his troops as they routed.

This was Napoleon's first victory, his first illustrations of the wars of manoeuvre to bring a superior force into position, albeit a local advantage, to crack the enemy's resolve by striking hard at that point. It was a technique that would take some years to perfect, but he had begun.

Napoleon followed up this victory by attacking Colli. On 13 April he seized Dego, then drove Colli all the way to Mondovi, where he beat him on 21 April. Just two days later, Colli sued for peace and on 28 April Piedmont was out of the war.

Beaulieu was similarly handled in Napoleon's first campaign, and at Lodi he managed to establish his reputation with his men. Five days after Lodi, Napoleon entered Milan in triumph. The 'little corporal' had arrived.

French cavalry in action against Austrian infantry. *Mario Tomasone*

The Battle of Lodi (1796)

Battle Name	Dates	Campaign
Lodi	10 May 1796	1st Italian Campaign
Troops Involved		
France	40,000	
	2,000 losses	Commanded by Napoleon
Austria	24,000	
	2,000 losses	Commanded by Beaulieu
Outcome:		
French victory		

The Austrian army had retired beyond the River Po and this was to afford Napoleon a glorious opportunity to prove his theories of manoeuvre. Ordering his army to concentrate around the towns of Tortona, Alessandria and Valenza, he intended to cross the Po and bring the Austrians to battle on his ground and at the time of his choosing.

He had three choices of crossing: Valenza, south of Pavia and Piacenza. Valenza would place the lead elements of his army at a considerable disadvantage as it would face the main Austrian force. Success was unlikely here as was the crossing to the south of Pavia, again within Austrian striking distance.

Remarkably, he chose Piacenza, 50 miles (80 km) west and well in the Austrian rear. This would place his army between Beaulieu and his supplies and the only route of escape.

Napoleon mounted a diversionary attack on the Valenza crossing. Dallemagne, with 3,600 grenadiers and 2,500 cavalry, would seize the Piacenza Bridge. The south banks of the River Po would be covered by other French troops, thus masking the manoeuvre. At 0400 on 7 May Dallemagne left Stradella and reached Piacenza by 2100. It was fortunate that he had been reinforced by La Harpe's division, as on 4 May Beaulieu sent

An Austrian square faces the French. Mario Tomasone

Liptay, with a division of infantry supported by cavalry, to cover the crossings at Pavia. Beaulieu himself, after the attacks at Valenza, had decided to pull the bulk of the army across the River Ticino. Beaulieu now knew of the attempt on Piacenza and was sending Wukassovitch, with 4,500 men, from Valeggio to cover it.

On 8 May, Dallemagne began to force the Piacenza crossing, facing Liptay's troops who were thrown back to Fombio. The next day Dallemagne and La Harpe attacked and pursued Liptay's troops for two hours. Meanwhile, Augereau's troops had crossed the Po further west, at Varetto, and Massena

and Serurier were close.

Beaulieu was retreating on the River Adda, but the leading French units were in sight of Lodi on the river by the early hours of 10 May. By this time nearly all of the Austrians had crossed and the Austrian rearguard consisted of 10,000 men under Sebottendorf.

The French cleared the town quickly and after two assaults on the bridge, they were over the river and the Austrians were running. They had done their job; Beaulieu and the Austrians had evaded an audacious plan, but Napoleon would perfect the technique in the years to come.

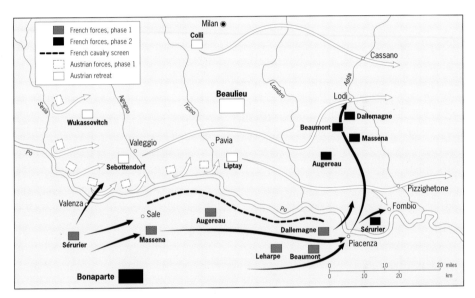

The Battle of Castiglione (1796)

Battle Name	Dates	Campaign
Castiglione	5 August 1796	1st Italian Campaign
Troops Involved		
France	27,500	
	1,500 losses	Commanded by Napoleon
Austria	25,000	
	3,000 killed or taken prisoner	Commanded by Würmser
Outcome:		
French victory		

Defeating the 12,700 Austrian garrison of Mantua would unlock their control of northern Italy and the siege, beginning on 3 June 1796, dominated proceedings for the next eight months.

By July, however, two Austrian armies were marching to relieve the garrisons, forcing Napoleon to order the abandonment of the siege in a desperate

attempt to concentrate his forces. Fortunately for the French, the Austrian advance was slow, but it was beginning to gather momentum as they forced Massena to abandon Verona. The two Austrian armies were not yet united and Napoleon still had a chance to deal with them.

On 3 August Massena moved against the smaller

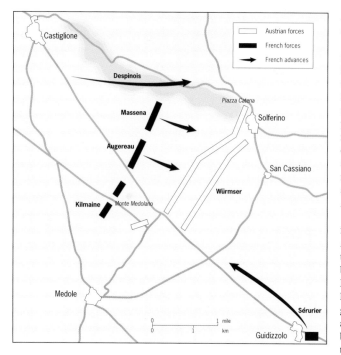

Austrians and cut off the enemy's retreat.

Unfortunately, not everything went according to plan. Sérurier was ill and the Corsican commander, Fiorella, took over his division and launched the flank attack prematurely. Napoleon's initial rearward movement to encourage Würmser to advance was in progress, but now he had to launch the assault to tie down the Austrians.

Napoleon urged his men forward with Massena and Augereau's troops striking the main Austrian line between Solferino and Monte Medolano. Marmont, still a low-ranking officer, was given command of the artillery, delivering telling bombardment on the left of the Austrian line as a prelude to the infantry assaults, led by the grenadiers.

of the Austrian armies at Lonato. Quasdanovich, the Austrian commander, suffered heavily and was thrown back in disorder. Napoleon now determined to deal with Würmser, who, if allowed to reach Mantua, would be sufficiently strong to beat his forces in northern Italy.

Napoleon began to concentrate his forces on the plain of Castiglione. Massena and Augereau, supported by Kilmaine's cavalry, would occupy Würmser frontally with an assault. Hopefully, Despinois, moving up from Brescia, would assist in this attack. Napoleon's ace was Sérurier's division, which he hoped would hit the left rear of the

Würmser's right collapsed as Despinois' men finally arrived and stormed through the Austrian line. Würmser, ordering a general retreat, managed to extricate the bulk of his army in the nick of time, saving it from the fate Napoleon had planned for it. Napoleon's troops had entered the combat exhausted and after the engagement pursued for some three hours before it was called off.

The Austrians' first attempts to relieve Mantua had failed and for the time being French control of northern Italy was secured. The Austrians, however, would surely try again.

Austrian and French infantry close to engage. Mario Tomasone

The Battle of Würzberg (1796)

Battle Name	Dates	Campaign
Würzburg	3 September 1796	War of the 1st Coalition
Troops Involved		
France	30,000	
	5,800 losses	Commanded by Jourdan
Austria	44,000–60,000	
	1,469 losses	Commanded by Archduke Charles
Outcome:		
Austrian victory		

Austrian infantry about to charge. *Mario Tomasone*

Following his victory over Jourdan at Amberg (24 August) Archduke Charles pursued him; he needed another victory and a quick one in order to turn south and deal with Moreau.

His main army pursued the French to Regnitz, then Bruberg and Würzburg. Jourdan had left 800 men here to garrison the town. A concerted Austrian attack seized the town, but the French garrison retreated to the citadel and denied the enemy victory. In the early hours of 2 September, Jourdan despatched Bonnaud from Schweinfurt to Würzburg and by noon the first French infantry arrived and launched an assault, pushing the Austrians from Steinburg and the Kunach Valley. Hotze's Austrians clung on to the town suburbs and Galgenberg.

Skirmishing and artillery fire continued during the rest of the day. Jourdan still thought he was just facing Hotze and Sztaray and expected to outnumber them. But Archduke Charles began to move in support during the night and in a despatch told Sztaray to expect him at 1000 on 3 September. Sztaray moved west in the night in anticipation of his arrival, but by the early morning he was sure that the French would attack before he arrived.

By dawn, the Austrians had concentrated around Lengfeld, immediately swinging in to attack the French. Sztaray claimed the hills around Lengfeld and Jourdan was forced to evacuate the Kurnach Valley. Here Sztaray would stay and await Charles.

Jourdan counter-attacked at 1000 and after seven assaults the Austrians were evicted from Lengfeld. Charles had been delayed by the fog, but he arrived at 1130. By noon fourteen infantry battalions were approaching and forty-two squadrons of hussars and dragoons had already arrived. Kray's infantry and cavalry had been ordered to head for Prosselheim and the French left, cutting the Schweinfurt road. He began running into French troops at 1100, by which time Jourdan had realised that his planned outflanking move was not going to work.

Sztaray's men continued to resist whilst Kray moved beyond Prosselheim and headed for Dipbach. The French were able to hold back the first assault, but they were overwhelmed. To the south Wartensleben had arrived, and Jourdan now knew the battle was turning against him. He began to mass his cavalry and sent a frantic message to Lefebvre, requesting his immediate help, but the despatch was slow in reaching him as Kray's cavalry had already cut the road to Schweinfurt. Bernadotte and Bonnaud's cavalry began to mass near the

Schweinfurt road, whilst Klein began to move against Kray's left. Archduke Charles hesitated, waiting for Werneck to come up before launching his assault. As a precaution, he ordered Lichtenstein to form up his cavalry on Wartensleben's right.

At around 1400 Klein charged Kray, Lichtenstein charged Klein and scattered him. At 1500 Werneck arrived and at about the same time Bonnaud emerged from Sperleholz Woods. After three attacks from Austrian cavalry, Bonnaud's men fled and headed for their own infantry squares.

Panic now spread through the French army, but Bernadotte had advanced as far as Lengfeld and was ready to launch his attacks. Jourdan had seen enough. Grenier was separated and the battle lost. He ordered a retreat towards Arnstein, north of Würzburg.

Archduke Charles ordered a general advance at 1600. Werneck was ordered to clear the area around Rotenhof and ensure that a link-up was made between Sztaray and Wartensleben. Werneck's grenadiers stormed Rotenhof in the face of grapeshot from the French defenders, and more of his troops took up positions in the wooded area beyond.

Meanwhile, Kray had impacted on Grenier's rearguard at Unterbleifeld and caused heavy casualties. The general pursuit went on through the villages in the Bleifeld area, the Austrian cavalry now finding it difficult to keep pace with their own infantry, let alone the French, owing to the uneven ground.

Near the Gramschatzer forest, three French regiments formed squares and tried to fend off the Austrian cavalry, but most were cut down. All along the advancing front French troops and guns were falling into Austrian hands. Kray was gradually forcing Grenier further away from Jourdan's scattered army, but after Charles crossed the Kurnagh Valley he halted his troops near Rimpar and officially ended the pursuit at 1900, content to bombard the retreating French with his artillery.

The French losses, given the confidence of Jourdan at the beginning of the battle, were immense. Some 2,000 men had been killed or wounded and 3,800 prisoners (including the Würzburg garrison) had been taken. Archduke Charles could be rightly proud of the 1,469 men of his own who had fallen at Würzburg.

Jourdan would have two other opportunities to beat Archduke Charles, at Ostrach and Stockach in March 1799, and both times he failed. Archduke Charles seems to have been such a figure of fear for Jourdan that in 1805, when he was destined to face him again, Napoleon replaced him with Massena.

The Battle of Arcola (1796)

Battle Name	Dates	Campaign
Arcola	15–17 November 1796	1st Italian Campaign
Troops Involved		
France	Day 1: 15,000	
	Day 2: 17,000	
	Day 3: 20,000	
	4,500–4,600 losses	Commanded by Napoleon
Austria	Day 1: 3,000–9,000	
	Day 2: 12,000	
	Day 3: 17,000	
	6,000–7,000 losses	Commanded by Alvintzy
Outcome:		
French victory		

With the Austrian garrison at Mantua bolstered by troops from Würmser's army, Napoleon renewed his siege on 24 August. In September, however, leaving 8,000 men to cover the city, he marched north to Trent. The Austrians were again mustering to relieve Mantua and Napoleon defeated Davidovich at Caliano on 4 September, driving him through Trent. Napoleon then defeated Würmser at Bassano on 8 September. The second Austrian attempt to relieve Mantua had failed.

By October, the Austrian garrison at Mantua had reached 28,000, held by just 9,000 French. A new attempt to relieve the city was launched by Alvintzy, who was moving on Vicenza, hoping to meet up with Davidovich at Verona. Napoleon sent Massena and Angereau to hold him up, but on 12 November they encountered his whole army at Caldiero and were pushed back. Napoleon then despatched Vaubois to hold off Davidovich whilst he moved to engage Alvintzy.

On 14 November Napoleon advanced along the south bank of the River Adige and crossed the river

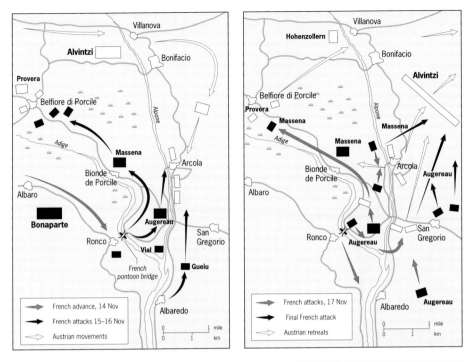

Napoleon leads French grenadiers across the bridge at Arcola under fire from Austrian artillery.

at Ronco, some 4 miles (6.5 km) south of Arcola. Alvintzy, still advancing on Arcola, sent reinforcements to the Austrian garrison and more troops to deal with Massena, who was protecting Napoleon's left flank, at Porcile. In turn, Napoleon sent Guieu via Albaredo to attack Arcola from the east.

On 15 November Massena held off Provera's men whilst Napoleon's main force attempted to force the bridge at Arcola. Even as Napoleon's troops were gaining the upper hand, news came that Vaubois was falling back. It was not clear how badly he had fared, but Napoleon called off the attacks, allowing the Austrians to reinforce Arcola and occupy Porcile.

On 16 November, Napoleon launched more attacks on the bridge but failed to take it. After a day's struggle, Porcile was finally taken. It was now clear that Alvintzy's main force was in retreat and renewed attacks on 17 November aimed to cut off what remained of the Austrians. Massena occupied the Austrians at Arcola whilst Angereau was ordered to swing east and capture the town from the rear. Massena managed to storm the Arcola Bridge, and meanwhile troops were sent across the River Alpone to distract the Austrians, allowing Angereau to advance north towards Arcola. Alvintzy now ordered a full withdrawal to Vicenza for fear that his whole army would be surrounded and beaten by the French. Another attempt to relieve Mantua had failed, forcing Davidovich also to retire, but in the new year another attempt would be made.

The Battle of Rivoli (1797)

Battle Name	Dates	Campaign
Rivoli	14–15 January 1797	1st Italian Campaign
Troops Involved		
France	Day 1: 10,000–20,500	
Day 2: 14,000		
	5,000 losses	Commanded by Napoleon
Austria	Day 1: 12,000–28,000	
Day 2: 20,000		
	14,000 losses	Commanded by Alvintzy
Outcome:		
French victory		

In mid-January, Alvintzy launched a series of attacks, aiming to crush Joubert in the Adige Valley and link up with Würmser. Bayalitsch had hit Verona, Provera had attacked Legnano, whilst Alvintzy's main force (some 28,000) was moving up the Adige Valley.

Six columns of Austrian troops were converging on Joubert on the Rivoli Plateau. Liptay, Koblos and Ocksay were attacking the northern end of the plateau, Quasdanovitch had pushed the French outposts away from the ridge of Mount Magnone and was coming up the Osteria Gorge. Lusignan was working around the west and Wukassovitch from the east to get around the French rear.

Napoleon joined Joubert at 0200 on 14 January, and by 0600 they had been reinforced by Massena. Napoleon ordered Joubert to hold off Liptay and Koblos on the Trombalore Heights, with one brigade placed at San Marco, and Massena would hold the left flank (the Tasso Valley) and hold the rest of his division in reserve at Rivoli itself.

The engagement began at daybreak as Joubert pushed his 10,000 men forward to attack the Austrians descending from the slopes of Monte Baldo. Koblos checked Joubert and Liptay began working around his flank; Napoleon immediately called up Massena's reserves to stem the tide. Whilst the French were preoccupied in the north, Wukassovitch had set up artillery on the eastern side of the River Adige, Quasdanovitch had seized the approaches to the Osteria Gorge and Lusignan's 4,000 had appeared to the south of Rivoli, cutting Napoleon off from his reinforcements.

It seemed that Liptay and Koblos were now exhausted and Napoleon took the opportunity to shift Joubert to deal with the Osteria Gorge. A lucky shot detonated an Austrian ammunition wagon and into the chaos French infantry, supported by cavalry under Leclerc and Lassalle, cleared the gorge. No sooner had this been done than the French redoubled their efforts to drive Liptay and Koblos aside. In the south, Massena's reserves held Rivoli until Rey's troops arrived; they trapped Lusignan and took 3,000 prisoners. By 1700, the victory was nearly complete, and Napoleon left Joubert to deal with the next day's engagement which would finally settle the issue.

Joubert renewed the attacks in the morning, driving the Austrians back, but as they streamed towards La Corona Murat and Vial took the vital passes and seized hundreds of prisoners. The remnants of the Austrian army fled down the Adige Valley; the last great Austrian offensive was over.

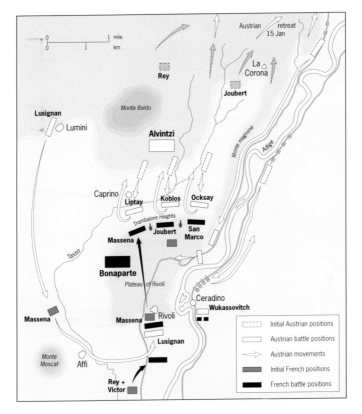

French cavalry attacking an Austrian square. Mario Tomasone

The Battle of Cape St Vincent (1797)

Battle Name	Dates	Campaign
Cape St Vincent	14 February 1797	
Troops Involved		
Spain	27 ships	
	3,000 losses	Commanded by de Córdova
Britain	15 ships	
	300 losses	Commanded by Jervis/Nelson
Outcome:		
British victory		

When Jervis spotted a Spanish fleet some 24 miles (38 km) from his positions at dawn on 14 February, he immediately ordered his own fleet to close with the enemy. The Spanish were in a 20-mile (32-km) column and Jervis proposed to cut off the leading ships with his two lines of attack.

The Spanish fleet consisted of the *Santissima Trinidad* (130 guns), the 112-gun *Conception*, *Salvador del Mundo*, *Manecano* and *Principe de Asturias*, plus one eight-gun vessel, nineteen 74s, seven frigates and a twelve-gun brig. Against these Jervis could deploy just fifteen vessels, amongst whom was Commodore Horatio Nelson, master of the 74-gun *Captain*.

At around 1040, Jervis signalled to pass through the enemy fleet. This was done, and ten minutes later the *Culloden* opened fire on the enemy's lead ships. The Spanish tried to manoeuvre to join up with the separated ships and get away, but Nelson pulled alongside de Córdova's own *Santissima Trinidad* and engaged. Soon he was facing the *San Joséf*, the *Salvador del Mundo*, the *San Nicholas*, the *San Isidro* and two other vessels. The *Culloden* came up to assist, then the *Blenheim* arrived. The *Excellent* engaged the *Salvador del Mundo* and the *San Isidro*, and the latter struck colours.

Nelson now concentrated on the *San Nicholas*, which he boarded and seized. The *San Joséf* came alongside and without a second thought, he boarded this Spanish vessel, which gave up after a few minutes.

There were still eighteen Spanish ships to be dealt with; the *Victory* rounded on the *Salvador del Mundo* and fired until she struck her colours. The *Santissima Trinidad* brought up the rear of the fleeing enemy and she was forced to strike her colours. She needed to be towed into Cadiz later.

The engagement, now a pursuit, lasted until around 1600. The last orders at 1700, were to form a protective line to cover the disabled British vessels and the four prize ships.

It is astounding to record that the *Captain* alone fired off 146 barrels of powder in the engagement, only beaten by the *Culloden* (170 barrels) and the *Blenheim* (180 barrels).

The British fleet put into Lagos Bay. The battle had made Nelson; he was given the Order of the Bath and the Freedom of London, and Jervis was knighted. The Spanish King Charles IV dismissed de Córdova and demoted the captain who had survived the battle of Cape St Vincent.

The Battle of Cape St Vincent.

The Battle of Camperdown (1797)

Battle Name	Dates	Campaign
Camperdown	11 October 1797	
Troops Involved		
Netherlands	15 ships of the line	
	11 smaller ships	
	6,000 losses	Commanded by de Winter
British	16 ships of the line	
8 smaller ships		
	1,000 losses	Commanded by Duncan
Outcome:		
British victory		

Duncan's fleet had been at sea for some eighteen weeks and finally put into Great Yarmouth for refitting and resupply. He left only two ships to shadow the Dutch and send word if they should make a move.

Nominally, the Dutch fleet's purpose was to support the proposed French amphibious landings in Ireland, but this plan never materialised. In any event, the Dutch set sail on 8 October and Trollope, commanding the shadowing force, sent word to Duncan. By contemporary standards, both the British and the Dutch fleets were somewhat obsolete. Only seven of the British ships sported seventy-four guns and just four Dutch ships were of this size. This was in stark contrast to the British ships which had fought at Cape St Vincent, where the majority of the vessels had been 74s.

Duncan set sail and began to hunt the Dutch fleet, and on 11 October at 1130 he spotted them off the coast of Holland, near Kamperduin (Camperdown). Duncan split his fleet into two groups, but by 1200 he was forced to slow his approach, owing to straggling. The Dutch vessels tried to break, but Duncan ordered the main group of his ships to engage immediately, whilst the second group was to close on the enemy's rear.

At 1230 the *Monarch* passed through the enemy line, the *Powerful* closed with the *Haarlem*, the *Monmouth* attacked the *Alkmaar* and the *Russel* tackled the *Delft*. At 1245, Duncan's main squadron began to engage the enemy. The flagship, the *Venerable*, the *Ardent* and the *Bedford* pounced on the *Vrijheid*, whilst the *Triumph* took on the *Wassenaer*.

The *Hercules* caught fire and struck its colours, and the *Venerable* became badly damaged and was forced to withdraw. Meanwhile, the *Triumph* forced the *Wassenaer* to strike, and then joined in against the *Vrijheid*. With four British ships pounding it, the *Vrijheid* was reduced to a wreck and quickly struck colours.

The battle was, effectively, over, with some eleven enemy ships being taken; most were badly damaged, and the *Delft* and the *Monnikedam* were scuttled *en route* back to England.

The French plan to invade Ireland was dealt a crippling blow by the lost fleet at Camperdown, coupled with the earlier defeat at Cape St Vincent. What remained of the Dutch fleet was lost when British troops landed at Helder in 1799. The Dutch sailors mutinied and surrendered to the British without a fight.

The Wexford Rebellion (1798)

The French and American Revolutions had convinced many in Ireland that only an armed uprising against the government would bring freedom and equality. To that purpose Wolfe Tone had convinced the French to launch an invasion of Ireland in 1796, which proved to be abortive.

The British government was alarmed, but instead of looking for a peaceful solution resorted to indiscriminate violence and repression. A rebellion was planned for 1798, but the United Irishmen

movement had been heavily infiltrated and many of the leaders were arrested.

Although there were uprisings in other parts of Ireland, Wexford's was the most important; its economy was in tatters and the United Irishmen were well organised in the area. The rebellion was sparked by an accidental engagement between local yeomanry and a group of rebels led by Father John Murphy. The brief skirmish set the countryside alight; Murphy had been waiting for news of the

British troops attack the Wexford rebels.

rebellion but had, in fact, started it himself.

His men raided local houses looking for guns and weapons, then headed for Oulart Hill, a prearranged meeting place. Other leaders followed, along with some 500 rebels. It was 26 May 1798, and the following day saw the first pitched battle.

The hated North Cork Militia were sent from Wexford to disperse the rebels, but they ran straight into an ambush and were slaughtered, the rebel pikemen surging out of the ditches and despatching the cavalry.

On 28 May, with the rebel ranks swelling, they descended on Enniscorthy, which was seized after a hard fight by the ploy of stampeding cattle through the town's gate. The defenders fled and on the next day the rebels took Wexford without having to fire a shot. This was the rebellion's high-water mark.

The rebels now sought to bring the rest of Ireland under their control, splitting the army into two groups; they fought and lost the battles of Bunclody (1 June), New Ross (5 June) and Arklow (9 June). After these defeats they were forced back to Vinegar Hill, where they faced the whole British army.

They mustered some 20,000 (many of whom were non-combatants) against an estimated 20,000 British and loyalist troops under Lake. The rebels were encircled by 21 June and under intense artillery fire, they gave way to the British infantry. There was a mass slaughter but many escaped, including Father Murphy. Reprisals were brutal in Wexford, and the rebellion was over.

The Battle of the Pyramids (1798)

Battle Name	Dates	Campaign
Pyramids (Embabeh)	21 July 1798	Egyptian Campaign
Troops Involved		
France	25,000	
	300 losses	Commanded by Napoleon
Mamelukes	21,000	
	3,000–5,000 losses	Commanded by Murad Bey and Ibrahim Bey
Outcome:		
French victory		

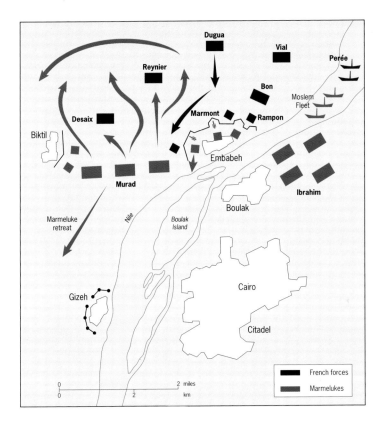

Dugua
Vial
Perée
Reynier
Bon
Moslem
Fleet
Desaix
Marmont
Rampon
Biktil
Embabeh
Murad
Ibrahim
Boulak
Marmeluke
retreat
Nile
Boulak
Island
Gizeh
Cairo
Citadel

French forces

Marmelukes

0   2 miles
0   2   km

Egypt was controlled by the Mamelukes, vassals of the Ottoman Empire, the country and army being led by Ibrahim Bey and Murad Bey. Napoleon had landed at Alexandria on 1 July 1798 and was soon *en route* to capture Cairo.

On 20 July, Napoleon received word that the Mameluke army was concentrating around 20 miles (32 km) from Cairo. He marched his worn out army, suffering from the heat and lack of water, to the village of Embabeh on the banks of the Nile. The Mamelukes had foolishly allowed half of their forces to be caught still on the opposite bank of the Nile and for the whole battle Ibrahim could only sit and watch. Murad Bey had deployed his questionable *fellahin* (poor-quality and poorly armed infantry) in a defensive position protecting the village. The main strike arm was his 6,000 mounted troops. Napoleon advanced in five divisional squares, with Bon and Vial on the river bank, Desaix and Reynier in the desert and Dugua in the centre, to act as a reserve.

Desaix detached troops to capture the village of Biktil and at around 1530 the Mamelukes began to mass their cavalry to strike at Desaix and Reynier. The two divisional squares only just managed to form up as the Mamelukes charged at them. The

three columns of cavalry swarmed around the Frenchmen, unable to break into its squares, constantly under artillery and musket fire.

It swirled around, now under fire from howitzers in the middle of Dugua's square (in which was also Napoleon himself). They then galloped back to try to deal with Desaix's detached troops, who had occupied Biktil. The Frenchmen clambered onto the rooftops to avoid being ridden down and sniped at the enemy cavalry.

Napoleon now launched Vial and Bon towards Embabeh, covered by his gunboats on the Nile. With the Mameluke cavalry occupied around Biktil, the French infantry fell on the Mameluke infantry and in a matter of minutes they were within the defence works. Resistance was futile and brief and the *fellahin* began to flee (some 1,000 were drowned trying to cross the Nile).

By around 1630, the battle was effectively over and the Mameluke cavalry were in full retreat. But although the Mamelukes were decisively beaten, they continued to harass Napoleon's troops. The French entered Cairo on 22 July, but they would not have very long to savour their victory, particularly after their fleet was destroyed at Aboukir Bay by Nelson on 1 August.

The Battle of Aboukir Bay (1798)

Battle Name	Dates	Campaign
Aboukir Bay	1 August 1798	Egyptian Campaign
Troops Involved		
France	13 ships	
	8,900 losses	Commanded by Brueys
Britain	14 ships	
	900 losses	Commanded by Nelson
Outcome:		
British victory		

The Battle of the Nile was one of the most decisive naval battles ever fought. At a stroke, it denied Napoleon of his eastern empire and crippled France's navy.

The British fleet blockading Cadiz was warned of a massive French expeditionary force leaving Toulon; Nelson, with just three ships, was sent to investigate. He was reinforced by ten new vessels and headed off into the Mediterranean to find his quarry.

He put in at Gibraltar and was caught by storms, but proceeded into the Mediterranean. The French, meanwhile, had sacked Malta and were heading for Alexandria. He arrived in Alexandria on June 28 but could see no sign of them. He arrived at Sicily on 28 July and Greek fishermen told him that they had seen the French south of Crete. Nelson turned back for Alexandria, but could still see no sign of the enemy. They were then spotted in Aboukir Bay. The fleet consisted of three 80-gun frigates, nine 74-gun battleships and the 120-gun *L'Orient*, Napoleon's flagship. It was protected by a shore battery, but Nelson was not to be denied.

At 1740, his ships sailed in amongst the French vessels, but the leading British ship, the *Culloden*, struck a shoal and was stuck there for the rest of the battle. The *Goliath* and the *Zealous* took up the lead and made for the first two French ships, the *Guerrier* and the *Conquerant*, both of which fired on the approaching enemy. The *Goliath* settled in place in front of the *Conquerant* and the *Zealous* to the front of the *Guernier*, and began raking with fire. The French guns were pointing away from the shore side of their ships and could not reply. With the French outwitted and desperately trying to shift their guns, the bombardments were merciless. In the first twenty minutes, three French ships had been silenced and by 2000 hours five had surrendered.

Nelson, aboard the *Vanguard*, was hit by flying

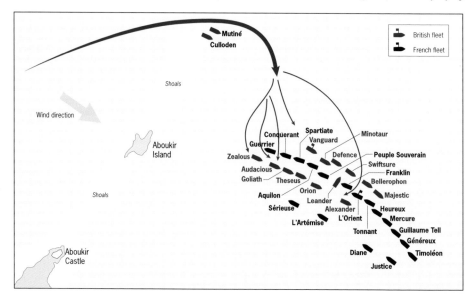

debris, a flap of loose skin falling over his one good eye. His men thought he was mortally wounded, but at 2145 he insisted on being brought up on deck. Three-quarters of an hour early, the *L'Orient* was well afire; when she blew up it could be heard 20 miles (32 km) away.

Three French ships fled, only two escaped, and not a single British ship was lost. Napoleon's men were marooned, his dreams of conquering India lying at the bottom of Aboukir Bay.

The Battle of the Nile.

The French Invasion of Ireland (1798)

Although the rebellions in Wexford and other parts of Ireland had been put down, a new force entered the fray on 22 August 1798. At Kilcummin Head, to the west of Killala Bay, 1,070 French infantry led by General Humbert, three cannons and a supply of 3,000 muskets landed.

The United Irishmen had continually lobbied Napoleon for support and this tiny gesture was to have long-lasting effects on Ireland. It also came close to succeeding. Humbert was no fool; he knew that alone and in conventional warfare, he had no chance against the British. He realised that the element of surprise was all he had. Above all, he wanted to impress the Irish with swift successes, for that meant willing recruits.

The first engagement took place that very afternoon, when 300 French grenadiers scattered the eighty-man garrison at Killala after a brisk firefight. On 24 August, Sarrazin led 500 French and Irish against Ballina. Here there were several hundred Prince of Wales Fencibles and yeomanry. The two armies clashed 1 mile (1.5 km) north of the town, trading volleys until Fontaine arrived on the British left flank with a group of musket- and pike-armed Irishmen, at which point the British fled.

The local British commander, Hutchinson, now expected Humbert to move on Castlebar and to this end he positioned a strong force at the River Moy. Over the next few days there were skirmishes along the Ballina – Castlebar road, so Hutchinson was content that he had done what was needed; he only had to wait for Humbert to march into his trap.

As it was, Hutchinson was replaced at midnight on 26 August by Lake, who would have little opportunity to react to what Humbert was actually planning. Castlebar was held by some 1,610 men. Humbert feigned a movement up the Castlebar road and then had his forces double back and take a trail west of Lough Conn, and by midnight he was at Lahardne. Here, an Irish priest who had spent time at Nantes gave him directions and food.

Humbert's command, consisting of 800 French, 15,000 Irish and a single gun, marched 25 miles (40 km) during the night and reached Castlebar at 0800 on 27 August. Total surprise had not been achieved as the British had been warned at 0700 by a local farmer. Consequently, Humbert found the British deployed and ready for him on Sion Hill, to the north-west of the town.

He deployed his Irish troops in the centre and covered his flanks with his own Frenchmen and began to advance. The British artillery drove off the first attack, but Humbert made a second attempt after a pause. This time, the British began to waver and the rebels overran the artillery and turned them on the British. Lake's army fled and for the next hour or so only Fraser's and Roden's troops tried to make a fight of it. The bulk of the army did not stop until they reached Tuam, some 34 miles (54 km) away. Because of this the battle is also known as the 'Castlebar Races'.

Humbert now incorporated some 250 deserters from the Longford and Kilkenny militias and attracted hundreds of new recruits. He knew that there would be stiffer opposition thrown at him.

By 2 September, Cornwallis had assembled 7,800 men at Tuam (four brigades) and Moore had another 2,800 at Boyle. When Cornwallis advanced to Castlebar on 4 September, he found a Franco-Irish rearguard holding the town. Humbert had only one chance and that was to continue to evade Cornwallis by continuing to march across Ireland. In that way, he could hope to attract more Irish troops and perhaps make an attempt on Dublin. He had therefore marched his army some 30 miles (48 km) north-east and fallen on loyalist yeomanry at Tobercurry.

Although he dealt with them easily, the garrison at Sligo had been alerted and on 5 September, Colonel Vereker marched out of the city with around 500 men. He took up positions to the north of Collooney with his right on a steep hill and his left protected by the River Ballysadare. Again, the loyalist force was routed.

Humbert now turned south, hoping to link up with rebels in Longford and Westmeath, but he was facing 17,000 British troops. Cornwallis barred his way to Dublin and Lake shadowed him. He was brought to battle at Ballinamuck on 8 September.

Humbert deployed his troops on Shanmullagh Hill with French grenadiers and an Irish battalion under Blake covering the road. The grenadiers were overwhelmed and Blake was forced to retreat. Lake now launched a frontal assault on the hill, which was repulsed twice, but a flanking move allowed the British to attack from three sides and it was all over. The French (about 800) were eventually repatriated, but most of the Irish were killed on the spot or later hanged.

The Battle of Marengo (1800)

Battle Name	Dates	Campaign
Marengo	14 June 1800	2nd Italian Campaign
		Marengo Campaign
Troops Involved		
France	23,000	
	7,000 losses	Commanded by Napoleon
Austria	28,500	
	14,000 losses	Commanded by Melas/Zach
Outcome:		
French victory		

The Austrian general Melas was centred round Alessandria and found his communications with Turin cut by the French. Ott's Austrians were attacked at Montebello on 9 June by Lannes and Victor and the whole of Napoleon's army could then advance towards Alessandria. They set up positions at Marengo. Napoleon sent Desaix to Novi to prevent Melas from escaping to Genoa and a further force north to hold the Po River crossings. Napoleon fully expected Melas to retire and was caught completely unawares when he launched a full-scale attack in the early hours of 14 June.

As the Austrians engaged Victor's division, Napoleon was still not convinced that Melas' attack was a full assault. By 1100 his mind was made up and he began to send increasingly desperate pleas to his commanders to move up immediately before the Austrians overran his positions.

Victor's troops were giving ground and as Ott's Austrians struck towards Castel Ceriolo, Napoleon

threw in his only reserve to stem the tide. At around 1200, the Austrians paused to reorganise, Melas confident that the battle had been won. By 1500, he handed over the command of the expected pursuit to Zach, returning to Alessandria to have a minor wound dressed. Fortune was not with the Austrians, however, and Desaix came to Napoleon's relief. He had begun his march but had been impeded by floods. Hearing cannons firing back at Marengo he literally marched to the sound of the guns.

His troops began arriving on the battlefield at around 1700 and Napoleon ordered him to counter-attack immediately, despite his men's exhaustion. Napoleon sent Marmont's artillery and Kellerman's cavalry brigade in support of the Desaix advance. Desaix was shot dead at the head of his troops and for a moment his men hesitated, but Marmont's artillery began blowing holes in Zach's Austrians.

The key moment came when an Austrian caisson exploded. The Austrian troops were stunned

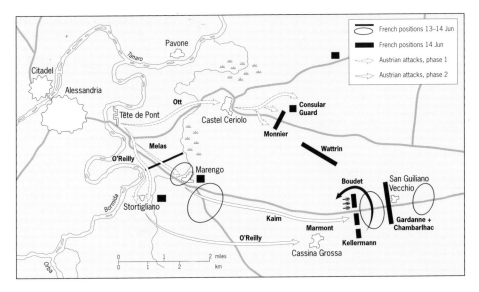

for a second, and at that moment Kellerman charged. Immediately, Zach's troops began to fall back and panic spread all along the Austrian line, which gave the weary French troops new heart. At first, the Austrian retreat was orderly, but it soon degenerated into a desperate rout.

On the evening of 15 June, Melas reluctantly signed an armistice agreeing to evacuate Lombardy. On 3 December, Moreau beat the Austrians once more at Hohenlinden, which forced them to sign the Treaty of Luneville (February 1801).

French Infantry form up at a Marengo re-enactment. *Mario Tomasone*

The Battle of Alexandria (1801)

Battle Name	Dates	Campaign
Alexandria	21 March 1801	Egyptian Campaign
Troops Involved		
France	20,000	
	4,160 losses	Commanded by Menou
Britain	14,000	
	1,468 losses	Commanded by Abercrombie
Outcome:		
British victory		

The British Expeditionary Force (BEF) under Sir Ralph Abercrombie moved to deal with the substantial French garrison under General Menou at Alexandria. On the night of 20 March, Abercrombie's troops had established their lines across the isthmus, with their right resting on the sea and the ruins of Nicopolis and their left on the lake of Aboukir and the Alexandria Canal.

The British troops faced the city from the south-west. Abercrombie posted Moore's division on the right; the Guards held his centre and three other brigades the left. In reserve were two infantry brigades and some cavalry.

No sooner had the camps begun to be established than the alarms were raised at 0300 as there was visible activity in the city. At 0330 the French came storming out and drove in Abercrombie's pickets. It seemed that the French, in their columns, intended to break the British line on Moore's portion of the position. The initial fighting fell on the Gloucestershire Regiment (28th), but the French attacks were repulsed. A second French column broke through and a vicious fight developed between them and the Black Watch (42nd) in the ruins of Nicopolis.

By now, the 28th was surrounded (later the regiment would be awarded the distinction of wearing its badge on the front and back of its headgear), but the French were driven off when three fresh British units were thrown in.

The 42nd, facing French cavalry, was under great pressure and it was at this point that Abercrombie received a mortal wound in the thick of the fighting. In the centre, the Guards drove off the French

whilst the British left was never under serious threat.

Attacks on the British right continued until around 0830; the 42nd alone had fought off two determined attacks by the French cavalry. As daylight illuminated the battlefield, British gunboats began to open up on the French, which in part accounts for the disproportionate losses during the battle. The French columns seem to have suffered a great deal of disruption from these boats, in additon to a large naval gun which had been added to the battery close to the Gloucestershires.

Abercrombie died on 28 March of his wounds; three other Guards and Moore had been wounded. After the battle, the city held out until August, at which point the whole of Egypt was given back to the Turkish Sultan Selim III.

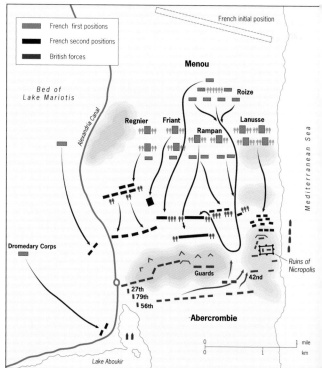

The Battle of Copenhagen (1801)

Battle Name	Date	Campaign		
Copenhagen	2 April 1801			
Troops Involved				
Denmark	18 vessels			
	3,700 losses (perhaps up to 6,000 killed, wounded or captured)	Commanded by Fischer		
Britain	33 vessels (12 engaged)			
	941 losses	Commanded by Nelson		
Outcome:				
British victory				

When Denmark refused to leave the Armed Neutrality of the North Coalition, the Royal Navy was sent in to deal with the Danish fleet at Copenhagen before Napoleon could make use of it. War had not been formally declared and this was something of a pre-emptive strike.

On the night of 1 April, Nelson's fleet anchored off Draco Point just 2 miles (3 km) from Copenhagen. In the morning, once the Crown Batteries had been silenced by Parker, who was commanding the whole operation, some 500 British soldiers and sailors would land to seize the position.

At 0930 Nelson's force weighed anchor and worked its way around the shoals, engaging the enemy at around 1005. Initially Nelson could not bring all of his guns to bear and the return fire from the Danes was so intense that Parker began to panic. Parker ordered a withdrawal and Nelson, it is said, put his telescope to his blind eye and exclaimed, 'I have only one eye; I have thus a right to be blind sometimes. I really do not see the signal!'

By now, the Danish ships were mastless wrecks, but for another hour the battle raged. By between 1300 and 1400 the British fire began to slacken. The Danish ships which had struck their colours came under fire from their own batteries. Nelson now fired off a despatch to the Prince Royal of Denmark, who had assumed command of Copenhagen, telling him that if he did not surrender then he would be forced to sink the crippled Danish ships.

Thesiger delivered the despatch and an armistice was agreed; shortly afterwards, the Danes agreed to suspend their cooperation with the Treaty of Armed Neutrality.

Nelson said of the Copenhagen engagement: 'I have been in one hundred and five engagements, but that of today was the most terrible of them all!'

Whilst he organised the refitting of the disabled ships, he constantly sought intelligence regarding the intentions of the Swedes. They had been rumoured to have set sail to aid the Danes, but when encountered, they offered a flag of truce. Tsar Paul had been murdered in Russia and his son, Alexander,

sought peace with Britain; the potential crisis of the treaty had now passed.

British deaths at Copenhagen did not exceed 300, but over 700 were wounded. The Danes originally admitted some 1,800 deaths, but later accounts suggest the casualties may have been as much as 6,000.

Nelson's famous signal at the First battle of Copenhagen.

The Battle of Ulm (1805)

Battle Name	Dates	Campaign
Ulm	8–21 October 1805	Ulm-Austerlitz Campaign
Troops Involved		
France		
	6,000 losses	Commanded by Napoleon
Austria	72,000	
	40,000 (30,000 captured) losses	Commanded by Baron Mack von Liebereich
Outcome:		
French victory		

Napoleon was in Paris on 13 September when he received news that Mack's Austrians had crossed the River Inn and were advancing on Munich. A week later, Murat confirmed that Mack had reached Ulm. Significantly, there was no sign of the Russian army heading to link up with the Austrians.

By 25 September, Napoleon had reached Nancy, and the next day he was at Strasbourg. On the same day 40,000 French, under Lannes and Murat left Strasbourg. Their first objective was Freudenstadt and their aim was to entice the Austrians further west. Napoleon did not need to be concerned that the Austrians would take flight and head east, as they seemed rooted to the spot at Ulm.

By 3 October, the French army had reached a line between Stuttgart and Ansbach, with Ney holding the pivotal position at Stuttgart; the armies could now swing around Mack's rear and head for the Danube. On 6 October, the French army was approaching Münster, Donauwörth, Neuburg and Ingolstadt on the River Danube, but still Mack remained stuck at Ulm and showed no intention of reacting. The crossing took place during 6 and 7 October. The French army now pivoted on Augsburg and moves were already underway to seize Landsberg and Memmingen, capturing the Austrian depots and preventing Mack from falling back towards Innsbruck.

The seizure of the crossings over the Rivers Lech and Isar effectively meant that the Russians were out of the equation; they would not reach Mack in time to provide any assistance.

The first real engagement occurred at Wertingen on 8 October, when nine battalions of Austrians were swept aside by Murat and Lannes. By the night of 11 October, Bernadotte was within 6 miles (9.5 km) of Munich and Napoleon now engaged Murat to close the trap and strike at Mack with the minimum delay.

The day, however, did not all go according to plan as far as the French were concerned. Murat was advancing towards Ulm on the south bank of the River Danube, sure that Mack's main army was directly ahead of him. Consequently, he ordered Ney to bring two of his three divisions over the Danube and join him. This left Dupont very exposed and when he found himself facing 25,000 Austrians, including 10,000 cavalry some distance to the east of Michelsberg Heights, he was in a serious situation.

In typical style, however, Dupont attacked the dithering Austrians and his 4,000 men held on to the village of Albeck (or Haslach) all day, before retiring to Brenz after dusk. Mack's army had missed the opportunity to break out, sever Napoleon's supply and communications and link up with the Russians.

Soult was now at Landsberg and Napoleon, with Murat, Lannes, Ney, Davoôt and the Imperial Guard at Augsburg. Napoleon ordered that 'not one is to escape' as the French began to march west.

By the morning of 13 October, Napoleon was near Ulm and as the day developed several engagements of varying size were fought. At Albeck Murat joined Dupont to see off a determined attack by Werneck's corps. This was achieved only after Ney had stormed the Elchingen Bridge against 9,000 Austrians. They had partially demolished the structure, but, under fire, Ney personally organised the repairs and then stormed the town. Any chance Mack had had of escaping now looked doomed.

Archduke Ferdinand had seen enough, and despite orders from Mack he broke out of the ring with 6,000 men. His cavalry force was ruthlessly pursued by Murat and only a handful managed to reach Heidenheim, where Werneck had retreated after his engagement with Murat and Dupont.

The climax of the operations took place on 15 October. Ney stormed the Michelsberg field work, allowing the French artillery to be set up to bombard Ulm itself. Mack sued for a temporary armistice. He offered to surrender in eight days if the Russians had not arrived. Napoleon refused and offered him five days' respite in the certain knowledge that Kutusov's Russians were still 100 miles (160 km) away.

On 19 October, Werneck was forced to surrender to Murat at Trochtelfingen. The French general then moved on to Neustadt, where he accepted the capitulation of 12,000 Austrians. In a day, he had taken 20,000 prisoners, including seven generals, 200 officers and 120 guns.

With these two new disasters, Mack offered his surrender on 20 October. Some 27,000 Austrian troops piled their arms and Austria was effectively out of the war in just twenty-six days. Ulm was a stunning victory and bought at the lowest possible cost in terms of French casualties.

Only 10,000 Austrians made good their escape from the disaster. As for Mack, he was later court-martialled and sentenced to twenty years' imprisonment.

Napoleon could be more than pleased with the results of the 'Ulm Manoeuvre' as it has become known. What he could not have known on 21 October was that his fleet was being destroyed at Trafalgar by Nelson on the very same day Mack surrendered.

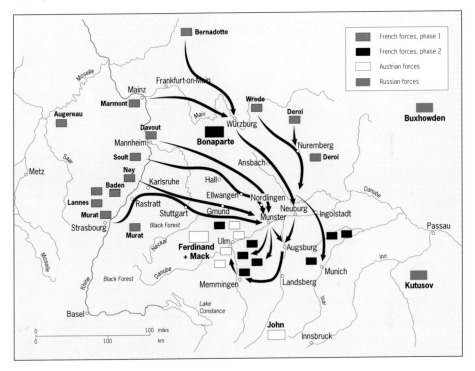

The Battle of Trafalgar (1805)

Battle Name	Dates	Campaign
Trafalgar	21 October 1805	
Troops Involved		
France/Spain	33 vessels	
	14,000 losses	Commanded by Villeneuve/Gravina
Britain	27 vessels	
	1,500 losses	Commanded by Nelson
Outcome:		
British victory		

Napoleon's naval strategy relied on great cunning and the supposed ignorance of the British. By March 1805 he had assembled some 160,000 men for his long-awaited invasion of England. The only thing that stood in his way was the Royal Navy.

British vessels controlled the English Channel and were effectively blockading all of the French ports. In order to slip across the Channel and deliver the troops onto English soil, these enemy ships would have to be decoyed.

The first part of the plan required the French fleet to escape from Brest and Toulon, join up with the Spanish (sailing out of Cadiz and Cartagena) and head for the West Indies. It was assumed that the British would follow, then the Franco-Spanish fleet would head back to the Channel and deal with British vessels which might seek to disrupt the invasion.

The plan was bold and many things could go wrong; perhaps the worst miscalculations concerned the tactical and strategic genius of the enemy commander, Horatio Nelson.

The plan got underway on 29 March 1805 when the French commander of the fleet, Admiral Pierre de Villeneuve, slipped out of Toulon and headed for Gibraltar. Nelson though tthat he would be heading for the Mediterranean and sailed to Sardinia to ambush him. The Frenchman had, in fact, passed Gibraltar and was at loose in the Atlantic, already with a good lead. Before committing himself to pursuit, Nelson made sure that Cornwallis (who was protecting the approaches to the Channel) was made aware of Villeneuve's escape, and he then sped off after the Frenchman.

Villeneuve had already rendezvoused with Gravina's Spanish fleet, which had sailed out of Cadiz and was heading back towards the Channel. Nelson, meanwhile, owing to poor intelligence reports, was heading for Trinidad. When he realised what had happened, he despatched a fast boat to the Channel (which overtook the Franco-Spanish fleet). As a result Calder's fleet, which had been blockading Brest, was able to engage the enemy off Cape Finisterre on 22 July. Although the action was indecisive, the French invasion plan had been contested and the Franco-Spanish fleet put into Corunna and Ferrol.

Nelson was still determined to tackle the fleet and deal with it, and the dangers it presented, in a single action. His opportunity came on 19 October 1805, when Villeneuve sailed out of Cadiz, heading for the Mediterranean. He had been roundly admonished by Napoleon for his lack of activity and now proposed to raid the supply convoys *en route* to Malta and then put in at Toulon. Little did he know that Nelson was waiting beyond the horizon and that he intended to prevent him from reaching the Mediterranean.

Nelson had mustered twenty-seven vessels for the task; they would face a combined Franco-Spanish force of thirty-three. At around 0600, the two fleets spotted one another off Cape Trafalgar. Nelson had already formulated his battle tactics, which involved attacking the Franco-Spanish fleet at right angles. From the outset Villeneuve realised that he could not even get to Cadiz without a fight, but he had not expected the disaster which was about to overwhelm his fleet.

Nelson's flagship, HMS *Victory*, led the first column of vessels and Collingwood's HMS *Royal*

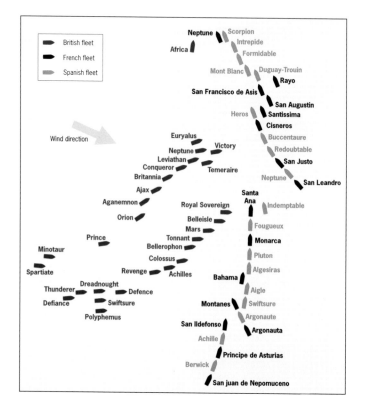

Sovereign the second. Collingwood broke through the enemy column at around 1200, closely followed by Nelson and three other ships, which made straight for Villeneuve's flagship, the *Bucentaure*. Quickly, superior British naval skills and gunnery did their work, cutting the Franco-Spanish fleet into digestible pockets of resistance.

By 1600 around fifteen Franco-Spanish ships had been crippled or forced to strike their colours. The *Bucentaure* and Villeneuve were captured, but as the Victory closed in on the *Redoubtable*, a French sniper shot Nelson and mortally wounded him.

The French Admiral Dumanoir attempted to help the main fleet with his ships at the head of the column, but lost two vessels and fled. The Spaniard Gravina (who was badly wounded) did what he could at the end of the fleet. When the French 74-gun ship *Achille* blew up at 1730, however, it marked the end of the resistance. Villeneuve had lost eighteen vessels and with them Napoleon's naval power, a blow from which it would never fully recover. The British, however, were subjected to a terrible battering from a storm that night which claimed all but four of the prize vessels still afloat. More cripplingly, they had lost Nelson, although his death ensured that Napoleon would never be able to invade England.

Nelson will forever be remembered for his signal that day: 'England expects that every man will do his duty' and for the command, 'Engage the enemy more closely.'

The Battle of Austerlitz (1805)

Battle Name	Dates	Campaign
Austerlitz (Battle of the 3 Emperors)	2 December 1805	Ulm-Austerlitz Campaign
Troops Involved		
France	66,800–73,200	
	9,000 losses	Commanded by Napoleon
Austria and Russia	85,400–85,700	
	15,000 losses (+ 11,000–12,000 captured	Commanded by Kutusov/Tsar Alexander I/Francis I
Outcome: French victory		

As early as 21 November, Napoleon had chosen the ground at which he would turn and face the Austro-Russian army, overlooking the village of Pratzen, with the towns of Krenowitz and Austerlitz in the distance. He decided that he would allow the allies to occupy the Pratzen Heights. His right would be weak and his left strong, with the bulk of his army hidden around Zurlan, a peak of 850 ft (260 m). At the right moment he would unleash his army against the enemy on Pratzen Heights and fall on their rear.

As far as the allies were concerned, they believed that Napoleon would not offer battle until he had reached Vienna. The Frenchman was happy to let them remain deluded and simply observed the snail-like allied advance, willing them to close. On 30 November, he gave the orders to evacuate the Pratzen Heights and lure the allies westwards. They began to occupy the exact positions he had anticipated between 1500 on 30 November and 0200 on 1 December.

Meanwhile, the French had massed some 60,000 men and were ready to move into position. Davoût occupied the Raigern Abbey. As far as the allies were concerned, the French left was thinly held, as was the line along the Goldbach Brook. The allies proposed that Docturov would hit Tellnitz at 0700 on 2 December, Langeron would advance between Tellnitz and Sokolnitz, and Prschibitschewski and Kollowrat would take Sokolnitz Castle. Once this had been achieved, Kienmaier would move to block the Vienna–Brünn road and Bagration would tackle the French left, linking with Kollowrat. Constantine's troops would be held back in reserve, to be thrown in where needed.

Matters were delayed, however, probably because of translation problems and the fact that the allied administration was not very professional, a factor which resurfaced and confused matters later.

At 0630 on 2 December, the French left and centre units began to occupy their positions and just after Buxhöwden threw Kienmaier at Tellnitz. After an hour's fighting, the village remained in French hands, despite the fact that Soult had sent cavalry in against Buxhöwden's right flank, which were driven off. At 0830, Docturov's Russians hit Legrand on the Goldbach Brook and forced him away. Buxhöwden

A detail from Bacler d'Albe's painting showing Napoleon inspecting his troops on the night of December 12 1805. The troops are bivouacked on the Pratzen plateau near Austerliltz.

now halted, waiting for Langeron to take Sokolnitz. Langeron had been held up by Lichtenstein, who had himself been blocked by Kollowrat.

Davoût's men had not left Raigern Abbey until around 0630. He then marched, as per orders, for Turas, but new orders directed him to march for Sokolnitz as soon as possible. Fraint's men moved to assist Legrand and managed to regain Tellnitz. Docturov and Kienmaier counter-attacked and retook the village but they were again ordered to halt by Buxhöwden.

By 0900, Langeron and Prschibitschewski had taken Sokolnitz and the castle, supported by allied artillery but by 1000 Davoût had retaken the area, after having marched north. The battle, however, was not being decided on this part of the front and at just after 0830 Napoleon had launched Soult at the unsuspecting allies.

St Hilaire headed for the high ground above Pratzen and Vandamme headed for the peak to the north of the village. Kollowrat had been following Prschibitschewski on the left, with Miloradovich on the right, also sending two battalions into Pratzen itself. These were immediately overwhelmed. Kutusov was at hand and ordered Miloradovich to face his right flank and for the Austrians to form up on Miloradovich's left. For a moment St Hilaire's leading units were stopped, then his second brigade emerged, supported by artillery. Kollowrat charged, was driven back and then charged again, this time supported by Russians. Vandamme then settled the issue by sweeping through Miloradovich's position, whose men promptly fled, followed by the

Austrians. Vandamme now swung around the peak.

Along the Olmütz road, Lannes carefully engaged Bagration, waiting for Murat and Bernadotte to form up beside him and fill the line towards Vandamme. Bagration was no keener to engage; he waited for Lichtenstein to reach his positions alongside him. Constantine, however, saw the group and hurried forward, leading the Russian Guard. He had, in his haste, committed the entire allied reserve, possessing now the village of Blasowitz and for now protecting Bagration's left flank.

Lichtenstein was now forced to work his way around Constantine to get to his ordered position. No sooner had he got in place than he was attacked by the French cavalry. His own cavalry beat them off and gave chase, straight into Lannes' infantry which had formed squares. With that, Kutusov told him to move south and he complied, leaving half of his men with Bagration.

Meanwhile, on the allied left, Langeron and Prschibitschewski were still fighting with Davoût for possession of Sokolnitz. The area changed hands several times and remarkably, given the allies' 400 per cent manpower advantage in this region of the battlefield, they made no progress either at Sokolnitz or at Tellnitz.

In the centre, the Russian Guard found itself unsupported, partly as a result of Lichtenstein's movement and the attack being launched by Soult. Rivaud's French stormed and took Blasowitz; the Russian Guard counter-attacked, but was brought to a halt and badly mauled by Rivaud and Caffarelli.

Kutusov ordered the Russian Guard to the plateau, but now they came under severe pressure from Vandamme who was firmly established and aggressive. In a matter of minutes, the Russian Guard was streaming back towards Krzenowitz. A counter-attack from the Russian Guard cavalry shattered Vandamme's over-exposed troops and the French advance here was stopped.

Bernadotte had been ordered to move up on Vandamme's left. Bessiere, at the head of the Imperial Guard cavalry, saved Vandamme after several charges. In the ensuing chaos, Lichtenstein was also swept away as Rivaud and Drouet (Bernadotte's corps) advanced to the edge of the Pratzen Plateau, watching the Russians streaming through Austerlitz.

Meanwhile, in the north,

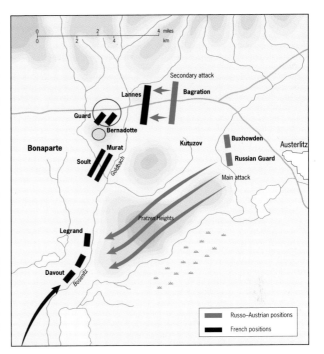

matters had not gone well for Bagration. He had tried to turn Lannes' flank and had advanced as far as Bosenitz, but he was stopped dead by artillery. The Russian artillery, however, opened up and ripped through the French ranks until Lannes counter-attacked. Despite numerous allied cavalry charges Caffarelli could not be stopped. Nansouty now charged on Murat's orders and soon after

Bagration's cavalry, and those which Lichtenstein had left him, were routing towards Austerlitz.

Bagration began a fighting retreat towards Posoritz, holding off Murat, but a determined all-arms attack by Lannes broke the Russians, who routed as far as Raussnitz. Under cover of darkness, he then headed south and retreated via Austerlitz.

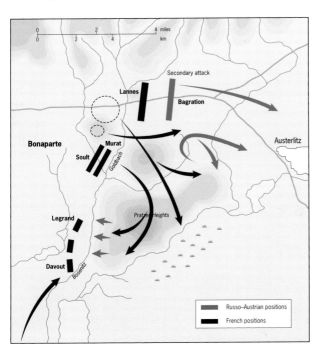

At 1300 St Hilaire attacked towards Sokolnitz Castle. Vandamme assailed Augeld, with elements of Legrand's, Oudinot's and Beaumont's forces filling the gap between. The Imperial Guard, around this time, reached St Anthony's Chapel. At the same time Davoût launched an all-out assault; the allies were trapped, only able to retreat between the ponds of Satschen and Menitz. Thousands ran the gauntlet and thousands fell. Kienmaier did his best to cover the flight, and Docturov tried to make a last stand at Tellnitz but was swept away by sheer weight of numbers and plummeting morale.

Austerlitz had been an allied disaster, fought on Napoleon's battlefield. The French were never seriously threatened by a chaotic and inefficient allied force which lacked the guts to fight.

The Battles of Buenos Aires (1806 and 1807)

Battle Name	Dates	Campaign
Buenos Aires	25 June 1806 and	
	5 July 1807	
Troops Involved (1806)		
Britain	1,500	
	1,500 captured	Commanded by Popham/Beresford
Spain	Unknown	
	Losses unknown	Commanded by Pueyreddon
Outcome:		
Spanish victory		
Troops Involved (1807)		
Britain	8,000	
	2,500 losses	Commanded by Whitelock
Spain	Unknown	
	Losses unknown	Commanded by Liniers
Outcome:		
Spanish victory		

The British made two unsanctioned attacks on Spanish-held South America; both commanders would later face reprimands from the British government.

Following the capture of the Cape of Good Hope, Admiral Popham gathered a scratch force, led by Beresford, to strike at Spanish-held Buenos Aires. The invasion fleet arrived off the South American coast on 8 June and on 25 June the expedition anchored off Point Quelmy à Ponichiou. The engagement opened at Reducción, against Spanish infantry backed by 2,000 cavalry, but the Spanish positions were stormed and on 27 June the Rio Chuelo was forced and Buenos Aires surrendered.

By the beginning of August, the Spanish had recovered and began massing in the area. Under Pueyreddon, at least 1,500 Spanish engaged Beresford and were initially beaten, but by 10

The Battle of Buenos Aires. Fighting in the streets as British infantry attempt to storm the city.

August he marched on the city and on the following day Buenos Aires fell and the British surrendered. The prisoners were to remain in Spanish hands until Whitelock invaded nearly a year later. Popham was to be reprimanded and replaced by Stirling.

In 1807, after taking the city of Montevideo for the loss of 600 men (1,200 Spanish killed or wounded and 2,000 captured) some 8,000 British began the march on Buenos Aires, reaching Reducción on 1 July 1807.

Montevideo had been captured with some dash by Auchmuty, but the Buenos Aires expedition was led by Whitelock, a less than brilliant commander as the outcome was later to prove. The British crossed the River Chuelo and Whitelock called on the governor to surrender; the response was an attack on the British picket lines. The assault was arranged, therefore, for 5 July. Auchmuty would take the Plaza de Toros and four other groups would storm the streets with the target being Rio de la Plata.

The Spanish resisted strongly, holding the rooftops of the houses in the city and showering the British with musket fire, stones, bricks and grenades. Auchmuty's troops took their objective, as well as 600 prisoners and 32 guns. Elsewhere, the other columns were being badly mauled. The left wing was stalled and Crawford's troops cut off, and he was forced to surrender.

Whilst Whitelock pressed the Plaza de Toros and the Residencia, much of the rest of the city remained in Spanish hands. On 6 July Liniers offered Whitelock a way out: in return for the British prisoners, he would evacuate the city. Whitelock grabbed the offer, but when he returned to England he was cashiered. Even twenty-five years later he would not find many men content to be in his company.

The Battle of Maida (1806)

Battle Name	Dates	Campaign
Maida (St Eufemio)	4 July 1806	
Troops Involved		
France	c8,000	
	4,000 killed or wounded	Commanded by Reynier
Britain	4,795	
	c326 losses	Commanded by Stuart
Outcome:		
British victory		

On 1 July 1806 a composite force under Stuart began landing in the Bay of St Eufemio on the coast of Italy. The plan was to support anti-French elements in the new French kingdom of Naples.

Barely had the British troops landed, than the fleet opened fire on the French-held castle of St Almanthea, which was quickly reduced, with 900 prisoners falling into British hands. Nine battalions with supporting artillery headed inland, through the forest, towards Maida, sweeping aside a blocking move by a French regiment which netted another 200 prisoners.

Stuart issued a proclamation inviting the Neapolitans to rise up against the French, a move which led to the creation of the Calabrian Free Corps. Meanwhile, Reynier, who was based at Reggio, was en route to intercept the invaders and the rebels. He took up positions at Maida with 4,000 infantry supported by cavalry and guns and awaited the arrival of reinforcements under Monteleone, which would give him a total force of some 8,000 men.

Stuart's first objective was to prevent the two French forces linking. Consequently, on 4 July, he marched for Maida hoping to get there ahead of Monteleone. In this he failed and Monteleone took up positions on the French right.

The two armies closed, with the French quickly moving forward as Stuart's troops deployed into line. Kemp's light infantry spread out whilst the British artillery began to open fire. Kemp held the right wing and engaged the French at 100 yards. To his left was Acland's brigade and to their left were a provisional battalion of grenadiers and the 27th Foot.

MacLeod's Highlanders stove in the French line held by the 42nd Regiment (Imperial Guard) and Kemp's light infantry charged as the French wavered and fled. Acland now reinforced with the 78th and the 81st and swept the French left wing aside.

Three hundred French dragoons tried to stem the rout, but they were slaughtered by steady British volleys. Reynier's right and centre withdrew in good order and the British pursued him for 3 miles (5 km) before stopping. Reynier retreated towards Crotona, still shadowed by the Calabrians and the Highlanders. Thousands of mountainmen flocked to aid the struggle against the French and this almost forgotten campaign was to continue for another two years.

By 1808, Reynier had regained control of most of southern Italy. Notable other engagements include the siege of Castle Scylla, which fell to Reynier in mid-January 1808 after a long and gallant defence under Robertson.

The Battle of Maida.

The Battles of Jena and Austerstadt (1806)

Battle Name	Dates	Campaign
Austerstadt	14 October 1806	Prussian Campaign Jena Campaign
Troops Involved		
France	27,000–28,800	
	7,000 losses	Commanded by Davoût
Prussia	63,000–65,000	
	25,000 losses	Commanded by Brunswick
Outcome: French victory		
Jena	14 October 1806	Prussian Campaign Jena Campaign
France	46,000–96,000	
	5,000 losses	Commanded by Napoleon
Prussia	38,000–53,000	
	25,000 losses	Commanded by Hohenlohe/Rüchel
Outcome: French victory		

When the Fourth Coalition (Britain, Prussia, Russia and Portugal) was formed against France in 1806, the Grande Armée was in southern Germany and Napoleon planned to invade Prussia. If Napoleon could strike quickly, the other allies would not have sufficient time to come to Prussia's aid before it was too late.

Napoleon could field a force of around 180,000, against which the Prussians could muster some 130,000. Napoleon launched his offensive from

Bavaria on 8 October 1806, advancing on a front of some 30 miles (48 km) in three columns, screened by cavalry. Soult, Ney and the Bavarians occupied the right, Lannes and Augereau the left and the centre consisted of the Imperial Guard, Bernadotte and Davoût. Even travelling through the Thuringian Forest, the French were covering some 15 miles (24 km) per day.

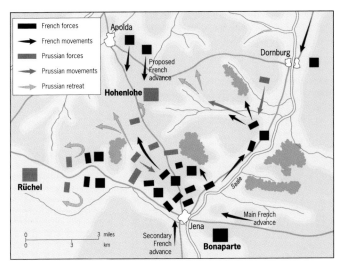

Napoleon had planned to bring the Prussians to battle near Leipzig, but they had not deployed in the area. The first contact was made at Saalfeld (10 October) when Lannes defeated a small Prussian force. On 13 October, however, he encountered a larger army at Jena.

Napoleon now ordered the whole army to head west and support Lannes, arriving himself at 1600. He believed that this was the main Prussian army, but, in fact, he was mistaken. Brunswick and the main Prussian force was actually heading for Auerstadt, some 15 miles (24 km) away, and what Lannes had encountered was a large covering force under Hohenlohe.

Still labouring under the assumption that this was the main Prussian army, Napoleon gradually began filtering troops into the area (they had been marching through the night and into the following morning). The first to come in support of Lannes was the Imperial Guard at 1000 on 14 October, by which time Augereau, Soult, Ney and the reserve cavalry were close. Napoleon had around 80,000 men at his immediate disposal.

He now despatched Davoût and Bernadotte on what he believed to be an enveloping manoeuvre around the Prussians. At Jena, Napoleon organised the line with Lannes in the centre, Augereau on the left and Soult on the right and sent them forward against the Prussians. Hohenlohe had just 33,000 men at this time and was sending desperate messages to Rüchel for assistance; Rüchel's 15,000 men were in the Weimow area.

In the meantime, as Lannes, Augereau and Soult advanced, Ney decided to launch his own attack on Hohenlohe against Napoleon's orders. His cavalry charged at the Prussians and was nearly surrounded. Napoleon had to quickly deploy Lannes and the reserve French cavalry to save him. His plans, for the time being, were ruined, but fortunately Hohenlohe failed to take advantage of the situation. His hopes seemed to have been resting on the arrival of Rüchel, so he chose to fight a delaying action. His infantry stood defiantly, and were shot to pieces for some two hours whilst the rest of the French army reorganised itself.

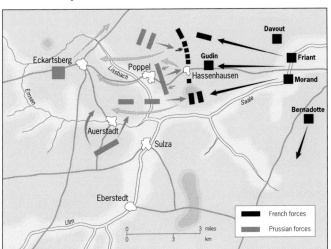

Napoleon finally got his troops in order before 1500 and immediately launched a full-scale attack on the Prussians. Hohenlohe had welcomed the arrival of Rüchel an hour before, but even together they could not withstand the assault. Soon after the advance got underway, the whole of the Prussian army was in full retreat, having suffered horrendous casualties and losing thousands of men as they surrendered to the French.

Whilst Napoleon was concentrating on what he 37

still believed to be the main Prussian army, Davoût had, in fact, contacted the larger Prussian force under Brunswick. He and Bernadotte had been sent on the enveloping march, but Bernadotte had actually marched south and did not become involved in either of the battles of 14 October. Davoût's corps of around 27,000 faced Brunswick's force of up to 65,000. Luckily for Davoût, the Prussian attacks were very poorly co-ordinated and he was able to defeat each of the assaults. So solid and determined was his defence that he was able to take the initiative and start an offensive at around 1100, when he broke the back of the Prussian resolve.

By this time, Brunswick and Mollendorf (his second in command) had both been mortally wounded. The Prussians found themselves commanded by their king, Frederick William III. He promptly ordered a retreat, but not until after his troops had suffered at least 13,000 casualties and a similar number captured. Davoût's corps had suffered proportionately heavy casualties, but was still intact and pressing the Prussian retreat when Bernadotte finally arrived on the battlefield. His sole contribution was to take over from the exhausted men of Davoût's corps in the pursuit.

With these two defeats the Prussian army had been shattered; and the country lay at Napoleon's mercy. He marched into Berlin on 24 October and the last Prussian army, under Blücher, surrendered at Lübeck on 24 November. It was seven years before the 'invincible' Prussian army could face Napoleon on the battlefield again.

The Battle of Eylau (1807)

Battle Name	Dates	Campaign
Eylau	8 February 1807	Prussian Campaign Jena and Friedland Campaign
Troops Involved		
France	71,000	
	25,000 losses	Commanded by Napoleon
Russia	67,000	
	15,000 losses	Commanded by Bennigsen
Outcome:		
Draw		

The Prussian army had all but collapsed after the defeats at Jena and Auerstadt, King Frederick William had fled to Russia and Napoleon was heading for Warsaw. All that stood before him was Bennigsen and remnants of the Prussian army, supported by a Russian army under the aged Kamenskoi.

Bennigsen had some 35,000 men at Pultusk on 26 December 1806, when Lannes and Davoût attacked them. The engagement was indecisive, Bennigsen losing some 5,000 for the loss of 8,000 French. Another engagement at Golymin between Murat and Augereau had been similarly indecisive and these two expensive battles convinced Napoleon that the campaigning season was over.

Poland was not the ideal resting place for an army in winter; supplies were, at best, unreliable – not that the French supply system had ever been anything but amateur. As it was, Kamenskoi was assassinated on 9 January and the full control of the Russo-Prussian army fell squarely on Bennigsen. He was clearly determined to make the best use of this opportunity and by the end of January was making attacks on the outlying French positions. Ney was immediately accused of having provoked the Russians during one of his many forays to pick up supplies by raiding, but the enemy's movement did seem to offer Napoleon an opportunity, perhaps, to deal with them decisively before the spring.

He first had to send couriers to the various corps' commanders, telling them to concentrate. Unfortunately, a copy of the orders and attack plans fell into the hands of Russian Cossacks, who immediately passed them on to Bennigsen. This information allowed him to escape from an indecisive battle fought at Ionkovo on 3 February.

With Napoleon in pursuit, Bennigsen turned to face him at Eylau on 6 February. He had some 67,000 men and 460 cannon; Napoleon had just 45,000 men and 200 guns. Close by, however, were Ney and Davoût, with a further 26,000 men. Bennigsen could only rely on 9,000 Prussian troops (under Lestocq), but these were engaged in operations against Ney.

On the afternoon of 7 February, Napoleon closed on Eylau. The battle began by accident when the French baggage train moved into Eylau, oblivious of the fact that it was held by the Russians. After the town had changed hands several times, Napoleon found himself in possession by nightfall.

Weather conditions overnight and early the following morning did not augur well for a major engagement. Napoleon was, in any case, facing the enemy without the troops of Davoût or Ney. It was his intention to hold and counter any enemy attack until such time that he was reinforced by the other two corps. Soult occupied the left, Augereau the right, with Murat's cavalry held in reserve to the rear.

The predominantly infantry line of Bennigsen was supported on each flank by cavalry, but he had placed two large batteries of guns in the centre to soften up the French or break up any attacks. As it was, Bennigsen's hand was forced at around 0900 when Soult launched a spoiling attack. This convinced him to throw his own troops at the French left, supported by the massed artillery. Although the Russians had a clear superiority, the French inflicted far higher casualties on the densely packed Russian columns.

Whilst the struggle continued, the advance units of Davoût's corps began to arrive; Bennigsen immediately moved to hold them in order to finish off Soult. In desperation, Napoleon threw Augereau's corps into a frontal attack on Bennigsen's centre. By now the driving snow was causing heavy casualties from friendly fire compounded by the fact that they marched straight at a 70-gun enemy battery.

Things looked utterly bleak at 1030; Augereau's corps had been shredded and the Russians were in full advance in the centre of the battlefield. Soult was still holding, but only just. Nearly all the regiments in Augereau's corps had been decimated; one of the 14th failed to retire with the rest of the troops and was engulfed by the Russian steam-roller.

Napoleon had but one option,

which was to commit his cavalry under Murat. The 10,700 men had to turn the tide or the battle would be lost. With Murat at the head, this was arguably one of the most glorious cavalry charges in military history. Murat's men swept through the Russian infantry, reformed in the rear and overwhelmed the Russian battery that had slaughtered Augereau's troops. Although Murat lost 1,500 men, Napoleon's army was saved.

A total French victory was snatched from Napoleon's grasp by the timely arrival of Lestocq and his Prussians. Finally Ney arrived and began an assault on the left, but by now darkness was closing in. The encounter had been extremely bloody, but inconclusive. If Napoleon wished to claim a victory and success he could; he had, at least, stopped Bennigsen's Russian winter offensive.

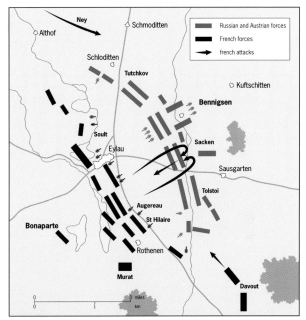

Napoleon and his staff at Eylau.

The Siege of Danzig (1807)

Battle Name	Dates	Campaign
Danzig	18 March–27 May 1807	Prussian Campaign
		Jena and Friedland Campaign
Troops Involved		
France	20,000–47,900	
	Unknown losses	Commanded by Lefebvre
Prussia	16,000 (plus 8,000 Russians)	
	Prussian losses possibly 9,000 1,500 Russian losses	Commanded by Kalkreuth/Kamenskoi
Outcome: French victory		

The continued Russian occupation of the port of Danzig offered the threat of a sea-borne reinforcement of the city and a potential counter-offensive. Equally, Danzig contained vital supplies of great use to the French. Napoleon therefore ordered Lefebvre to begin a siege on 11 February, although it was not until 18 March–2 April that a full investment of the city was completed.

The first parallel (siege entrenchment) was completed opposite the bastion called Hagelsberg on 2 April, and the second was constructed between 11 and 14 April. The latter construction coincided with a sortie by the garrison on 13 April, which was driven back after the Prussians had gained the French trenches. Another similar sortie took place on 29 April. By far the most dangerous threat to the French siege came on 10 May, when a Russian fleet, supported by the Royal Navy, landed 8,000 Russian troops, under Kamenskoi, at the Prussian outpost of Neufahrwasser, on the western side of the mouth of the River Vistula.

The French had occupied Hulm Island, which lay between Neufahrwasser and Danzig, which dissuaded the Russians from making an immediate attack. By the time they did so on 15 May, Lannes had moved up to assist Lefebvre. The four Russian columns fell on Schramm and Gardamme, holding the Frische-Nehrung (to the north-east of Danzig). The fighting was intense, but Kamenskoi was repulsed, leaving 1,500 dead, wounded or captured and by 25 May he had evacuated Neufahrwasser. Kalkreuth had failed to support the Russians; had he done so, the fate of Danzig and its garrison may have been different.

On 20 May, before the Russians withdrew, Kalkreuth launched another sortie which destroyed some of the French trenches, but he was repelled and forced back into the city. On 21 May, Mortier's 12,900 arrived to reinforce Lefebvre and Lannes. Kalkreuth now knew that the assault on Hagelsberg was inevitable and that it was certain that Danzig would fall.

The French batteries were nearing completion, which meant that Danzig would be nearly levelled before the French assault. Kalkreuth earnestly wished to avoid this and any unnecessary bloodshed in his gallant garrison.

Lefebvre was also aware of the realities and when he approached Kalkreuth under a flag of truce on 22 May, a deal was struck. On 27 May, the garrison marched out and headed for Pillau with full military honours. Over the next few days the other Prussian outposts also surrendered. Napoleon had Danzig and had released the three corps that had been tied up at the siege.

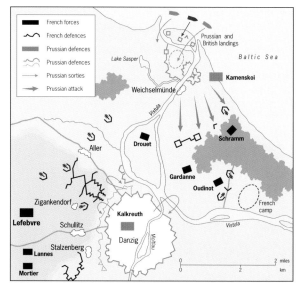

The Battle of Heilsberg (1807)

Battle Name	Dates	Campaign
Heilsberg	10 June 1807	Jena and Friedland Campaign
Troops Involved		
France	50,000	
	10,000 losses	Commanded by Soult/Lannes
Russia	80,000	
	8,000 losses	Commanded by Bennigsen
Outcome:		
Indecisive		

In mid-April Napoleon moved his headquarters to Finkenstein and it seemed possible that the Russians would attempt to relieve the garrison at Danzig. As it was the attack was ineffective. Napoleon knew he held the upper hand with 220,000 men against Bennigsen's 115,000, but despite the numerical disadvantage, it was the Russians who moved first, on 5 June when their infantry swarmed through Heilsberg to attack the French at Spanden and Lomitten. These attacks were a ruse and the main force fell on Ney at Deppen.

Napoleon sent reinforcements and by the end of the day the Russians were falling back. The Emperor now contrived to fool Bennigsen by allowing a despatch, ordering Davoût to attack the Russian rear with 40,000 men, to fall into his hands. His real target was the Russian camp at Heilsberg.

On 8 June, Napoleon decided the time was ripe for a counteroffensive and he was determined to hit the enemy hard before they could retreat to Königsberg, it was understood that they were already falling back to Güttstadt.

Bennigsen had intended to face Napoleon at Güttstadt, but he was unconvinced by the strength of his position and fell back to Heilsberg. Napoleon's troops began to close on Güttstadt, with Soult's corps engaging Kamenskoi's rear guards and Murat

contacting Bagration at Glottau. Platou's Cossacks covered the withdrawal over the River Alle, burning the bridges as they went. By the evening of 9 June, Soult had occupied Altkirch and Davoût had taken the left bank of the River Alle near Güttstadt, which now quartered Ney, Murat and the Imperial Guard.

Bennigsen had taken up strong positions on either side of the River Alle at Heilsberg. Murat found him first and managed to ease the Russians out of Lanau, but he was stopped short of Bevernick by Russian artillery. With Soult's help Bevernick was taken at 1530, but Murat was counterattacked by Russian cavalry, who scattered the French. The latter were only saved by two infantry regiments and a handful of guns.

Soult now attacked the left-bank positions, but the position favoured the Russians and casualties were high. Napoleon was determined to beat the enemy and launched Lannes at 2200; he was heavily defeated and lost 2,284 men.

Heavy Russian artillery fire prevented new French attacks on 11 June, but by nightfall Bennigsen was in retreat and at 0400 on 12 June French troops took the heights of Heilsberg unopposed.

Napoleon did not have another chance to beat the Russians until they met at Friedland on 14 June.

The Battle of Friedland (1807)

Battle Name	Dates	Campaign
Friedland	13–14 June 1807	Prussian Campaign
		Jena and Friedland Campaign
Troops Involved		
France	80,000	
	8,000–10,000 losses	Commanded by Napoleon
Russia	60,000	
	20,000–25,000 losses	Commanded by Bennigsen
Outcome:		
French victory		

After the indecisive and costly battle of Heilsberg, Napoleon decided to withdraw and threaten the Russian flank. Bennigsen retired toward Friedland, his forward supply base and the River Alle. Napoleon followed, despatching troops to cut him off from Königsberg, where he believed the Russians were retreating. Instead, he received word that Bennigsen was concentrating his forces around Friedland on 13 June. By the morning of 14 June Napoleon was severely outnumbered, but troops were arriving all morning. Without waiting for Murat and Davoût to move up, he decided to launch an attack that day, the anniversary of Marengo.

Bennigsen had not chosen his ground well. If pressed, the entire army would have to cross the River Alle at Friedland, no doubt with the French hard on their heels. The Russians occupied a vast 4-mile (6.5-km) arc with their backs to the river; if disaster struck, the whole army could be lost.

Napoleon waited as long as he dared without running the risk of the Russians shipping across the River Alle during the night. At 1730 a preliminary bombardment signalled the first assault. It was to be made by Ney on the Russian left. As the Russians were forced back to the river, the French came under fire from batteries sited on the opposite bank; Ney's men were stopped for the time being.

Napoleon now committed Victor to attack in support of Ney, falling on the Russian cavalry which had just been sent in to support Bagration's left. By now, a mass of Russian troops were streaming back towards the single bridge. A remarkable feat from Sénarmont (Victor's artillery commander) snarled the Russian cohesion. He leap-frogged his batteries forward, bombarding the milling host and freeing up Ney to continue his advance.

Bennigsen tried to relieve the pressure on his left by launching his right and centre at the French. The attacks faltered and he threw in the Imperial Guard, again to no avail. Luckily for the Russians, a ford was found to the north of Friedland which served most of his right wing, but by 1100 the battle was over and only a Russian battery on the opposite bank of the River Alle covered the disordered rout. Bennigsen had narrowly avoided complete disaster, but on 19 June the Russians sued for peace.

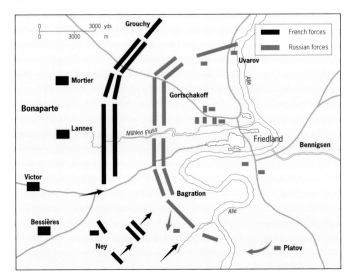

The Seige of Copenhagen (1807)

In 1806 a British expeditionary force was organised to seize the Danish fleet before the French could claim it for themselves. Technically, Denmark was neutral, but the French had convinced her to cease trade with Great Britain. In order to pre-empt any decision by the Danes to join the French, it was proposed to strike and eliminate the threat.

Twenty-seven ships of the line and ninety other vessels would convey Carthcart's 17,000 men to blockade, but not assault, the Danish capital of Copenhagen. Carthcart would be supported by 8,000 men of the King's German Legion.

Carthcart's force began disembarkation on 16 August at Vedbeck, halfway between Copenhagen and Elsinore. Operations began at 0500 and an advance was ordered until the early evening. At daybreak on 17 August Carthcart began moving on Copenhagen. There were only minor skirmishes on the first full day of operations and by 18 August the Danish outposts had retreated and the British were in control of the suburbs of Frederiksborg.

Copenhagen was, at the time, surrounded by no

British artillery bombard Copenhagen.

less than 5 miles (8 km) of earthen ramparts, with some twenty-four bastions. The ramparts were protected by a broad and deep ditch fed by water from a lake. On the north side of the city were the double ramparts of Fredericshavn. The city was therefore ably protected, but Carthcart had no intention of assaulting the defences.

Gradually, the British blockade, both sea and land, began to make its presence felt on the city. On 1 September a summons to surrender was ignored and on the following day the British opened fire. The devastation was immense, but even after a day's lull in the firing, the garrison and population still defied Carthcart. By the time he opened fire again on 4 September, the city was in a pitiful state.

On the morning of 5 September, after at least 2,000 people had died and 500 houses had been levelled, the Danes asked for a 24-hour truce in order to negotiate surrender. Meanwhile, a force of Danish troops had formed up at Kioge, 3_ miles (5.5 km) from Copenhagen. Wellington was sent with the reserve to deal with them. It was a brief and decisive action; the Danish militia were scattered in minutes and 1,100 prisoners taken.

This served to accelerate the surrender of Copenhagen; the price was nineteen ships of the line, fifteen frigates, six brigs and twenty-nine gunboats, the whole of the Danish navy including their ammunition and stores.

Copenhagen was occupied on 7 September and by 20 October all but the Brigade of Guards and the 4th Regiment had re-embarked.

The Battle of Rolica (1808)

Battle Name	Dates	Campaign
Rolica	17 August 1808	Peninsular War
Troops Involved		
France	3,000	
	500 losses	Commanded by Delaborde
Britain	4,000	
	400 losses	Commanded by Wellington
Outcome: British victory		

This was the first major engagement between the British and the French in the Peninsular War. Wellington had landed with a hastily organised army at Mondego Bay around 100 miles (160 km) north of Lisbon. His force, including some 1,700 Portuguese, amounted to some 15,000. Ranged against him were Junot's 25,000, but these were split up into various garrisons around Portugal. His effective moveable troops consisted of just 3,000 men.

Junot's plan was simple: he expected an attack either on Loison's 6,500 or Delaborde's 5,000. Both were little more than 40–50 miles (65–80 km) from Mondego Bay and each would support one another whilst Junot marched up to deal the decisive blow.

Wellington chose the closest French force, that of Delaborde, who was positioned at Alcobaca. The Frenchman fell back to better ground around Rolica as Wellington approached. Wellington split his forces into three columns, the left commanded by Ferguson, and the right by Trant, whilst he retained the centre. Both Ferguson and Trant were despatched to work around Delaborde, who was waiting on a hill blocking the road to Lisbon.

Seeing the enemy advance, Delaborde threw out pickets and then fell back to a better position on a ridge some 300 feet (90 m) high, with steep sides. He intended to stay there until Loison came to his aid.

Wellington regrouped to approach the three gullies which led up the ridge, but the 29th Regiment (under Lake) found itself isolated as the battalions staggered through difficult country. It was the first to come under fire from the ridge and Lake ordered it straight up the gully and into the face of the fire from the French. He was killed and the regiment suffered huge casualties. The French then counter-attacked and for two hours Wellington's lead troops could not make any headway.

When Ferguson's men got around the French rear, the pressure slackened and Delaborde began an

British infantry under French artillery fire. Lynn Holmes

orderly withdrawal. He fell back to the Zambugiera Pass, where the British, in hot pursuit, captured half of his guns. Still unbroken, he then retired to Cazal de Spraga, where he reformed.

Wellington now broke off his pursuit, angered that he had been unable to finish off Delaborde. As for Loison, he was still at least 10 miles (16 km) away to the east. Delaborde, meanwhile, fell back towards Lisbon.

Rolica set Wellington on the path to greater things and, as importantly, gave the army a much-needed boost.

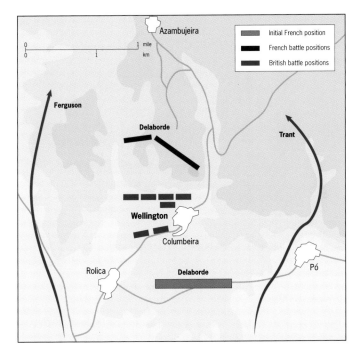

The Battle of Vimeiro (1808)

Battle Name	Dates	Campaign
Vimeiro	21 August 1808	Peninsular War
Troops Involved		
France	13,000	
	2,100 losses	Commanded by Junot
Britain	17,000	
	720 losses	Commanded by Wellington
Outcome:		
British victory		

Just four days after Rolica, Junot marched out of Lisbon to attack the British at Vimeiro. Wellington had been reinforced, but he also had to contend with the political appointment of Sir Harry Burrard as overall commander of the army. Burrard told Wellington that no further offensive actions were to be undertaken until Dalrymple and Moore arrived, both of whom were senior to Wellington.

Wellington had deployed his six brigades and eight guns on a ridge parallel to and south of the River Maceira; a battalion guarded the eastern ridge. Two further brigades and six guns protected the village of Vimeiro, atop a flat hill. During the night of 20 August, reports arrived warning him of Junot's approach, but at dawn there was still no sign of the enemy. At around 0900, the first signs of the approaching Junot were seen on Wellington's left flank.

Wellington immediately transferred three brigades from the western to the eastern ridge and as he watched the French approach, it seemed that the first attack would be made on Vimeiro itself, held by just 900 British infantry. They would face the onslaught of Thomière's 2,400 men supported by cavalry and artillery.

As shrapnel cut into the advancing columns, the French soon came within musket range and the first stopped dead as they desperately turned to form line. The second column of 1,200 men fared no better, although it had suffered fewer casualties in the advance to musket range. With the fleet-footed British infantry firing into the front and sides of the column, it, too, faltered then fell back, leaving seven guns to the enemy.

The French were not finished and launched two more grenadier columns at Vimeiro, but once again they were stopped by the 2,000 British defending the village. One of the columns, however, had worked its way to the south and stormed in. There was intense house-to-house fighting, but despite being outnumbered, the British forced the French out and regrouped.

This was Wellington's opportunity to attack, but he had barely 250 cavalry under Taylor. Although they met with initial success, they galloped ahead of the support and suffered 50 per cent casualties, including Taylor himself.

Another attack by Solignac's 3,000 men on the east ridge failed, as did another by Brennier's 3,200. The latter gained ground but before noon all were fleeing, completely disordered and broken.

The Battle of Sahagun (1808)

Battle Name	Dates	Campaign
Sahagun	21 December 1808	Peninsular War
Troops Involved		
France	8th Dragoons/1st Provincial Chasseurs	
	157 losses	Commanded by Debelle
British	10th and 15th Hussars	
	14 losses	Commanded by Paget
Outcome:		
British victory		

Amongst the tales of the big battalions facing one another across several miles of battlefield, the incredible story of the Battle of Sahagun, by comparison a skirmish, bears consideration.

By mid-October 1808 Moore was advancing on Salamanca with some 30,000 men. He was assured that the Spanish would rise against the French and swell his army. His troops entered Salamanca on 13 November, but on the 28th he heard the shattering news that Napoleon's vast army of 200,000 had slaughtered the Spanish. Baird had been due to join him at Salamanca with 10,000 men, but he still had

French artillery protected by skirmishers. Lynn Holmes

not arrived. Rather than retreat into Portugal, Moore decided to march straight across Napoleon's front and help the Spanish at Madrid. He did not know, at this stage, that the capital had already fallen.

It soon became apparent that there would be no Spanish support and Moore reluctantly headed for safety, hoping to be picked up at Corunna. By 20 December his army, now including Baird, was headed for Mayorga. On the following day Paget's cavalry was in action against the French.

A French cavalry force was discovered at Sahagun, just 9 miles (14.5 km) from the British camp and just before dawn on 21 December the 10th and 15th Hussars rode out to catch them unawares.

The French commander, Debelle, had only placed guards on the main road; these were swiftly overcome and only one trooper escaped to raise the alarm. Within minutes the French cavalry had mounted up, but Paget sent in the 10th under Slade to storm the town whilst he rode around the rear with the 15th to cut the enemy off.

Paget got into position first and charged into Sahagun, the Chasseurs (1st Provisional) were scattered and the 8th Dragoons fled. Although outnumbered two to one Paget lost only fourteen men to 157 French killed, wounded or prisoners.

Not content with this, Paget struck again on 29 December, this time at Benavente against Lefebvre-Desnouettes. The Frenchman commanded the cavalry of the Imperial Guard, hard on the heels of the British rearguard; he had crossed the River Esla with 600 men and headed confidently for Benavente. Paget deployed some 650 Hussars, who ambushed the French and chased them for 2 miles (3 km), causing over 100 casualties for the loss of fifty men.

This second action cemented Paget's reputation as a cavalry commander. His victory at Benavente was watched by an angry and exasperated Napoleon, who would not forget him.

The Battle of Corunna (1809)

Battle Name	Dates	Campaign	
Corunna	16 January 1809	Peninsular War	
Troops Involved			
France	16–17,000	Commanded by Soult	
	900 losses		
Britain	16,000	Commanded by Moore	
	900 losses		
Outcome:			
French victory			

The so-called Corunna Campaign had been a near disaster. Moore's retreat through the inhospitable countryside in the height of winter was a nightmare. The Spanish were reluctant to assist as this army of liberation had liberally helped themselves to anything that had not been nailed down. The French, under Soult, were in hot pursuit, eager to eliminate the British. At times, as the chasing hounds caught up with their quarry, it would turn and fight, but for the most part, the British had little fight or resilience left to resist.

On 31 December, Crawford's Light Division split off from the retreat and headed for Vigo, where it was safely picked up by the Royal Navy. Although he now had fewer mouths to feed, Moore was exposed to a much greater extent than ever before.

Between 11 and 15 January 1809, his troops managed to stagger into Corunna, hoping for a quick exit from the Peninsula and escape from the pursuing French. However, although Corunna afforded some protection by the River Mero, the San Christobal heights were quickly seized by Soult.

As 16 January dawned, the French launched a massive attack along the whole of the British defensive ring. With a 400 per cent advantage in guns, Soult's men desperately tried to throw the British into the rear. The heaviest attacks, supported by artillery, hit the British right flank. Initially, at least, the British gave ground, but they stubbornly refused to be beaten. In the centre, the strategic village of Elvina was captured, won back, lost again and regained. Everywhere along the front, the last reserves were thrown in to hold the positions.

At the very height of the engagement, Moore was hit by a cannonball and mortally wounded. His second, Baird, was also wounded and by the evening the command had passed to Hope. By this stage, the battle had been reduced to an artillery duel, with both sides exhausted.

The British now seized the opportunity to withdraw to the waiting ships and they were not molested again by the French. When the remnants of the army arrived back in England, they were disembarked during the night in order to avoid

The Battle of Corunna.

alarm. For three months there would be no British field army on the Peninsula, but soon they were back. Meanwhile, the only British in all of the Peninsula were the 10,000 men in garrisons at Lisbon.

The Battle of Medellin (1809)

Battle Name	Dates	Campaign
Medellin	29 March 1809	Peninsular War
Troops Involved		
France	16,000–18,000	
	700 losses	Commanded by Victor
Spain	24,000–35,000	
	10,000 losses (many captured)	Commanded by Cuesta
Outcome:		
French victory		

The infirm and frankly incompetent Spanish General Gregorio Cuesta had taken command of the Galician army in July 1808. Bessières had crushed him at Medina del Rio Seco on 14 July 1808, but the surrender of Dupont's 17,500 men had helped to stimulate Spanish resistance. Junot was isolated in Portugal and when he was defeated at Rolica and Vimeiro in August, the Spaniards were beside themselves at the prospect of getting to grips with the French again.

When Moore arrived in Spain in September 1808 with some 35,000 men, he found the Spanish armies to be vast but useless. They were little more than a rabble of ill-trained and ill-disciplined opportunists. Then Napoleon took command of the 200,000 French troops in Spain and Moore was compelled to attack

them for the sake of Anglo-Spanish relations. Ultimately, he retreated to Corunna and Soult dealt the British a heavy blow in January 1809. The British evacuated and Napoleon thought that the Spanish campaign was as good as over. When Wellington returned to command the British forces at Lisbon, and train the rapidly improving Portuguese units, he found Cuesta a liability.

As was to be seen at Talavera, when the odds were against him, Cuesta chose discretion as the better part of valour, but at Medellin it appeared that he had a ready advantage in terms of manpower and it was here that he impudently chose to attack Victor. Victor's 18,000 men took up positions to the south with the River Guadiana at their backs. The Spaniards advanced with confidence, a force of at least 24,000, perhaps as many as 36,000. The French, outnumbered as they were, had more artillery and cavalry than Cuesta.

Cuesta advanced on a 4-mile (6.5-km) front, hoping to flank the French on both sides. Victor simply retired to a better, prepared position and made ready to make a stand. The engagement opened with French cavalry sweeping away the advancing Spanish lancers; they then charged home into the distracted and ill-organised infantry. Within a short period, the whole Spanish force was fleeing and Cuesta nearly fell into French hands.

The mass of routed Spanish troops were easy prey for the French, who apparently took at least 10,000 prisoners, in addition to those who had fallen in the initial, brief period of fighting.

The Battle of the Basque Roads (1809)

Battle Name	Dates	Campaign
Basque Roads	11–12 April 1809	
Troops Involved		
France	15 vessels	
	5/6 vessels lost	Commanded by Allemand
Britain	17 vessels	
	No losses	Commanded by Gambier/Cochrane
Outcome: Britain victory		
British victory		

By 1809, the French fleet was effectively refusing to engage the Royal Navy. The enemy vessels needed to be eliminated or neutralised, however, so an audacious raid was planned on French shipping in the Basque Roads near Rochefort. Admiral Willaumez left Brest in February with eight vessels; he intended to link up with the Lorient and Rochefort squadrons and head for the Caribbean. The Lorient squad was intercepted and three frigates were captured. Willaumez fled to the only safe anchorage, the Basque Roads, where he knew he could join up with the Rochefort squadron.

Willaumez now had some eleven ships of the line and four frigates, but immediately Gambier sailed to blockade him with eleven ships of the line, eight frigates and eighteen other ships. Theoretically, the French should have been safe, as the area was riddled with shoals, a cable stretched across the entrance to the Charente estuary and there were forts on the Ile D'Aix and the Ile Madame.

Gambier sent a despatch to the Admiralty asking that Cochrane be sent to him immediately to lead the attack. The proposal was that the Basque Roads be taken with the use of fire ships. He arrived on March 26 in his own frigate, twelve fire ships and William Congreve, with a supply of rockets.

Gambier assigned six frigates, eleven brigs, eight fire ships and three small vessels, with 1,500 barrels of gunpowder, to Cochrane to launch the attack, which was planned for 11 April. Cochrane made the approaches to the cable with a fire ship on each side. The two 'bomb ships' drifted into the cable and destroyed it when they detonated, then twenty fire ships were sent (with skeleton crews) towards the French fleet lying behind the cable's remains. Three of his frigates followed and, in turn, the French cut their cables and drifted back.

The net result of this chaos was that by dawn on 12 April only two French ships of the line and one frigate could manoeuvre; the others were stuck fast on banks. Cochrane now attacked two French ships, which immediately struck their colours, and three others were burned. At high tide, the remaining French ships refloated themselves and made for the Charente estuary. Cochrane did not dare to follow for fear of coming upfire from the guns on the Ile Madame or getting stuck himself as the tide receded. One of the French commanders was to pay for the defeat with his life; half of the fleet was gone and he was court-martialled and shot.

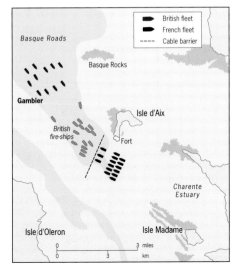

The Battle of Eckmühl (1809)

Battle Name	Dates	Campaign
Eckmühl	22 April 1809	Danube Campaign
Troops Involved		
France	50,000	
	6,000 losses	Commanded by Napoleon
Austria	75,000	
	12,000 losses	Commanded by Archduke Charles
Outcome:		
French victory		

On 16 April Napoleon arrived in Stuttgart to take command of operations in Germany. Berthier had had some 176,000 men under his command in the theatre and as far as Napoleon was concerned, had achieved precious little with them. He found the situation chaotic. The Austrians were on the offensive and very much had the initiative. Napoleon seized the opportunity to strike at the over-extended Austrians first, hitting Archduke Charles' centre at Abensberg on 20 April and the next day at Landshut. Davoût was sent in pursuit of what was believed to be an inferior force, but instead, at Eckmühl, he encountered Archduke Charles' main force of some 75,000. At his immediate disposal Davoût had barely 20,000 men; not surprisingly the Austrians seized the chance to crush this smaller force before more French could move up in support.

Around 40,000 Austrians struck Davoût's left flank, whilst the balance of the force marched around to cut the French off from the River Danubube. By 1300 on 22 April, Davoût was in dire straits, but help was at hand in the form of Lannes and his 30,000 troops, marching north from Landshut.

Whilst Lannes' troops attacked the Austrian left, Davoût rallied his men to hold the enemy frontally, giving his fellow general the chance to deploy. More French troops arrived on the battlefield in the shape of Lefebvre, who attacked the Austrian right. This new pressure made the Austrian positions untenable and with his flanks exposed and wavering, Archduke Charles ordered a withdrawal towards Ratisbon on the River Danube.

Fortunately for the Austrians, the French troops were exhausted and unable to pursue. Archduke Charles left 6,000 men at Ratisbon which, on the next day, fell under pressure from the French. The action opened with a cavalry battle, fought outside the walls of the city, but Napoleon was determined to strike at the city immediately and not subject it to a siege.

Lannes' corps assailed the city at 1300 and was repulsed. During the afternoon it was widely believed that Napoleon had been shot, which caused the French to waver, but after showing himself to the army they took new heart, launching a second assault at 1700. Three attempts were made on this occasion to breach the walls and eventually, after losing 1,000 men, the city fell at 1900. By then, Archduke Charles and his army had escaped.

French infantry ready to advance. Mario Tomasone

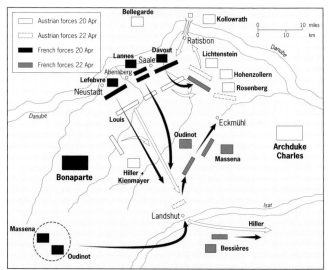

The Battle of the Douro (1809)

Battle Name	Dates	Campaign
The Douro (Oporto)	12 May 1809	Peninsular War
Troops Involved		
France		
	1,800 losses	Commanded by Soult and Victor
Britain		
	121 losses	Commanded by Wellington
Outcome:		
British victory		

British infantry firefight. Lynn Holmes

The Lisbon garrison left behind on the Peninsula amounted to some 10,000 men under the command of Craddock. On 22 April, Wellington arrived and soon launched a devastating offensive. He faced three French armies; Soult at Oporto, Victor at Ciudad Rodrigo and Lapisse at Talavera. Soult was the most exposed and it was here that Wellington proposed to deliver his first blow. He split his 33,000 men into three forces; he, at the head of 18,400 men would head straight for Oporto. MacKenzie was to stay at Lisbon with 12,000 men and Beresford's 6,000 men would cut Soult's line of retreat at Amarante.

By 8 May Wellington had encountered French outposts to the south of Oporto and these were swept aside in three days. Relentlessly, he followed them to the River Douro, Soult destroying the last pontoon bridge when they were safely across.

With the last bridge gone, Soult was understandably confident that the only attack could come from the west. Consequently, his defensive positions were orientated in that direction and the bulk of his troops were in Oporto awaiting such a move.

On the morning of 12 May, Wellington began to survey the French (north) bank of the Douro. It seemed to him that they were ill prepared for a forced crossing. It was then that he noticed a bend in the river, out of sight of Oporto. On the opposite bank was the Bishop's Seminary, which, if taken, would provide cover for his army to cross the river.

As luck would have it, there were four unguarded wine barges on the French bank. They were appropriated with the aid of five local people and the river crossing could now begin. Before the French realised what was happening, Wellington had 600 men across the river.

Soult initially, dismissed the news, but then sent Foy with three battalions of infantry to push the British out of the seminary. The supporting French artillery was quickly silenced by British guns on the opposite bank. The locals now responded by bringing their own barges to help the British across, but by the time these arrived Foy was already in retreat.

Wellington pursued the retreating Soult and caught his rearguard at Salamonde. Soult was forced to destroy his artillery and make good his escape into Spain. Wellington now turned his attention to Victor, but not before he had returned to Oporto to consider his options and re-supply his forces.

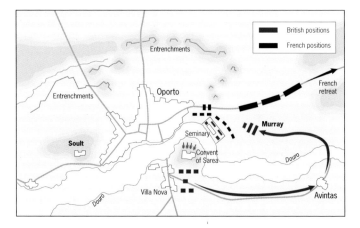

The Battle of Aspern-Essling (1809)

Battle Name	Dates	Campaign
Aspern-Essling	21–22 May 1809	Danube Campaign
Troops Involved		
France	Day 1: 23,000–31,400	
	Day 2: 62,000–70,000	
	19,000–21,000 losses	Commanded by Napoleon
Austria	Day 1: 95,900	
	Day 2: 90,800	
	23,400 losses	Commanded by Archduke Charles
Outcome:		
Austrian victory		

Napoleon had firmly established himself in Vienna, but Archduke Charles' army was still intact. The greatest problem, however, was getting at him, as the Danube lay between them and the bridges in the area had been destroyed by the Austrians. The opportunity to build a bridge at Nussdorf was lost when the Austrians occupied Stammersdorf and Gerasdorf. The only viable option was Kaiser-Ebersdorf, although this would entail building a series of bridges to the Loban Island and then a further bridge between Aspern and Essling.

The immediate area for the bridge-building was secured on 18 May and on 19 May Loban Island was cleared of Austrian troops. By the next day both Molitor's and Lassalle's divisions were across the Danube. Cavalry crossed at 1700, but a large boat launched from upstream broke the bridge and it was not until 0300 on 21 May that it was repaired.

Napoleon threw more infantry across the bridge at dawn, but again the structure collapsed. The French, however, now occupied strong positions, protected by dykes. Aspern was not occupied and when the Austrian infantry appeared at 1430 they made a quick dash for the village. By 1500 it was in Austrian hands; Molitor would have to take it back, which he did, holding it against growing pressure from Hiller and Bellegarde. The bridge had now been repaired once more and further elements of the French army were making their way across. At 1900

French troops crossing the Danube at the island of Lobau prior to the battle of Aspern-Essling.

Charles led Hiller's and Bellegarde's corps against Aspern, clearing Molitor from the village. Massena counterattacked, taking most of the village back.

During the night, more French troops braved the bridge whilst, with the exception of the Austrians still in parts of Aspern, the whole army had retired. Charles erroneously believed that come the morning, Napoleon would be gone.

At 0300 the French began their attempt to clear Aspern, and had done so by 0500. Rosenberg then attacked Essling, but Napoleon's infantry struck between the two villages at 0700. They drove the Austrians back for 2 miles (3 km), but their line maintained its integrity. All that remained was for Davoût's men to finish them off, but by then the bridge had been destroyed once more.

Without reserves, the French fell back and at 1330 Charles launched his assault. Desperately short of ammunition, Davoût was getting a trickle across the river by boats, but it was Bessiere's cavalry that held and countercharged. Charles then resorted to artillery, and by 1400 the battle was over. By 0500 the following morning Napoleon had returned back across the river.

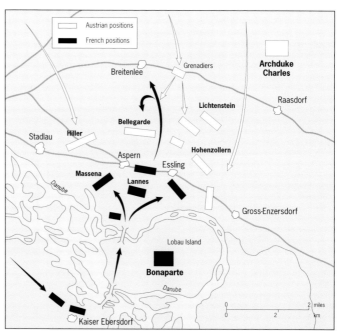

53

The Battle of Raab (1809)

Battle Name	Dates	Campaign
Raab	14 June 1809	Danube Campaign
Troops Involved		
France	24,000–31,000	
	3,000 losses	Commanded by Eugéne/MacDonald
Austria	35,000–40,000	
	5,000–5,500 losses (2,000 prisoners)	Commanded by Archduke John
Outcome: French victory		

Gradually, Eugéne had pushed Archduke John back from northern Italy and into Hungary. He was buoyed with the news that the French had won victories at Abensberg and Eckmühl. Equally, Archduke John was given new confidence by the news that Napoleon had been defeated at Aspern-Essling. He now resolved to turn and face Eugéne.

The Archduke marched past Vienna, along the south bank of the River Danube, and took up positions in front of the Raab fortress in a strong location, ideal for defence. His troops outnumbered the French, but were of dubious quality, being 'insurrectionist' troops, raised quickly.

The Austrian cavalry was positioned on the plain below the main positions, good cavalry country, but it was also of poor quality. John had interspersed his regulars amongst the insurrectionist troops, with infantry in the north and centre and the cavalry occupying the south.

The French moved up to engage, bombarding the Austrian centres as a prelude to the inevitable infantry assaults. The farm of Kis-Megyer lay at the heart of the Austrian centre and in the vicious fighting this was to change hands five times. The French assaults proved insufficient to dislodge Archduke John, but then Grouchy found a ford and successfully engaged the Austrian cavalry. The enemy cavalry were driven off and John's battle line was buckled in the south.

At this point, Eugéne launched another infantry assault on the centre, supported by his carefully husbanded reserves. MacDonald had now joined him, bringing his total effectives up to 33,000. This time, the assault swept over the farm and threatened to break the Austrian line in two. The Austrians were now threatened by encirclement, held in the centre by Eugéne's infantry and harassed by the cavalry under Grouchy from the south. Archduke John chose the only option available to him and retreated to the Raab fortress.

Eugéne swiftly invested the fortress and in just eleven days the garrison surrendered. He then headed off to link up with the main French army and was in attendance at the Battle of Wagram.

The Battle of Raab had lasted for just five hours, but it shattered the 'insurrection' and cleared the whole of the south bank of the River Danube of Austrian troops. Indecision and poor battlefield tactics had given the French yet another victory over the Austrians.

The Battle of Wagram (1809)

Battle Name	Dates	Campaign
Wagram	5–6 July 1809	Danube Campaign
Troops Involved		
France	Day 1: 110,000–136,500	
	Day 2: 170,500	
	32,000–34,000 losses	Commanded by Napoleon
Austria	Day 1: 130,000	
	Day 2: 146,000	
	40,000–43,000 losses	Commanded by Archduke Charles
Outcome: French victory		

After the disaster at Aspern-Essling, Napoleon still held Loban Island; this time he determined not to be hamstrung by a single bridge, but to cross it in force with a secure reinforcement and resupply route to his rear.

The Austrians had thrown up fieldworks from the banks of the Danube through Aspern, Essling and Gross-Enzersdorf, but just beyond the town the defences abruptly finished.

On 29 June, a new bridge was built at the old crossing point and a brigade was thrown across to reconnoitre the area. The defence works were thinly manned and prisoners reported that Charles had returned to Pressburg. In fact the Austrians had taken up positions on the higher ground along the River Russbach with elements stretching out through Gerasdorf, Stammersdorf and Langenzerdorf to the Danube.

On the night of 3/4 July, French troops began crossing the Danube, mainly heading out towards Wittan. The crossing was carefully planned for maximum surprise, but Bernadotte's troops were still crossing at daylight and Charles now knew that the French were attempting another attack from the Aspern-Essling area.

He had deployed his troops to ensure that he could strike at the French from any direction and cut them off from their bridgeheads. The troops holding the defence works would be expected to hold as long as possible, their inevitable retreat covered by cavalry.

At 2000 on 4 July Oudinot moved to secure the crossing and an hour later French batteries opened up and destroyed an Austrian battery on the Hansel Ground. The area was secured by 2300 and the French opened up on Gross-Enzersdorf. The old bridgehead was reopened immediately by St Cyr and Molitor, Legrand quickly following. Davoût crossed at 0600 and took Wittan. Gross-Enzersdorf and Wittan were chased out by 1000 and by 1230 the French were established on the opposite bank in force. Elements of Austrian infantry between Aspern and Essling had been rooted out by French cavalry and were streaming away.

At 1300 Oudinot, Lasalle and Marulaz advanced on Rutzendorf, which they captured at 1400. Massena, meanwhile, cleared the remnants of Austrian opposition from the Aspern-Essling area.

By 1800, the French army was ready and poised for an attack on the main Austrian line; the Russbach

Painting by Adolphe Roehn showing Napleon dozing on the night of July 5-6 1809 before the battle of Wagram.

itself was little more than a stream and should prove to be no real obstacle. Before the Austrians could move to consolidate their positions Napoleon launched an all-out attack. Both elements of Eugéne and Bernadotte's corps broke into Wagram but were ousted. Other elements of Eugéne's corps broke through the Austrian lines, but were thrown back when Charles committed his reserves and Oudinot gained a temporary foothold in Baumersdorf. The day's fighting was over temporarily, but hostilities began again in the early hours of the next day. Napoleon ordered Massena to concentrate around Aderklaa with only Boudet covering the left. Davoût, meanwhile, was to muster around Grosshofen, Napoleon clearly thinking that Charles would anchor his defence for the next day on Wagram.

The last French attack of the day had convinced Charles to change his plans, however he had intended to hold the Wagram–Markgrafneusiedl line, but it now fell to him to take the initiative. He ordered Klenan to strike from Stammersdorf against Aspern and Kollowrat from Hagenbrünn to hit Leopoldau and Breitenke. He planned that both attacks would get underway at 0100, but neither marched out of their camp until 0400. Charles had also planned for Prochaska's grenadiers to hit Süssenbrünn at 0300, but instead of being at Gerasdorf as he believed, Prochaska was, in fact, at Sauring. In conjunction with this planned move Bellegarde would link up with Prochaska (of Lichtenstein's corps) by moving to Aderklaa. It would then be Hohenzollern's turn to advance and engage the French (Charles reckoned around 0400). John's corps was then expected to move up to take Leopoldsdorf. If the plan had come to fruition, the French army would have been surrounded and solidly beaten, but as it was, with the delays in relaying orders, it was the moves of Rosenberg that first alerted the French to the danger.

Rosenberg had been ordered, as part of the plan, to attack Grosshofen and Glinzendorf. Massena had been moving on Aderklaa with Nansouty and Arrighi following, and Davoût was moving west when he encountered Rosenberg's troops. Nansouty's artillery and Arrighi's cavalry helped him force Rosenberg back over the Russbach by around 0600. More bad news arrived at Napoleon's headquarters at Raasdorf; the whole of the French left was in danger of crumbling; it was 0900.

Bellegarde had occupied Aderklaa and awaited Prochaska's arrival at 0730; then they waited for Kollowrat. It was around this time that Massena arrived to occupy Aderklaa, which Bernadotte should have already occupied. St Cyr seized the village, then lost it again and as Bernadotte's troops moved up, they broke and fled. Napoleon arrived

and told Massena to recapture Aderklaa as it was pivotal for the French left. Massena duly obliged when Molitor's men stormed the village.

Offensive action now rested on Davoût and he was ready by 0930. Austrian cavalry were dispersed from Siebenbrünn and he set up his artillery there to bombard Markgrafneusiedl and the heights.

On the French left, Boudet had been driven back to Aspern, so at least part of Charles' plan was working. Pressure was building elsewhere, Molitor was evicted from Aderklaa at 1100 and the bulk of Massena's corps was heavily engaged to the south of the village.

Meanwhile, back on the French right, Davoût's troops were storming through the field fortifications, having silenced Rosenberg's artillery. The mêlée surged through Markgrafneusiedl, now the Austrian rear was exposed and threatened by Grouchy and Montbrun's cavalry. Charles moved quickly to cover with troops from Hohenzollern's command facing Oudinot.

Napoleon now planned to switch the axis of attack; Massena would swing south to cover Klenan and Kollowrat, supporting Boudet and protecting the bridges. Eugéne would occupy Massena's positions and hold both Lichtenstein and Bellegarde. Around noon Massena was in place and Davoût was making steady progress in the west; it was time for MacDonald's troops (of Eugéne's corps) to advance.

After a preliminary bombardment from his own guns (eighteen), Wrede's artillery (twenty-four) and Lauriston's guard artillery (sixty guns), MacDonald advanced in a curious open-ended oblong of 8,000 men. The advance took place at 1230, and was first hit by Lichtenstein's cavalry, but these were beaten off. Both Bellegrade and Kollowrat threw everything they had at him, but they both failed. MacDonald's men were not halted until 1345, by which time they were over halfway to Süssenbrünn. Davoût was still pushing Rosenberg back, Oudinot struck at Hohenzollern and snarled his line, and linked up with Davoût.

Klenan began to retire to Stammersdorf and Bellegarde to Hagenbrünn. MacDonald pushed on once more, this time taking Süssenbrünn and Gerasdorf and reaching the outskirts of Jägerhaus; here he was stopped by a reserve brigade of Austrians.

Meanwhile, at 1600 John finally arrived on the battlefield at Siebenbrünn and pushed towards Markgrafneusiedl before Reynier, who had been held in reserve, saw him off.

The casualties on both sides had been vast, probably as a result of the large numbers of artillery pieces on the field. Charles' men were beaten, but many managed to retire in reasonably good order.

The Battle of Talavera (1809)

Battle Name	Dates	Campaign
Talavera	27–28 July 1809	Peninsular War
Troops Involved		
France	46,000	
	7,268 losses	Commanded by Joseph Bonaparte
Britain/Portugal/Spain	55,600 (20,600 in combat)	
	5,365 losses	Commanded by Wellington/Cuesta
Outcome:		
British/Portuguese/Spanish victory		

Soult had been forced out of Portugal by June 1809, leaving Wellington clear to strike out into Spain with the intention of linking up with the Spaniards. It was agreed that the allied forces would meet to the north of the Tagus at Plasencia.

The French, meanwhile, had three large forces still in Spain. Joseph Bonaparte was in Madrid with 12,000, Sebastiani had 22,000 men at Madridejos and Victor, who was moving up from Mérida to Talavera, commanded another 20,000 men.

For Wellington and the Spanish General Cuesta, there was an opportunity to take on each of the French armies and defeat them. Unfortunately, the two men could not agree and with the Spanish contributing 35,000 of the 55,000 strong combined force, Wellington found it difficult to pin his ageing ally down.

The two men had met on 20 July and had missed their opportunity to fall on Victor by the time they had agreed tactics on 23 July; Victor was falling back to Madrid on the following day. Cuesta would not be denied, however, and he set off in pursuit, his troops receiving a bloody nose on 25 July, when the French turned to face them.

Wellington's troops, meanwhile, had reached the River Alberch, just to the east of Talavera on 27 July. Whilst viewing the French from a position at Casa de Salinas Wellington was nearly captured by enemy light infantry, but managed to make good his escape. The day saw several skirmishes but little more than probes from both of the armies.

During the night Wellington organised his deployment. His line stretched from Segurilla in the north to Talavera in the south. Cuesta's chastened 35,000 were on the right flank (Talavera) and the allied left flank rested on Cerro de Medellin, a large hill 1 mile (1.6 km) from the heights of Segurilla.

Shortly after 2200 a French division approached from the Cerro de Cascajal facing the Cerro de Medellin. It crossed the valley and the Portina, a stream running along the valley. The British and German troops on the Cerro de Medellin were caught completely unawares. It was a close run thing as they tried to beat off the French columns who had

reached the summit. Eventually the French gave up, leaving 300 dead, but having inflicted similar casualties on the enemy, as well as having thoroughly destroyed their night's rest.

At 0500 on 28 July the French artillery began firing at the Anglo-Spanish positions. The sixty or so guns were answered by British gunners. The French attack consisted of 4,500 men in three columns, led by Ruffin. They advanced steadily despite stubborn defences. The main force seemed to be heading for Stewart's, and Tilson's brigades which they outnumbered. Steady British fire stopped the attacking columns and with little hope of returning effective fire, the assault broke up and soon Ruffin's men were streaming back to the French lines; by 0700 it was over.

The battle descended into a one-hour artillery duel, followed by a five-hour lull. The French artillery opened up once more at 1300. This time the 4,500 men of Laval's division were heading for the Pajar, a fortified farmhouse at the junction of the British and Spanish troops. Campbell's division drove them off, forcing them to leave behind seventeen artillery pieces. No sooner had the attack petered out than eighty French artillery opened fire as 1,500 French, under Sebastiani and Lapisse, marched forward. Even these veterans could not withstand the British fire power and began to fall back. Some of the British troops were over-zealous in their pursuit, however, and a gap opened up in the line, towards which 22,000 French infantry and cavalry headed. The gap was plugged by a single battalion and then three more, amounting to 3,000 men. British artillery began to plough into the advancing French then, almost as one, the 3,000 British muskets fired. The French columns were again shattered, with Lapisse alone leaving 1,700 men behind, as he fled back across the Portina.

The French now turned their attention to the Medellin itself. Ruffin's division began to advance across the valley under British artillery fire. Wellington threw Anson's cavalry brigade at Ruffin, whose men promptly formed the square. A disaster struck the lead cavalry regiment, the 23rd Light

Dragoons, who ploughed into a dry river bed and then were attacked by French cavalry; casualties were high. The second regiment, the 1st Light Dragoons (King's German Legion) failed to penetrate the French squares, which were still under artillery fire.

Ruffin's men, however, were beginning to waver and they finally pulled back to Cascajal. The fighting petered out and Wellington's troops remained in position, awaiting more attacks in the morning. At dawn Wellington could see that the French had had enough and had retired.

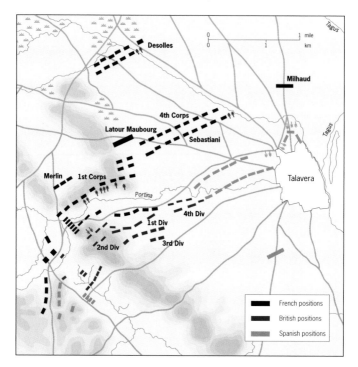

The Battle of Busaco (1810)

Battle Name	Dates	Campaign
Busaco	27 September 1810	Peninsular War
Troops Involved		
France	66,000	
	4,600 losses	Commanded by Massena
Britain	50,000	
	1,252 losses	Commanded by Wellington
Outcome:		
British victory		

When Ciudad Rodrigo and Almedia fell into French hands, Wellington was forced to retreat into Portugal, taking up positions on a ridge at Busaco overlooking the River Mondego. The British positions covered a 9-mile (14.5-km) front from Busaco to Mondego, the French could be seen well in advance and the ridge was difficult to climb.

At 0530 on 27 September French skirmishers began to engage the British pickets, then emerging out of the fog came Merle's troops, who hit

Lightburne's brigade but were driven off by volley fire. Four more French battalions tried their luck further south but they, too, failed. Seven more, under Foy, made their way up the ridge. It was 0645 and the fog had been burned away by the early-morning sun. It took the intervention of Leith to help fend off Foy's attack and the French eventually fell back, Foy himself wounded.

At 0830 the French attacked again. Ney sent Loison's division to tackle Crawford's part of the line, which occupied the village of Sula. The French took the village and ran straight into British artillery. Loison refused to be stopped; his troops overran the guns and stormed the ridge. Crawford quickly counterattacked with the 43rd and 52nd; Loison's men were routed, leaving over 130 dead. In the attack he had lost 1,200 men out of his force of 6,500.

To the south, Marchand led eleven battalions against Pack's Portuguese, but they were roughly handled by the defenders and sent reeling back.

By noon, all of the French attacks had been comprehensively dealt with and they did not seem to have any more stomach for a determined assault on Wellington's positions.

Massena had seen all his attempts fail and, what was more, he had lost the highest proportion of officers to men in any action in the Peninsular War. Aside from those captured (which included General Simon of Loison's division), no fewer than 300 men had been killed, captured or badly wounded.

Massena was not done; the next day he threw his cavalry around Wellington's flank and the British force retired to Torres Vedras, Massena's next major obstacle.

It had been a bloody encounter and despite Wellington's previous suspicions about the quality of the Portuguese troops, they had acquitted themselves well and would remain a solid addition to his British regulars for the campaigns to come. Pack's men had come of age in one of Wellington's well-won victories.

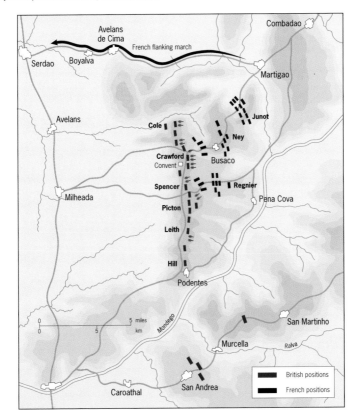

British infantry under pressure form a square. *Lynn Holmes*

The Battle of Barossa (1811)

Battle Name	Dates	Campaign
Barossa	5 March 1811	Peninsular War
Troops Involved		
France	9,000	Commanded by Victor
	2,062 losses	
Britain	5,000	
	1,238 losses	Commanded by Graham
Outcome:		
British victory		

After the battle of Busaco, Wellington occupied the lines of Torres Vedras, three defensive barriers protecting Lisbon, a mixture of natural and man-made fortifications. Massena's troops closed on the area, unaware of their defensive strength until they saw them; they instantly realised that an attack would be pointless and expensive.

Wellington could sit and wait in the certain knowledge that not only would he be able to feed his troops, thanks to the Royal Navy's sea supremacy, but they would also deliver him reinforcements. He could therefore afford to let Massena's men try to live off the land.

By November 1810, the unequal supply situation had wreaked havoc on the French. When Massena recrossed into Spain, in April 1811, he had lost 25,000 men. Throughout this period, he was leeching reinforcements from Victor, who was laying siege to Cadiz. Soult, meanwhile, had moved to besiege Badajoz. This meant that the 25,000 allies bottled up in Cadiz were now only facing 15,000 of Victor's men. An opportunity for offensive action against the French now presented itself.

Some 14,000 Anglo-Spanish troops were shipped to Tarifa, where they were to attack the French besieging Cadiz from the rear after a march north to the city. Another 4,000 Spaniards from Cadiz were to launch a simultaneous sortie out of the city.

Graham's troops were forced to land at Algeciras instead of Tarifa owing to poor weather on 23 February, with the Spanish troops arriving on 28 February. From the outset, the Spanish general Manuel La Peña, a man not noted for his abilities, claimed command, which Graham reluctantly conceded.

By 5 March, the force had reached Barossa where it engaged a French force under Villatte. Villatte's men withdrew to deal with the Spanish sortie from Cadiz, which persuaded La Peña that victory was at hand.

Graham's men had occupied the Barossa ridge, but La Peña ordered him to join him and launch another attack on the French. Prudently, Graham left a battalion on the ridge. No sooner had he moved forward than Leval's and Ruffin's divisions began to move on the ridge.

Five Spanish battalions which had been retained on the ridge fled at the sight of the French, so Graham began to order his troops to return to there. Browne, who was commanding the battalion on the ridge, hit the French first, soon supported by the Brigade of Guards, and together they swept Ruffin's men off the ridge. Meanwhile, Whealley's brigade had defeated Leval's division, making the British victory complete without a shot being fired by La Peña's troops.

The Battle of Fuentes de Oñoro (1811)

Battle Name	Dates	Campaign
Fuentes de Oñoro	3–5 May 1811	Peninsular War
Troops Involved		
France	50,000	
	2,192–2,250 losses	Commanded by Massena
Britain	36,000	
	1,400–1,500 losses	Commanded by Wellington
Outcome:		
British victory		

Wellington had launched two armies to attack the French in Spain; one under William Carr Beresford headed towards Badajoz, whilst his own forces took the more northerly route, via Salamanca.

He discovered that the Portuguese town of Almeida was held by the French and he determined to lay siege to it. Massena left Ciudad Rodrigo to relieve it, but Wellington marched into strong positions behind Fuentes de Oñoro, just inside the Spanish border.

The first clash came on 3 May, when five French battalions were sent to dislodge 2,000 British troops in the village itself. After heavy fighting, the defenders were pushed out, but Wellington committed a further three regiments and seized it back. Casualties at this point had been relatively low, with around 259 British and 650 French killed or wounded. The next day was restricted mainly to skirmishing in the area, and gave both sides a vital breathing space for reorganisation and redeployment.

Hostilities resumed on 5 May, when Massena's cavalry (some 4,000) charged Wellington's 1,500 Spanish and British mounted troops. The attack drove in the British pickets and burst through the right wing of the army. Crawford was sent to cover the right and the 7th Division despatched to the village of Frenada. With the line re-established, the French attack petered out and Massena brought up his artillery to duel with the British guns.

Meanwhile, the battle for Fuentes de Oñoro was in full swing, with both sides bringing up fresh infantry to contest the ground. By 1200, it had been raging for over eight hours and the British were running out of ammunition. Already, the French had taken the churchyard and the chapel, where there was heavy hand-to-hand fighting.

Wellington threw in the 71st and 79th Highlanders along with the 88th just as the French seemed to have secured the village. Together they cleared it at bayonet point.

The struggle continued into the evening, with the British finally gaining the upper hand, and by nightfall the French were in retreat. At 2400 on 11 May there was a huge explosion at Almeida where the garrison commander blew up a mine to allow his troops to escape the town, knowing that after Massena's defeat he could not expect to be relieved.

Massena was recalled to France, Wellington would now temporarily face Marmont; for the moment he had seized the initiative.

A Black Watch column moving to the field. Courtesy of the 42nd 1815 Re-enactment Association. Mario Tomasone

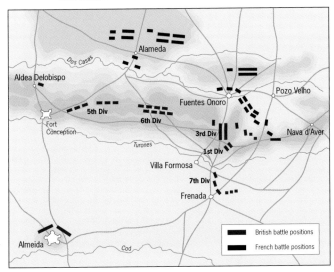

The Battle of Albuera (1811)

Battle Name	Dates	Campaign
Albuera	16 May 1811	Peninsular War
Troops Involved		
France	25,000	
	7,000 losses	Commanded by Soult
Britain/Portugal/Spain	32,000	
	6,000 losses	Commanded by Beresford
Outcome:		
British/Portuguese/Spanish victory		

Whilst Wellington was completing his victory at Fuentes de Oñoro on 5 May 1811, around 130 miles (200 km) to the south, Beresford was beginning to lay siege to Badajoz. No sooner had he begun his operations than he heard that Soult was on the march from Seville with 25,000 men, intent on driving him off.

By 13 May, Beresford was marching south to intercept Soult and on the 15th he reached Albuera. He positioned his troops with the town anchoring his centre and the other troops occupying heights to the west. The French arrived from the south-east on the morning of 16 May and drew up their lines facing west.

The first attacks hit Albuera itself, which was held by Alten; more probes were made to the south of Albuera Bridge. The real threat faced the Spaniards holding the right of the allied line. Soult had discovered that the River Albuera was fordable in several places and had crossed with a considerable number of infantry and cavalry, shielded by a heavily wooded area. The Spaniards, under Blake, were ordered to meet the French with the promise of British regulars in support. Beresford was sure that Soult's main attack would come from the east, but Soult was about to throw 8,400 men at him. Supported by the British, however, the Spaniards stopped the French columns, but then it began to rain.

Out of the smoke and gloom rode the French cavalry. Colborne's brigade, which had inflicted heavy casualties on the French infantry, were cut to pieces; only 300 of 1,600 survived. The 7,800 French swept on, but Beresford checked them with two fresh British brigades (3,700 men). The vicious and ruinous firefight lasted for over an hour, but the French numbers began to tell.

Around midday, Beresford ordered Carlos de España's Spanish brigade forward, but they refused. Instead, and against orders, Lowry Cote advanced in support with 4,000 fresh British and Portuguese troops. This turned the tide. He beat off repeated French cavalry charges and fell into line with Stewart's remaining men. The French began to waver under fire, exhausted and now under pressure. They streamed to the rear, but the heavy rain denied the British the opportunity to pursue. After four hours of heavy fighting, Beresford's men had grabbed victory from the jaws of defeat. Even Soult recognised that the steady British infantry had refused to accept that they had been beaten. It was a pyrrhic victory, however, with 6,000 dead and wounded.

The Battle of Albuera.

The Battle of Arroyo de Molinos (1811)

Battle Name	Dates	Campaign
Arroyo de Molinos	28 October 1811	Peninsular War
Troops Involved		
France	4,000	
	1,600 losses (1,300 prisoners)	Commanded by Girard
Britain	10,000	
	71 losses	Commanded by Rowland Hill
Outcome:		
British victory		

The action at Arroyo de Molinos, although not massive by comparison with other conflicts during the period, illustrated the effects of surprise on an unsuspecting enemy.

By September, the British blockade had been established around Ciudad Rodrigo; Hill and Spanish troops were engaged in tackling Drouet's and Girard's corps. Hill had driven Girard from Morena on 26 October and now the British commander sought to cut him off from the bridge at Mérida.

Whilst on his march, Hill heard that Girard had stopped at Arroyo de Molinos and that he had left a rearguard at Caceres. This meant that the Frenchman had no idea where Hill was and expected him to come up the road through Caceres. Hill then force-marched his troops to Alcuesca, some 3 miles (5 km) short of Arroyo de Molinos by the early hours of 27 October.

The British took up their positions and rested; the French were oblivious to the peril. At 0200 on 28 October, the order was given to advance on Arroyo de Molinos. The force consisted of two infantry columns, with a third cavalry column in the centre. Quietly, they moved onto a ridge ½ mile (1 km) from Girard's headquarters. The left column was to take Arroyo de Molinos and the right was to seize the Truxillo road. At 0400 a French brigade was on its way up the Medellin Road. The village was held by Dombrouski and Briche, and Girard was still there when two British officers suddenly charged.

There was a ferocious fight as the French were driven through the village. Just outside, the French infantry formed squares expecting cavalry, but British infantry volleyed them from the houses.

It was now growing light and the French were swarming back to the road to Medellin. Spanish cavalry were sent to block off the retreat, while British cavalry dealt with the scattered French horsemen. Girard had been wounded and his men were surrendering in their hundreds.

The French headed for the rocky area, Montanches, but the British and Portuguese troops outpaced them and began to round up increasing numbers of prisoners; virtually the whole of the French 34th Infantry were taken.

Girard, Dombrouski and Briche made good their escape and on 9 November joined up with Drouet at Orellana with fewer than 600 men. Hill had stirred up a hornet's nest and the French, for some months, were desperate to avenge the humiliating defeat.

The Second Battle of Ciudad Rodrigo (1812)

Battle Name	Dates	Campaign
Ciudad Rodrigo	8–19 January 1812	Peninsular War
Troops Involved		
France	2,000	
	2,000 losses	Commanded by Barrie
Britain	40,000	
	1,111 losses	Commanded by Wellington
Outcome:		
British victory		

Marmont took command of French troops in Spain on 11 May 1811, following Massena's recall to France. Wellington, using a spy network, gave exaggerated reports of allied dead, sick and wounded, giving the impression that he would not be mounting any offensive operations until at least the spring of 1812.

Meanwhile, of course, he was preparing to take Ciudad Rodrigo and later Badajoz. Troops assigned to the siege operations mustered at Almeida and the advance began on 4 January; four days later they were before the walls of the town. Ciudad Rodrigo was no easy target, fully enclosed as it was by 30-ft (9-m) walls and ramparts, lying on a high hill on the right bank of the River Agueda. To the north, however, there was a low ridge (Lesser Teson), but more importantly a second, higher ridge (Greater Teson). Importantly, the ridge was higher than the town walls and could command the area. On the first night, British and Portuguese troops stormed the French redoubt on Greater Teson and the scene was set for the siege.

Despite the appalling weather, the siegeworks progressed well, so much so that the French garrison commander became alarmed and launched a sortie at 1100 on 14 January. The attack was driven off, but not before the French had filled in some of the entrenchments and taken tools. That night, however, Wellington's troops took the San Francisco convent, which was still occupied by the French.

The sortie had set back the operations, but by 19 January the allied guns had succeeded in blasting two breaches in the walls. In preparation for the assault, the gunners continued to blaze at the town in the hope that they could prevent the French from building new defences to cover the breaches.

Wellington ordered O'Toole to launch a diversionary attack on the outworks in front of the castle, whilst the main blows were aimed at the breaches. The Light Division, under Cranford, was to hit the smaller breach and Picton's 3rd Division the larger.

As the diversionary attacks drew French troops away, Picton's men stormed towards the Great Breach under a hail of fire. The French had set up strong defences and the breach was covered by two guns. They only managed to fire twice, however, before Picton's men overran them.

Meanwhile, Crawford's troops had managed to take the Lesser Breach, although he was hit and died five days later. The French struggled on, but the main defensive works were Wellington's and so, too, was the town.

The Second Battle of Badajoz (1812)

Battle Name	Dates	Campaign
Badajoz	16 March–6 April 1812	Peninsular War
Troops Involved		
France	5,000	
	5,000 killed, wounded or	
	captured	Commanded by Phillipon
Britain	5,000 losses	Commanded by Wellington
Outcome:		
British victory		

Badajoz was the strongest French fortress on the Portuguese border, with nine bastions, walls up to 46 ft (14 m) and a castle within its precincts. On the right bank of the River Guadiana there were three impressive outworks and on the left bank there were three more. Having captured Ciudad Rodrigo, Wellington now fixed on taking the fortification, deciding to launch his first attacks on the south of the city.

On 16 March his men began to dig in, and the French launched a sortie three days later. Each side prepared for the inevitable assault, the French even creating a dam to make a lake that would force the British to march across in front of their main batteries.

Considerable progress was made on 25 March when the British took Port Picurina on the left bank and it was immediately occupied by British guns. News that two French armies were on their way to relieve the garrison forced Wellington's hand; he knew that he must launch his attack soon or all of his efforts would be for nought.

He gave orders for the assault to begin on the night of 5 April, but the breaches in the Santa Maria and Trinidad bastions were insufficient for success, so he postponed for twenty-four hours. On 6 April, the French feverishly shored up the beaches and prepared.

The British, too, were ready and at 2140 the attack was underway. Wilson's troops took San Roque on the left bank, then the storming parties headed for the beaches. The French had placed mines, set up killing zones and placed sharpened stakes to prevent them from getting through. Despite making forty attacks on the beaches, not a single British soldier got into the town and 2,000 were killed or wounded.

Meanwhile, Picton had been trying to storm the castle itself, crossing around the dam to approach the walls. He, too, had been denied, but Colonel Ridge managed to get some of his men onto the ramparts. More British troops poured over the walls and soon the castle was in British hands.

Phillipon had relied on the castle holding and had intended to use it as a last line of defence should the British carry the beaches. He and his men were now faced with disaster and by 0200 on 7 April resistance had collapsed and Badajoz was in Wellington's hands.

The Battle of Almaraz (1812)

Battle Name	Dates	Campaign
Almaraz	19 May 1812	Peninsular War
Troops Involved		
France	Unknown total numbers	
	400 losses (259 captured)	Commanded by Aubert
Britain	6,000	
	181 losses	Commanded by Rowland Hill
Outcome:		
Inconclusive		

Whilst Wellington prepared to attack the French in Spain, Hill was despatched to take the pontoon bridge over the River Tagus at Almaraz. It was of strategic importance as it was the main crossing point for the French west of Toledo. Its capture would sever the communications between Soult and Marmont. To achieve this Hill had some 6,000 men (many of whom had been with him at Arroyo de Molinos).

He got underway on 12 May, knowing that the bridge was well protected. It was overlooked by Fort Napoleon, situated on top of a hill on the southern bank, the rear of which was covered by a ditch and a loopholed tower. On the northern side was Fort Rugusa, a five-sided structure with a 25-ft (7.6-m) high loopholed tower. This was covered by fieldworks closer to the bridge.

The French defensive positions also included covering the road from Trujillo, 6 miles (9.5 km) from Almaraz, at Sierra de Mirabete. Here the road entered a mountainous region covered by an old castle, which had been improved to house eight guns. There was also a fortified house here and two small forts, Colbert and Senarmont. The only other way around the mountains was to take the Pass of La Cueva, 2 miles (3 km) to the east.

Hill divided his force into three columns; the first under Chowne would storm the castle at Mirabete, the second would force the pass itself and the third would take the route through La Cueva. Delays hampered the advance and it was not until the evening of 18 May that the troops were ready to march. At dawn his

troops had passed through La Cueva and were within ¼ mile (1 km) of Fort Napoleon.

Chowne's guns opened up at dawn on Mirabete, at which point Hill threw nearly two regiments at Fort Napoleon, coming under intense fire immediately from the defenders and from Fort Ragusa. The British sprinted in with ladders and ascended the wall, and after a vicious hand-to-hand fight the fort was taken. Aubert had refused to run or surrender and was killed.

The French on the south bank fled across the river, but soon the defenders in Fort Ragusa also retired, heading for Naval Moral. In just forty minutes Hill had secured the crossing. He had the pontoon bridge and the fortifications destroyed, but discovered that Mirabete was still in French hands. Wrongly believing that Soult was en route, he fell back to Truxillo.

French artillery and infantry. Lynn Holmes

The Battle of Salamanca (1812)

Battle Name	Dates	Campaign
Salamanca	22 July 1812	Peninsular War
Troops Involved		
France	50,000	
	14,000 losses	Commanded by Marmont
Britain/Portugal	48,000–48,600	
	5,214 losses	Commanded by Wellington
Outcome:		
British/Portuguese victory		

On 13 June Wellington advanced from Ciudad Rodrigo and marched into Salamanca four days later. The three small French-held forts were besieged and fell on 27 June, but the French army closed in on the area and remained close at hand.

Bizarrely, on 18 July, both armies marched, shadowing one another on either side of the River Guarena. On 21 July, they crossed the River Tormes and set up camp within a few hundred yards of each other; battle now seemed inevitable.

The following morning saw the two armies heading south in parallel; it was a race for the supply routes from Ciudad Rodrigo. The French troops collided with the leading Portuguese brigade at Los Arapiles, and the Portuguese were driven off, leaving the French in possession of a 100-ft (30-m) high hill, the Greater Arapil, to the north-east of the village.

The bulk of the two armies swung south-west. Marmont assumed that Wellington was retreating back to Ciudad Rodrigo, but the dust he saw in the distance was, in fact, Pakenham's 3rd Division coming up to Aldea Tejada to protect his right flank.

By early afternoon, most of Wellington's troops had stopped near the Lesser Arapil, ¼ mile (1 km) north of Marmont's vantage point. By now, intent on cutting off Wellington, the French were strung out over 4 miles (6.5 km), with the divisions under

British infantry charge a French column. Lynn Holmes

Thomières, Maucune and Clausel in the lead. Wellington was having his lunch at Los Arapiles, peering at the French through his telescope. Seeing how stretched the French army was, he realised that this was his opportunity. Instantly, he remounted and galloped off to Pakenham with instructions that he should attack at the earliest opportunity.

Around 1530, Pakenham's troops, supported by 1,000 cavalry, appeared on Thomière's right flank. The 6,000 British and Portuguese poured heavy rocketfire into the dense and confined French. Thomière himself and the two leading French battalions were wiped out, leaving his division leaderless.

Just after 1700, Bradford's Portuguese (8,500 men) hit Maucune's division which had been following Thomière. Maucune had seen the British attack on Thomière and expected a cavalry presence; consequently he ordered his 5,000 men into square. Unfortunately, it was the wrong division, and although his artillery wreaked havoc on the allies, Maucune's squares were decimated by three well-controlled and devastating volleys from the infantry. As the French ran, the allied cavalry were finally unleashed; nearly five battalions of Maucune's men were slaughtered.

Brennier had been quickly moving his 4,300 men up, and as he saw the onrushing dragoons he, too, formed square. However his men were either too exhausted or simply scared, and their volleys did nothing to break the charge. They too were swept aside and were running men.

The allied dragoons, under Le Marchant, were completely out of control, pursuing the French in every direction. In forty minutes, three French divisions had been accounted for but Le Marchant was killed during the pursuit.

To the east of Los Arapiles things were not going so well for Wellington. East of the Greater Arapil, Cole's 4th Division had been beaten off by two fresh French divisions. At the Greater Arapil itself, Portuguese troops under Pack had also been flung back.

Marmont had been badly wounded and so had his next in line, Bonnet. Overall command therefore now lay with Clausel, who still firmly believed that a victory could be won. He ordered Sarrut's division to hold Pakenham whilst he launched 12,000 men across the plain between the Greater and Lesser Arapils. The manoeuvre was doomed; this was exactly what Wellington had expected.

Clinton's 6th Division held the centre, with Anson's brigade (of Cole's 4th Division) on the left and Portuguese troops under Spry on the right. The whole line was reinforced by more Portuguese under Rezende. In the face of allied artillery fire from the Lesser Arapil, the French marched on in column. When they reached musket range the heads of the columns were blown away with carefully aimed volleys. They tried to return fire but the volleys were too effective and they were driven back, shattered and depleted.

By sunset Clinton's troops had taken the Greater Arapil but ran into 5,500 fresh French troops under Ferrey. Unlike his compatriots, Ferrey deployed well and drove Clinton back, only being forced to retreat himself when his flanks were exposed.

The whole of the French army should have been lost, as the Alba de Tormes Bridge was supposed to be guarded by Spanish troops. These men, under Carlos de España, however, had withdrawn. Nevertheless, hundreds of French were taken, including twenty guns, and on 12 August Wellington marched in triumph into Madrid, which had been occupied by the French since December 1808.

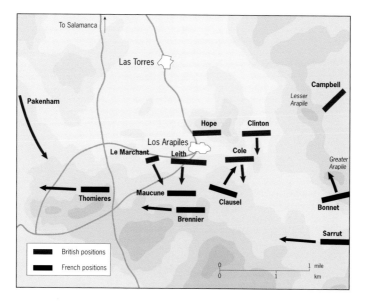

The Battle of Mogilev (1812)

Battle Name	Dates	Campaign
Mogilev (Saltanovka)	23 July 1812	Russian Campaign
Troops Involved		
France	26,000	
	1,000 losses	Commanded by Davoût
Russia	49,000	
	4,000 losses	Commanded by Bagration
Outcome:		
French victory		

The 2nd Russian Army was steadily moving east, pursued by Poniatowsky, Latour-Manbourg and Jérôme Bonaparte. Further to the east was Davoût and it was now time for a vast turning movement to trap the Russians and stop their eastward flight. Davoût headed for Mogilev to close the door and entered the city on 20 July. It was imperative for the Russians that Bagration's troops should be able to cross the Dneiper. Raevski was at Stary Bykhov and headed for Mogilev to support Bagration. Just outside the city, his advance guard cavalry had a sharp fight with French horsemen, whom he managed to overwhelm.

This new threat alarmed Davoût and he determined that he would have to fight to hang on to Mogilev after all. He despatched up to 28,000 men to the nearby village of Saltanovka and prepared for the attack. Meanwhile, Bagration was making all speed to Mogilev and by the morning of 23 July his advance guard reached the edge of the forests to the south of Saltanovka. Initially Dessaix engaged Paskevich, each trying to turn the other's flank in the thick woodlands. Raevski had established himself on the right wing and proposed to attack as soon as all of his troops had moved up. He then received a despatch from Paskevich telling him of his failure to turn Dessaix and the fact that Davoût was said to have five divisions (two of cavalry) at his immediate disposal. It was now evident that Raevski was not strong enough to handle the French at Mogilev. Whilst he held as long as he could, Bagration made for the Dneiper, constantly harassed by the pursuing French. Reluctantly, Raevski returned and headed for Novoselky and then for Stary Bykhov.

By 23 July all significant forces were over the Dneiper and the Russian armies reunited at Smolensk on 3 August.

Davoût had held firm at Mogilev. There was every chance that Raevski could have broken through and linked up with the Russian 1st Army under Barclay de Tolly, but as it was he had bought Bagration the time he needed to escape the trap set for him by the French.

Of particular note at Mogilev are two interesting facts: first Bagration (and presumably Raevski)

Napoleon enters the Russian capital.

thought that they were facing at least 60,000 French, which implies that Davoût's powers of manoeuvre were particularly strong; second, and especially interesting, was the presence of Raevski's sons, the elder claiming the flag of a Smolensk regiment and the younger always at his father's side.

French and Russian infantry melée. Mario Tomasone

The Battle of Smolensk (1812)

Battle Name	Dates	Campaign
Smolensk	17–19 August 1812	Russian Campaign
Troops Involved		
France	50,000	
	9,000 losses	Commanded by Napoleon
Russia	60,000	
	10,000 losses	Commanded by Barclay de Tolly/ Bagration
Outcome: France		
French victory		

The Battle of Smolensk by Peter Von Hess.

Ney and Murat had driven Neverovski from Krasny on 14 August and Russian prisoners reported that Smolensk was weakly held. Meanwhile, Barclay had ordered Bagration to Nadva and had here received urgent requests for assistance from Neverovski to cover his retreat. Bagration was reluctant, but detached his rearguard (Raevski) to march back to Smolensk.

Smolensk's defences were in a poor state of repair, surrounded by a brick wall and a ditch with some eighteenth-century fortifications. There was, however, a new citadel in the south-west corner of the city. Barclay ordered Bagration to move his whole army south of the River Dneiper; instead, he was content to follow the river on the north bank, believing that Smolensk, and Neverovski's and Raevski's commands were in imminent danger. Barclay placed Docturov's corps under Bagration's control; they were also to attempt to cover the city. By midday on 15 August Raevski was just to the west of Smolensk, but retired towards the city as light began to fail.

Around the same time, Murat arrived some 3 miles (5 km) from Smolensk, but failed to notice Raevski. Instead of heading for the city, he despatched troops to search for a rumoured bridge at Katan. Shortly after midnight, however, Murat and Ney received orders from Napoleon to strike at Smolensk. Davoût was to stay east of Krasny, Eugéne was to repair the bridges at Khomino and Pajol was sent off to try and find Barclay's main army.

Around 0700 on 16 August, Junot, Poniatowski and part of the Guard were also sent up to Smolensk, where Murat had already scattered Raevski's cavalry. By the afternoon, Napoleon had arrived and by 1700 Poniatowski had joined him, but Raevski had been reinforced.

Barclay and Bagration were concerned that Napoleon would try to cut them off from Moscow, so Bagration retired on Dorogobuzh, leaving Barclay to hold Smolensk. During the night Raevski was replaced by Docturov in Smolensk.

At 1230 on 17 August the French launched attacks on the city, primarily on the south, where Barclay's artillery could not interfere. After four hours of heavy fighting, the suburbs had fallen and much of the city was aflame. The assault was called off at 2000.

A new attack was planned by Davoût for 0200, but by 2300 Barclay had ordered that the city be evacuated. The French spotted the Russian withdrawal and at 0230 Davoût, Poniatowski and Ney found the city empty and the bridges on fire.

The Battle of Valutino Gora (1812)

Battle Name	Dates	Campaign
Valutino Gora (Lubino)	19 August 1812	Russian Campaign
Troops Involved		
France	30,000	
	7,000 losses	Commanded by Ney
Russia	40,000	
	7,000 losses	Commanded by Barclay de Tolly
Outcome: Fench victory		

Following his abandonment of Smolensk, Barclay's army still held the heights beside the River Dneiper, but started to withdraw through Prudishta and Gorbunovo. His abiding fear was that the French would send troops across the Dneiper and cut the route at Shein Ostrov. Consequently, he sent Tutchkov and Karpov to make sure the planned line of march was clear.

As it was, Ney had begun crossing the Dneiper at Smolensk at around 0400. His orders were to follow the Russian rearguard if he could find it, or if it had withdrawn to advance on Stabna. Incredibly, Barclay had got himself lost during the night; instead of finding himself at Gorbunovo at 0600, he actually emerged at Gedeonovo, near to Ney's outlying pickets.

He quickly left Eugéne's division as a rearguard on the Gedeonovo–Gorbunovo road and marched the

The Battle of Valutino Gora by Peter Von Hess.

rest of his troops away from the French. Eugéne's division came under increasing pressure from 0800, but at around 0930 Nansouty's cavalry burst onto the Gedeonovo–Gorbunovo road. Here it was forced back by Russian cavalry (Kiorf and Tutchkov). This gave Eugéne a chance to fall back at 1100 towards Gorbunovo, screened by the cavalry.

To the south, at Prudichevo, Junot had crossed the Dneiper to cover the construction of a pontoon bridge. With Davoût steadily advancing along the east bank of the River Dneiper from Smolensk, past Shein Ostrov, Ney was probing along the road to Gorbunovo. Meanwhile, Murat was advancing from Smolensk to where the Russian army had been the night before.

Tutchkov, after covering Eugéne, took up positions between the Kolodnia and Stragan rivers, covering the road to Lubino. Ney's troops began to engage him at 1330 and Tutchkov was eventually pushed back after an hour beyond the Stragan River.

By now Junot had moved up and was confronted by light cavalry under Orlov Denisov and Ney had moved to the Stragan River, but could not clear the Russians off the crest on the opposite bank. The bulk of Barclay's army was across the river and he was determined to hold off the French.

At around 1900, night was drawing in and Ney threw his men across the river in one last attempt to catch the Russians. It took until nearly 2300 to clear the crest, by which time Barclay had organised another rearguard which steadfastly help up the French advance. Had Junot known, he could have cut Barclay off.

The Battle of Borodino (1812)

Battle Name	Dates	Campaign
Borodino	7 September 1812	Russian Campaign
Troops Involved		
France	133,000	
	30,000 losses	Commanded by Napoleon
Russia	120,000	
	44,000 losses	Commanded by Kutusov
Outcome:		
French victory		

From mid-afternoon of 5 September, the Russian army began occupying and preparing fortifications around Borodino. The new overall Russian commander was Kutusov, who realised that in a war of manoeuvre, strategy and tactics, he had little hope of beating Napoleon. None the less, he had been charged with protecting Moscow from the French, and he first needed to postpone the inevitable battle and then be prepared to meet Napoleon on ground that favoured defence.

The Borodino site was well chosen; to begin with it was on higher ground. The town itself was strongly held, although in advance of the main line. The left flank rested on Utitza then ran through woodlands to the Fleches, south of Semyonovskaya. Beyond the village was the Great Redoubt, the pivotal point of the line. The Russian defences then covered the higher ground above Borodino, continuing past Gorki behind the Kalatsha River to its junction with the Moskvo River.

To crack the impressive defence works, Napoleon decided to try to force the Russians into a cul-de-sac between the Kalatsha and Moskvo Rivers. Consequently, Davoût would move first against the Fleches and Poniatowski would press up the old Smolensk road and take Utitza. Ney was to attack Semyonovskaya, and Eugéne would then take Borodino and move on the Great Redoubt. All Kutusov could hope for was that his men would stubbornly hold their ground, as he had little in the way of reserves to commit should the need arise.

At 0600 on 7 September the French attacks got underway with a bombardment of the Russian left. Ney's artillery began to strike at the enemy centre and Eugéne began to soften up the Russians in Borodino.

Davoût's troops got underway shortly after Poniatowski started to move. Unfortunately, Poniatowski chose to cut across country to the old Smolensk road, with the result that his troops did not get into action until around 0800. By this time, Eugéne had launched Delzons at Borodino.

Bagration's troops held the Russian left and he sent Tutchkov to help hold off Davoût. More Russian infantry were committed, then cavalry, and Davoût was stunned by a shell and Dessaix badly wounded.

At Borodino, Delzons had forced out the Russian Guard and began to advance towards Gorki; here he was met by thousands of Russians and driven back with high casualties. The Russians then launched a counterattack to take back the town, but they only managed to destroy the bridge to the east.

The Battle of Borodino by Franz Alexseevitch Rubo.

Morand was leading the assault on the Great Redoubt and had so far driven in the light infantry covering the fortification. At 0700 Ney moved to attack and Junot and Murat advanced to offer closer support. Bagration began to panic when he saw the fresh French troops, and pulled Raevski's reserves to the front. Meanwhile, the long process of getting Bagavout's troops from the far right wing had begun.

Shortly after 0800 Ney's troops stormed two of the three Fleches, and the third was also overrun when it was abandoned. Bagration launched a counterattack with cavalry and took back all but the northern Fleche, which was now held by Württemberg's infantry under the temporary command of Murat, who had ridden forward to reconnoitre the area. He was supported by Nansonty, who in turn supported Ney's renewed attacks. By 1000, the whole of the ridge below Semyonovskaya was in French hands.

Meanwhile, Poniatowski had eventually taken Utitza and was heavily engaged in the surrounding wooded area. At 1000 Eugéne made an attempt on the Great Redoubt, but this was repulsed. After Bagration's counterattack, Junot was pushed into the line between Ney and Davoût, and was then ordered further south to link up with Poniatowski to help push the Russians out of the woodlands.

Platov's and Uvarov's cavalry had not yet been committed and these were ordered to cross the Kalatsha River and fall on Eugéne's left flank; they would go into action some time after 1200. The Fleches were taken back by another of Bagration's counterattacks, but Ney and Davoût had regained them by 1130. The Russian left now held a line on the Semoyonovskaya Creek, where they rallied and

held off attempts to take the village. At around this time, Bagration was mortally wounded. Fresh French troops were moving up to support the attacks on the Semoyonovskaya area. Napoleon despatched Friant's division to reinforce Ney as Murat threw Nansonty and Latour-Manbourg across the creek to give Friant an opportunity to storm the village. Nansonty suffered heavy casualties and was forced to retire, but Latour-Manbourg cleared the Russian infantry and Friant duly took the village. The heights were now in French hands and from here their artillery could do much damage to the massed Russians.

By 1200 Tutchkov had pushed Pomatovski back to Utitza and was holding off Junot, but as the Russian centre was pushed back both Junot and Pomatovski resumed their attacks. This time they succeeded and the Russians fell back on the old Smolensk road.

Meanwhile, in the Great Redoubt area, the position was finally taken by Morand at 1100. Desperately, Russian artillery was trained on the French, followed by a counterattack by Raevski, who snatched back the redoubt.

Uvarov and Platov now made their presence felt on the French left, initially causing much panic. Delzon's infantry formed squares to block Uvarov and French baggage guards held off Platov. None the less, the move caused enough consternation to draw in Grouchy and Lecchi, giving Kutusov time to reorganise his lines.

Ostermann's troops reinforced Raevski, Bagavout now held the Russian left and Docturov took the right, resting his flank on Gorki. The redeployment was made just in time as Eugéne 73 redoubled his efforts to throw the Russians out of the Great Redoubt. His infantry forced out Raevski's troops and Caulaincourt (who had replaced the dead Montbrun) scattered the Russian cavalry that had been committed. His command was brief as he, too, fell near the Great Redoubt.

Ostermann now counterattacked but was roughly handled and fell back. Grouchy now swept forward to mop up the fleeing Russian infantry, but was stopped by the Russian Guard cavalry.

The Russians now occupied the next ridge stretching from Gorki down to the old Smolensk road; only a massive and co-ordinated attack would shift them. The French Guard had not been committed, but Napoleon decided not to risk his last reserves. The battle now rested on artillery fire; a solid pounding from the French would dissuade any attacks from the Russians.

Napoleon fully expected battle to resume in the morning, but after having written to the Tsar proclaiming a great victory, Kutusov ordered a retreat in the early hours of 8 September. He had promised to defend Moscow but Napoleon pursued him vigorously, leaving Junot on the battlefield at Borodino. Murat caught him on 9 September and captured 10,000 wounded men, pausing to the west of Moscow on 13 September Kutusov quickly realised that the city was indefensible and began to retire towards Koloman as Poniatowski had already taken Kaluga. Murat reached the gates of Moscow on 14 September.

Another view of the Battle of Borodino by Franz Alexseevitch Rubo.

The Siege of Burgos (1812)

Battle Name	Dates	Campaign
Burgos	19 September–20 October 1812	Peninsular War
Troops Involved		
France	1,800	
	600 losses	Commanded by du Breton
Britain	12,000	
	2,000 losses	Commanded by Wellington
Outcome:		
French victory		

After Salamanca Wellington was persuaded by the Spaniards to move to Burgos and seize the castle. His advance through the Arlanzon Valley was uneventful, as the French were not willing to risk giving battle at this point.

He entered Burgos, situated on the right bank of the River Arlanzon, on the road from Madrid to Bayonne on 19 September. As his troops arrived, the garrison set fire to houses around the castle to give them better fields of fire. The castle itself lay on a hill and had no fewer than three lines of defence: the old wall, palisade field works and the white church and the old castle keeps. It had a battery of guns called the Napoleon Battery on the hill of San Michael.

The siege was entrusted to the 1st and 6th Divisions, but only eight guns were available for use as siege artillery. None the less, the first assault was made that night. The 79th Highlanders and Pack's Portuguese attacked San Michael and were reinforced by the 42nd Highlanders. It was a costly failure, with 400 killed or wounded for the loss of 150 French.

Wellington resolved to starve the garrison out, and left 12,000 men to besiege the town with a further 20,000 as a covering force. There were also assaults on 21 and 29 September and on 4 October the outer line of defences fell. It looked hopeful that the castle would fall. Another attack was planned for 8 October. A mine was exploded under San Roman, the castle church, at 0430. Spanish and Portuguese troops poured in, but many were killed by a French counter-mine.

The Foot Guards were thrown into the breach and managed to break into the second defence line and then the third, by which time the French had recovered. German troops had by now come to reinforce the British but a French bayonet charge, led by du Breton, forced the British to retreat.

The order to abandon the siege came on 21 October and the British retreated. It was a timely decision, as Souham had amassed 44,000 men and was en route to relieve du Breton.

In the event, Burgos was abandoned by the French as they pursued Wellington back across Spain in their move on Madrid. Ten months after the siege Burgos fell to Wellington after just two days' fighting. Du Breton was to meet Wellington again after the Restoration when he presented his garrison at Strasbourg in more peaceful times.

The Battle of Maloyaroslavets (1812)

Battle Name	Dates	Campaign
Maloyaroslavets	24–25 October 1812	Russian Campaign
Troops Involved		
France	15,000	
	5,000 losses	Commanded by Eugéne
Russia	20,000	
	6,000 losses	Commanded by Doctorov
Outcome:		
French victory		

The French retreat from Moscow started on the 120th day of the Russian Campaign. Loaded with booty, thousands of camp followers and an endless stream of carts and wagons, it took five days to cover just 60 miles (95 km). Despite the fact that the Russians had superiority in cavalry, no attempt was made to block the troops' passage. On 22 October, however, Doctorov's corps left Tarutino and shadowed the French column. He then marched ahead and seized the road junction at Maloyaroslavets.

Mortier had been given the responsibility of covering the retreat and had been told not to leave Moscow until 23 October. The task of leading the way had been assigned to Eugéne's IV Corps, but Doctorov had beaten him to Maloyaroslavets.

Belatedly, Kutusov was on the move and by 1300 on 24 October he had reached a post some 25 miles (40 km) north of Kaluga (in the Afonassova and Gontsharavo region).

Meanwhile, for Eugéne and the French, there was the small matter of Doctorov and his occupation of Maloyaroslavets. More importantly, he also controlled the bridge on the River Lusha just to the north. On 23 October, the situation had seemed to be under control; Delzon's 13th Infantry Division had found Maloyaroslavets unoccupied and reported it as such to Napoleon. Admittedly, he had had to drive off Cossacks in the area. What he had failed to do, however, was to leave a presence at the town and in the night Doctorov had arrived in force and driven him back over the bridge. Having secured the town and the vital bridge, Doctorov now positioned artillery on the ridges and effectively commanded the bridge approaches. At first light on 24 October, Eugéne sent Delzon back across the bridge, but progress was difficult because of the accurate Russian guns. Only when French artillery arrived did Delzon gain a real foothold on the south bank.

He now took the town in a desperate bayonet charge, but Doctorov took it back. Possession see-sawed for the rest of the morning, with new troops arriving on both sides. When it seemed that

The Battle of Maloyaroslavets by Peter Von Hess.

Doctorov's men could be finally overwhelmed, Raevski's corps arrived to support him.

Eugéne now committed his last reserves under Pino and this time the assault on the town proved successful; the Russians finally abandoned their positions around 1200. Russian batteries remained on the ridges and continued to fire for some time later, but the crossing had been won.

The Battles of Krasnyi (1812)

Krasnyi, on the road from Smolensk to Orsha, had been the scene of a battle on 2 August 1812, when Murat and Ney had engaged Neverovsky at 1500. The Russian troops had occupied the wide road lined with birch trees in an attempt to stave off the French cavalry, but the action had ended in a French victory. Now it was to be the site of a series of battles and manoeuvres from 14 to 18 November, following the French withdrawal from Smolensk.

On 13 November, Junot and Poniatowski advanced towards Krasnyi just as Kutusov ordered Miloradovich to move to block the road. Cossack units and partisans were also directed to converge there.

Napoleon had decided to organise his retreat in five columns, leaving Smolensk from 13 to 17 November, so holding Krasnyi gave the Russians an opportunity to deal with the French one at a time.

On 14 November, four Russian corps left Shekanovo and by the next day they were to the south-east of Krasnyi, between Shiloud and Novoselki, taking up a flank position and opening

fire on the French columns. Meanwhile, at Pzhavka, Miloradovich attacked the rearguard of the Imperial Guard, capturing several hundred French troops. Elsewhere, Borozdin and Orlov-Devslov were attacking French troops on minor roads near Krasnyi. Partisans were also very active along the whole of the road from Smolensk.

The heaviest fighting around Krasnyi took place between 16 and 18 November; Eugéne attacked Miloradovich on the 16th and was able to slip around the Russian left. The following day Napoleon attacked with the Guard, hoping to clear the road for Ney and Davoût. Kutusov was wary of tackling Napoleon and called off his advance, but the major danger still lay on the road and Miloradovich inflicted heavy casualties on Davoût (some 6,000 prisoners had been taken so far on the road from Smolensk).

Ney finally left Smolensk on 17 November, with some 6,000 men. He reached Miloradovich's roadblock on the 18th and tried to bypass it just as Eugéne had done. The movement was a disaster and the Russians took hundreds of prisoners. By the time that the last of the organised French units had worked their way around Krasnyi at least 12,000 French troops had either been killed or forced to surrender.

At first Napoleon's gradual retreat from Smolensk had appeared sensible in an attempt not to bunch the whole army together and to make the withdrawal more organised. In the event, it simply conspired to help the Russians beat him comprehensively.

The Battle of Kransniy by Peter Von Hess.

The Battle of Berezina (1812)

Battle Name	Dates	Campaign
Berezina	26–28 November 1812	Russian Campaign
Troops Involved		
France	49,000–89,000	
	50,000–60,000 losses	Commanded by Napoleon
Russia	75,000	
	10,000 losses	Commanded by Wittgenstein/Tshitshagov
Outcome: Russian victory		

Following the retreat from Moscow, it seems that Kutusov reasoned that the Russian winter would do as much harm to the Grande Armée as a pitched battle. Equally, the weather's harshness would save many Russian lives in the battlefield.

By 23 November, Napoleon was considering how to get his troops across his next barrier, the River Berezina. Russian forces held the Borisov bridges, but on that day Corbineau found a ford at Studienka and by 24 November had informed Oudinot.

As far as Napoleon was concerned, there were two major Russian armies to contend with: Kutusov's 65,000 men were approaching, but too far away to impede him; of greater concern was Wittgenstein's 30,000 harassing him from the north-east, but more importantly, Tshitshagov was based at Sembin and had 34,000 men on the west bank of the Berezina.

Napoleon organised a series of diversionary attacks, both to confine and to draw off the Russians. Feints were to be made against Borisov and Vcholodi located to the south, which should draw off Tshitshagov. Only then could Corbineau send a

A watercolour of the crossing of the Berezina River (November 26-29 1812). General Éblé's engineers stand in lines, the only formed unit in the retreat.

cavalry screen across at Studienka to cover the building of three bridges by Elbé. Meanwhile, Victor would hold off Wittgenstein at Kostritsa and Davoût would contain Kutusov's advance guard, now at Bobr.

On 25 November, the apparent display of bridging operations at Borisov convinced Tshitshagov to abandon his positions at Studienka. With this Corbineau crossed and dispersed a Cossack rearguard, and a battery was set up to cover the crossing. At 1300 on 26 November, 11,000 men began crossing the first bridge. The second was completed at 1500 and more troops pressed across.

The crossing continued until 1300 on the 27th, when the second bridge collapsed. This caused a panic and hundreds died in the rush to cross the remaining bridge. Late on 26 November,

Tshitshagov had realised that he had been duped and he retraced his steps towards Studienka, where he encountered Oudinot. Meanwhile, Victor had been driven back towards Borisov.

The 28th dawned and at 0800 Wittgenstein drove Victor back to Studienka. A charge by Ney held off Tshitshagov, causing 2,000 Russian casualties.

There was, however, terrible panic on the bridges and by now thousands had fallen into the icy waters of the river. Victor still held and was finally given permission to cross at 2100, a feat he did not complete until dawn on 29 November. Now the remaining refugees and stragglers attempted to cross just as Elbé was ordered to fire the bridges at 0900. Some managed to cross, but many blocked the river with their frozen corpses for weeks.

The Battle of Berezina by Peter Von Hess.

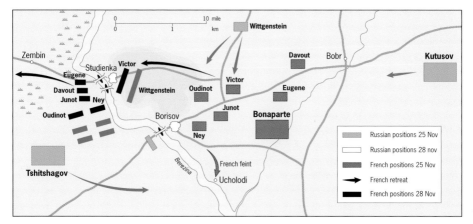

The Battle of Lützen (1813)

Battle Name	Dates	Campaign
Lützen	2 May 1813	Leipzig Campaign
Troops Involved		
France	45,000–110,000	
	20,000 losses	Commanded by Napoleon
Russia/Prussia	73,000	
	18,000 losses	Commanded by Wittengstein/Blücher
Outcome: French victory		

Napoleon was on the move and the allies began concentrating between Leipzig and Altenburg in preparation to attack his right flank near Lützen if he continued to advance over the River Saale. From 1 May, the French advance came under increasing pressure and at Weissenfels Bessières was killed in a heavy engagement.

As the French began to advance towards Lützen, the allies planned to move to engage at 0100 and complete their manoeuvres by 0700 on 2 May. This was optimistic and by 1100 they had reached Gross-Görschen, where they could only see scattered groups of French.

Wittengstein was confident of victory and ordered Blücher to attack at 1145. Instead of encountering a small force, however, they found themselves up against two divisions; the French occupied Gross-Görschen and Starsiedel to the west and Marmont was already on his way to support.

By 1200, Souham's troops in Gross-Görschen had been driven out by artillery, but Girard, at Starsiedel, held. Ney now arrived on the scene and organised a counterattack to stop Souham's retreat and a general action got underway, the sound of which attracted Napoleon's attention. He was deeply concerned about the developments on his right. He needed to buy time to allow Marmont to move up, whilst MacDonald swung his corps southwards to attack the enemy right over the River Flossgraben. The Guard would move up to Kaja to deliver the main infantry attack.

Napoleon reached the battlefield at 1430. Ney's men were exhausted and in dire straits, Bertrand's advance on the enemy left had been halted by the arrival of Russian troops, and all along the front the French were under heavy pressure. Finally, the Guard arrived at Kaja, but Napoleon did not commit them immediately. All that was required was to hold,

Russian foot and horse artillery from an engraving dated 1814.

as MacDonald was coming up on the enemy right and Bertrand had resumed his advance on their left.

Blücher was wounded and Yorck took over. The Russian reserves were slow in advancing, so Wittengstein decided not to rush Yorck's men to support Blücher's exhausted troops. Finally, at 1600, the reserves arrived and Yorck charged Kaja only to be stopped by the Young Guard.

At 1730 MacDonald stormed Eisdorf and Bertrand linked up with Marmont and at 1800 the whole French army attacked. They swept through Rhana, Klein-Görschen and Gross-Görschen and the allies began to withdraw. In the growing darkness the French continued, Marmont being marked by Prussian cavalry at 2100; it had been a costly victory.

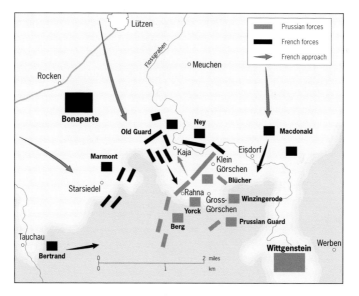

The Battle of Bautzen (1813)

Battle Name	Dates	Campaign
Bautzen	20–21 May 1813	Leipzig Campaign
Troops Involved		
France	Day 1: 115,000	
	Day 2: 96,000	
	20,000 losses	Commanded by Napoleon
Russia/Prussia	Day 1: 20,000–50,000	
	Day 2: 96,000	
	20,000 losses	Commanded by Wittgenstein
Outcome:		
French victory		

Bautzen saw the allies at a distinct numerical disadvantage throughout the battle. Napoleon intended to turn their right and seize the village of Hochkirch, which would give him control of the road leading to Görlitz. Marmont, MacDonald and Oudinot would attack the enemy's centre, Ney would turn the Allies right and make Wittgenstein commit his reserves. At this point Bertrand would launch a major assault against the centre, wherever it appeared to be weakest.

Unfortunately, Ney had not got into position by 19 May, so Napoleon decided to spend the 20th wearing down the enemy and delay his attack by a day. Meanwhile, the allies had their own plans; they intended to wear down the French attacks and then launch their own counterattacks against the enemy's left. The Russians were convinced that Napoleon's main strength would be in the south, so their own right was weak.

Just after 1200 on 20 May, Napoleon's artillery began bombarding the allies and at 1500 the French attacks began. Pontoon bridges were thrown over the

River Spree and French infantry stormed the first line of the enemy positions. By 1800, Bautzen was in Napoleon's hands. Ney was fast approaching the River Klix, but still the allies did nothing to move troops to the north to check his advance.

Early on 21 May, Napoleon realised that Ney would not be in position until 1100 and that Lauriston would be even further behind. None the less, he urged Ney to engage the enemy right at his earliest opportunity, whilst Lauriston was to move to cut the Görlitz road to the rear of the allies. Marmont, MacDonald and Oudinot would continue to batter the Allied centre. Soult and Bertrand were to deliver the major blow when the chance appeared. The French reserve would move up to the Baden area and be committed in the event of an emergency.

As the engagement got underway again in the morning, it was Oudinot who faced the greatest difficulties. Gortschakoff, holding the allied left, had been reinforced by Miloradovich and they were pursuing Oudinot very hard. MacDonald and Marmont were equally pressed by determined lines of allies intent on not being dislodged. By noon, however, Marmont had reached the River Blossaer-Wasser and Napoleon reinforced him with a division of the Young Guard.

Sounds of battle off to the north convinced Napoleon that Ney was now fully engaged and it was time for Soult and Bertrand to be committed. The 'grand assault' consisted of some 20,000 infantry, 1,000 cavalry and 30 guns, with the immediate objective of capturing the area between Kreschwitz and Pliskowitz. Napoleon also committed a Young Guard division and deployed as many guns to support the attack as possible. At 1400, the blow fell on Blücher, the first target being a fort, the linchpin of his defences. Napoleon had redeployed sixty guns to the west of Basankwitz, and they opened fire on Kreschwitz. The bombardment lasted until 1500, by which time Blücher's fort was in Soult's hands. The

assault was, however, stalled by intense resistance.

What of Ney and his attack on the allied right? By 1000 he had taken the redoubt at Gleinau, but he was still only approaching Preititz, which Napoleon had expected him to reach by 1100. As a result Blücher was able to extricate his troops and avoid being surrounded. Ney began attacking him around Klein-Burschwitz instead of going around his forces and trapping the Prussians.

On the central front, the French attacks now concentrated on dislodging the Russians in the Senkwitz and Bauschutz areas, but this line doggedly remained unbroken until 1700.

An hour earlier, Tsar Alexander had ordered a limited withdrawal, which encouraged Oudinot's exhausted men to resume their attacks. Whilst Soult was still trying to struggle forward, Napoleon decided to commit the Imperial Guard. It hit Blücher's left flank and finally he began to retire, still in good order. Shortly after Ney finally took Preititz and Lauriston seized Baruth, but the door was not shut and the allies began to retreat, still under pressure. The Prussians headed for Weissenberg and the Russians for Löbau.

Napoleon could not apply pressure with any great vigour, partly because the men were so exhausted, but also because a ferocious storm hit the area at around 2200. It had been a tarnished victory; Ney and Lauriston had not fulfilled their orders and across the whole of the army the fact that many of the men were recruits and conscripts and not the grizzled veterans of old had begun to tell.

The pursuit began on 22 May, but caused another brief engagement at Reichenbach, which prompted Napoleon to call it off. Wittgenstein resigned his post, to be replaced by Barclay de Tolly and Blücher argued with the Russians when they proposed to fall back to Poland. In the end, the allies returned to Schweidnitz in Silesia, hoping to link up with the Austrians.

The Battle of Vittoria (1813)

Battle Name	Dates	Campaign
Vittoria	21 June 1813	Peninsular War
Troops Involved		
France	66,000	
	8,000 losses	Commanded by Joseph Bonaparte
Britain	80,000	
	5,100 losses	Commanded by Wellington
Outcome:		
British victory		

Wellington was keen to convince the French that his 1813 campaigns would be aimed at central Spain, when, in fact, he intended to march through northern Portugal and aim for Burgos, then the

Pyrenees and into southern France. There were enormous benefits to this as he would be able to open up the northern Spanish supply ports and not have to rely on Lisbon as his main source of material.

By 3 June, his army had reached the Douro, catching the French entirely by surprise. Burgos was abandoned on 13 June and by the 19th he was to the east of Vittoria.

Joseph Bonaparte was hurrying to intercept, followed by a second force of 14,000 men, under Clausel, who did not arrive in time to fight. On the morning of 21 June, the French line was in position, with the commanders sitting on Arinez hill at their centre.

Wellington sent Hill's 20,000 men to take the south of the valley, which they did at 0830. Two hours later Graham's troops (British, Portuguese and Spanish) probed west and became embroiled in stiff fighting for several hours on the north bank of the Zadotra River.

Just after noon Kempt's brigade seized the Tres Puentes Bridge over the Zadorra. He was swiftly supported by the rest of the Light Division, who stormed the bridge at Villodas, whilst Picton took the Mendoza Bridge. Together, they now swept the French off Arinez.

By 1500, the British were pressurising the French at the village of Margarita, on the right flank of the French line. French infantry, under Gazan, supported by artillery, held the south of Arinez but Margarita fell and the line was compromised. With D'Erlon being pulled back by Picton, Kempt and Dalhousie, Hill's troops surging from Puebla and Graham's troops closing the net from behind, the French were in a perilous position.

At 1700 Cole's 4th Division smashed in Gazan's troops and the gap separated d'Erlon, who was still being pushed back. As the time passed Gazan realised that he would be cut off. Joseph was viewing all of this with increasing alarm and finally ordered a general withdrawal.

Instead of a measured retreat, the French army disintegrated, and 151 or 153 guns were captured. Joseph's army was saved from complete capture as the allies fell on the accumulated French plunder. It is said that no greater amount of treasure has ever fallen into enemy hands.

The Siege of San Sebastian (1813)

Battle Name	Dates	Campaign
San Sebastian	28 June–31 August 1813	Peninsular War
Troops Involved		
France	3,000	Commanded by Rey
	2000 losses	
Britain/Portugal	10,000	Commanded by Graham
	2,376 losses	
Outcome:		
British/Portuguese victory		

British and Spanish troops storm San Sebastian.

San Sebastian was the third of the successful sieges carried out by the British during the Peninsular War. Although Wellington was nominally in command, the operations were actually carried out by Graham. Unlike the frenetic sieges at Ciudad Rodrigo and Badajoz, the one at San Sebastian did not risk being broken by the French as Soult was safely bottled up beyond the French border.

The town was dominated by Monte Orgullo, a rocky mountain on which was built a castle. Below, the town sat on a sandy peninsula bounded by the Bay of Biscay on three sides. The only approach was from the south.

Graham chose the eastern side for his breaching attacks. This lay beyond the River Urumea, which could be crossed at low tide. His artillery bombarded the town until 25 July. Then Oswald's 5th Division and Bradford's Portuguese troops made the first assault, which failed.

Shortly after this, Soult attempted to force his way through the Pyrenees to relieve the garrison, but his attempts were repulsed. On 26 August, additional siege guns arrived from England and by this time the British were able to use the northern ports of Spain for resupply. It now seemed that San Sebastian could not hold out much longer.

By 30 August, Rey's artillery had been virtually silenced and Graham could look contentedly on the wrecked eastern wall. Unfortunately, because of the tides, Graham would have to launch his attack in broad daylight; it was timetabled for noon on the 31st. Graham had his men paraded at dawn; Bradford and Oswald would storm the main breach, and the second, smaller one would be attacked by 800 Portuguese.

The leading waves of allies were decimated; all along the defence works the French desperately threw everything at them. With the assault wavering, Graham ordered Dickson, who commanded the artillery, to open fire over the heads of his leading columns. The allied troops threw themselves to the ground and waited for 20 minutes as the artillery ripped the town and defences to pieces. There was an enormous explosion as the town's magazine was hit, which claimed many French lives.

As the bombardment lifted, the allied troops stormed forward, seizing the town and rounding up the survivors. The allies had lost 1,520 wounded and 856 kills during the operations. The castle held out until 8 September, by which time the whole of the town had been destroyed.

The Battle of the Pyrenees (1813)

After his victory at Vittoria, Wellington could now plan his invasion of France, but he faced two seemingly insurmountable obstacles: the Pyrenees and a new French commander, Soult. Pamplona and San Sebastian were both still held by strong French garrisons and would have to be taken before Wellington could attempt to cross the Pyrenees. He therefore began a blockade on Pamplona and moved his siege equipment up to tackle San Sebastian. Whilst 10,000 men under Graham began the siege, Wellington had just 60,000 men between San Sebastian and Pamplona, covering a 50-mile (80-km) front.

He concentrated the bulk of his troops at Irun, expecting that Soult, who had replaced Joseph Bonaparte, would make an attempt to raise the siege of San Sebastian. Soult, however, had other ideas, and planned to advance on Pamplona and then march on San Sebastian, forcing Wellington to raise the siege or face the prospect of being cut off on the north-east coast of Spain.

Wellington had set up his headquarters at Lesala. Hill held the right at Roncesvalles-Maya, the 7th Division held Echellar, the Light Division was based at Vera and the left was held by Spanish forces. Cole's division was held in reserve at Roncesvalles and the 6th Division was based at Estevan.

Soult planned his attack for early morning on 25 July, with two columns of 20,000 men, one under Reille and the other commanded by Clausel. Clausel's three divisions hit Byng's brigade on the east of the pass at Roncesvalles at 0600. Despite the vast numerical superiority, the French were held up for some four hours. The attacks began again in earnest at 1200, but it took a further three hours to sweep Byng aside and force him to retreat to even better positions on the Altobiscar mountain. Clausel could now move to outflank the allies. Reille's troops assaulted the western ridge at 1400, but by 1600, with heavy fog cloaking the battlefield, they had made little progress.

Meanwhile, D'Erlon's columns attacked the pass at Maya, dominated by the Gorospil and Alcorrunz mountains. Holding the pass were two brigades of Stewart's 2nd Division and at 0600 a large French force began its assault on Gorospil, which was held by just a single British company. Although it was reinforced by four more companies, and the 350 men held out for four hours, the 7,000 French troops finally swept them away. Despite valiant attempts, the French now held the east of the road and by 1630 they had control of the pass. It now seemed that they would be able to break through to Pamplona, but at 1800 Barnes arrived with reinforcements and stopped their advance. In this area alone, the French had lost

2,000 men for the cost of 1,500 British.

On 25 July Cole retreated from Roncesvalles towards Pamplona, but Wellington was unaware of this until 2000 on the 26th. None the less, he still hoped to stop Soult at Zubiri. On the morning of the 27th, however, he discovered that Cole was still retreating. Post-haste, he rode to Sorauren to take personal command of Cole's troops.

He drew up his 20,000 men on a steep ridge running east–west to the south-east of Sorauren. His line covered some 1_ miles (2.5 km) and at points the ridge was as high as 2,000 ft (600 m). Soult had moved some 35,000 men to a ridge to the north. To the south-east of Huarte, a second ridge was held by Anglo-Spanish troops under Picton, O'Donnell and Morillo.

Wellington expected the 6th Division, under Pack, to join him by dawn on 28 July, but poor weather delayed them and he finally came into view at 1000. Paradoxically, Pack's men were the first to engage the French as Soult launched columns against them from Sorauren, but they managed to throw them back.

At 1200 Soult launched a major attack against the ridge but was stopped dead on the ridgeline and his troops fell back in chaos. Some progress was made on the left of Wellington's line, but a timely counterattack cleared Soult's troops from the area around a small chapel. To the east, Morillo's Spaniards had been forced off the Zabaloica hill, but British troops came to the rescue and swept the French attacks with devastating volleys.

Soult called off the offensive at 1630, by which time he had lost around 4,000 men. Wellington's casualties were 2,652. Soult did not withdraw; he hoped for support from D'Erlon, whilst Wellington awaited the arrival of Hill and Dalhousie. There was little combat on 29 July, but by early light on the 30th Soult was in retreat.

Wellington immediately ordered an artillery bombardment and sent in troops to storm Sorauren. By 1200 Soult's men were running towards France. Wellington was now free to reduce San Sebastian and plan his invasion of France. Soult's offensive lay in tatters and with it France's ambitions in Spain.

The Battle of Dresden (1813)

Battle Name	Dates	Campaign
Dresden	26–27 August 1813	Leipzig Campaign
Troops Involved		
France	Day 1: 35,000–70,000	
	Day 2: 150,000	
	10,000 losses	Commanded by Napoleon
Russia/Prussia	Day 1: 120,000	
	Day 2: 170,000	
	38,000 losses	Commanded by Schwarzenburg
Outcome:		
French victory		

The French commander of the city of Dresden, St Cyr, had improvised defences around the suburbs and created five redoubts. The city's two bridges would have to be held at all costs, both to provide reinforcements and supplies, and as an escape route if needed. The allies approached the city at around 0500 on 26 August. Wittgenstein would cover the area closest to the River Elbe, whilst Prussian units would take the Great Garden on the outskirts of the city.

As it was, the Prussians did not take the Great Garden until 0730, Wittgenstein coming up against heavy French artillery fire from the east of the river. At around 0900 combined Prussian and Russian pressure succeeded in taking nearly all of the Great Garden, whilst the Austrians to the north-west stormed the villages of Plaüen and Löbtans. By 1100 St Cyr's men had only been pushed back to their main defensive positions; now Napoleon arrived and

it was hotly debated whether the allies should retire. As it was, the main allied attack had been planned for 1600; and perhaps against their better judgement it went ahead.

Wittgenstein was stopped in his tracks by French artillery; the Prussians had taken the Great Garden, but faltered before the city's walls. The Austrians, however, managed to storm some of the outlying redoubts and break into the suburbs of the city.

At 1730, Napoleon launched his counterattacks, with all of St Cyr's men committed to the defence. Mortier took back the Great Garden and swept Wittgenstein aside, and Ney struck at the allied centre. There was feverish work to be done overnight reorganising the allied lines.

At 0600 on 27 August Nansouty, Ney and Mortier struck the allied left, clearing the Blasewitz Woods, Seidnitz, Gruhna and Strehlen. St Cyr moved up to establish his line at the latter village.

Murat's attack was launched at 0630; he quickly overran the village the Austrians had taken the day before and pinned a large enemy force against the River Weisseritz at Dölzschess. The vital Pläven Bridge had fallen and the men were trapped and by 1500 the allied left was shattered.

On the French left, Napoleon ordered an assault on Reick, which was taken at the second attempt by bayonet with Wittgenstein's men returning to Torna. St Cyr was repulsed three times in his attacks against Leubnitz. Whilst Napoleon was planning a new assault on the allied positions, they decided to retreat as they were short on food and ammunitions, but, above all, their morale was at breaking point.

French Marshall. *Courtesy of Ondrej Tupy, The Club of Military History, Novy Jicin, Czech Republic*

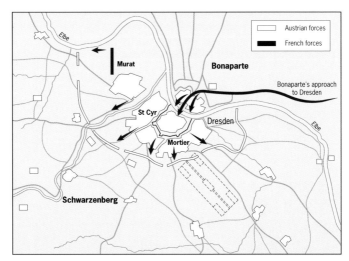

The Battle of Kulm-Priesten (1813)

Battle Name	Dates	Campaign
Kulm	30 August 1813	Leipzig Campaign
Troops Involved		
France	32,000	
	13,000 captured	Commanded by Vandamme
Austria/Russia/Prussia	44,000–54,000	
	11,000 losses	Commanded by Ostermann-Tolstoy/Kleist
Outcome:		
Austro-Russian/Prussia victory		

Early on 28 August, French patrols had found only scattered elements of the allied army which had opposed them at Dresden. Napoleon realised that he could trap them in the mountains if the pursuit was swift and determined and Vandamme was despatched in pursuit.

Matters were not going well for Napoleon, however. Oudinot had been defeated by Bülow on 23 August and now he received news that MacDonald had crossed the River Katzbach intent on pursuing Blücher, but the wily old Prussian had taken the opportunity to turn and give him a bloody nose on 26 August. MacDonald had lost 15,000 captured men and 100 guns. The whole strategic situation was beginning to unravel and turn against Napoleon. He faced the prospect of losing the fruits of his victory at Dresden, but there was worse to come.

Regardless of the defeats, he left the pursuit to others and returned to Dresden in the afternoon. But whatever hopes for peace he may have had were rudely shattered just two days later. The French pursuit was robust, but uncoordinated and the inevitable result was that opportunities presented themselves for the allies to turn and fight. This happened on 29 August when Vandamme's corps found itself isolated and facing a turning enemy at Priesten, 5 miles (8 km) from Teplitz. Ostermann-Tolstoy attacked him vigorously and by the end of the day the French had fallen back to Kulm.

Kleist, at the head of 10,000 Prussians, suddenly appeared to Vandamme's rear on 30 August whilst retreating from St Cyr. He happened on the scene just as Ostermann-Tolstoy's 44,000 men were heavily engaged with Vandamme and the French now faced 54,000 allies. Vandamme desperately tried to fight his way out of the trap, but succeeded in extricating just half of his forces. He and 13,000 men fell into enemy hands.

In a few short days the allied victories at Grössbeeren, Katzbach and Kulm had reduced the impact of the defeat at Dresden. It was to inspire the allies and raise their hopes and morale for their meeting with the French en masse at Leipzig.

The Battle of Leipzig (1813)

Battle Name	Dates	Campaign
Leipzig	16–19 October 1813	Leipzig Campaign
Troops Involved		
France	Day 1: 170,080	
	Days 3/4: 195,000	
	73,000 losses	Commanded by Napoleon
Austria/Prussia/Russia/Sweden	Day 1: 257,000	
	Days 3/4: 365,000	
	52,000–54,000 losses	Commanded by Blücher/Schwarzenberg/Bennigsen/Bernadotte
Outcome:		
Austrian/Prussian/Russian/Swedish victory		

The French missed their opportunity to crush the shattered allies after Dresden and only Vandamme's corps pushed them with any real vigour. Vandamme tried to cut off the Austrian supply and communications at Kulm on 29–30 August, but ran into a large Austrian force. The outcome was inevitable and only part of his corps managed to escape; he was captured along with 13,000 of his men. This disaster was a double blow for Napoleon; Vandamme had been an able and aggressive general and would be sorely missed, equally it gave the Allies fresh hope and helped eradicate the memory of the defeat at Dresden.

There were to be more disasters; at Dennewitz Ney collided with a Swedish force under Bernadotte and was severely mauled on 6 September. Napoleon was now determined to concentrate his forces, choosing Leipzig on the River Elster as his base of operations. Again things did not go well for the French. Blücher and Bernadotte were moving on the city from the north and the Austrians, commanded by Schwarzenberg, were approaching from the south. Napoleon's Confederation of the Rhine was now under dire threat of being crushed. This was not helped by Bavaria switching sides in early October and declaring war on the French.

Napoleon had gathered some 122,000 men at Leipzig by 15 October; he hoped that he could smash each successive allied army that dared to assail his forces. This was destined to be the largest battle of the era and would become known as the 'Battle of the Nations'. The engagement opened on 16 October when Barclay de Tolly's 78,000 Austrians struck against the south of the city. The attack was poorly co-ordinated, however, and the French were able to hold their counterattack. Meanwhile, in the north, the Prussians, under Blücher, attacked Marmont's positions around Mockern, but although they enjoyed a two-to-one advantage, they could make little headway.

The Austrians launched another assault to the west of the city before the end of the day; this time the front was held heroically by Bertrand's troops. Although all of the assaults had ended in failure, what was clear was that the city was almost totally surrounded. Equally, the allies could confidently expect additional reinforcements to move up during the night; Napoleon would have to face even greater odds in the coming days. For once, the initiative lay with the allies. Napoleon could not dare to concentrate a strong strike force to assail one of the allies and knock them out of the conflict for fear that

French General Drouot is charged by a Bavarian cavalryman in the retreat after Leipzig. Detail from a painting by Horace Vernet.

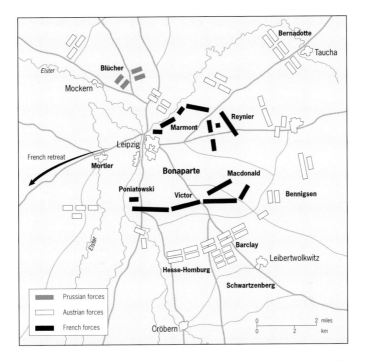

another would exploit the weaknesses made in his defences by the concentration.

On 17 October, there was little real fighting along the perimeter; the allies were redeploying their forces and welcoming the arrival of Bernadotte's Swedes and the Russians under Bennigsen, amounting to a further 100,000 men. The ring around the French now consisted of Austrians and Russian to the south, Swedes to the east and Prussians to the north, but they had not yet closed the route to the west. Despite this lifeline, however, the French were in great need of ammunition; each day of conflict depleted their low reserves even more as would be a telling factor as the engagement developed.

On 18 October, the allies were finally redeployed; Napoleon had spent the previous day shoring up his defences and the perimeter. The allies' assault called for the co-ordination of some 350,000 men. The pressure along the whole of the perimeter was intense, but the breaking point came when the Saxons, hitherto Napoleon's allies, defected. Napoleon's only hope now was to extricate as much of his army from the perimeter as possible and conduct a fighting withdrawal to the west. For nine hours, the allies battered the French, eventually penetrating the city itself. Only then did Napoleon order a retreat. As if the position was not perilous enough, the French conspired to do themselves an even greater injury. With some 20,000 men still manning the rearguard on the Leipzig side (east) of the River Elster, the only bridge was demolished by French engineers. Also trapped on the wrong side of the river were Lauriston and Reynier (who were both captured) and MacDonald and Poniatowski (the latter drowned whilst swimming across the Elster).

The Battle of Hanau (1813)

Battle Name	Dates	Campaign
Hanau	30–31 October 1813	Leipzig Campaign
Troops Involved		
France	70,000–80,000	
	6,000 losses	Commanded by Napoleon
Bavaria/Austria	45,000–50,000	
	10,000 losses	Commanded by Wrede
Outcome:		
French victory		

After their defeat at Leipzig, it was imperative that the French quickly extricate their army from Germany, particularly given the fact that Saxony, Wurtemberg and Bavaria were now enemies. The chosen route took the French through Erfurt, Eisenach, Fulda, Frankfurt, Geinhausen and Mainz.

It was between Geinhausen and Mainz that Napoleon's former ally, Wrede, decided to block the retreat with his Austrian-Bavarian force of 45,000–50,000. His advance guard had seized Hanau on 28 October and by the following day the bulk of his army was deploying around the town. He knew that he could expect the French to arrive at any time. By the night of 29 October, Napoleon was aware of Wrede's presence. For the present he had Sébastiani, MacDonald, Victor, Nansouty and the Old Guard, in all some 20,000 men. Marmont was a day away, Bertrand two and his first and second corps was forming his rearguard. By 0200 on 30 October, he had formulated his plan, he would attack Wrede's right through the Lamboi Forest and then envelop his left.

At 0800 some 3,000 French began to work their way through Lamboi Forest, clearing the Bavarians out until they reached the edges of the woodland. Victor reinforced the effort with 2,000 more and Sébastiani attack with cavalry in support. By 1200, the Austro-Bavarian troops had been driven from the forest and fell back to the main line. The French were unable to follow up because of heavy artillery fire and steady musketry. This situation remained a stalemate for some hours.

Meanwhile, as Napoleon moved up the Geinhausen road near the forest at 1500, he was unable to deploy on the plain, so resolute was Wrede's stand and weight of fire. The French were determined to force their way through, however, and fifty guns were brought up to cover part of the Old Guard. Behind them the guard cavalry formed up ready to mount a charge. The artillery opened fire, but Wrede threw his own cavalry at the French guns, some 7,000 men. Most got to within 50 yards before the weight of the French fire was unleashed, cutting down hundreds. Although a few managed to get in amongst the French guns, they were thrown back by French counterattacks.

By 1600 the allied cavalry was in full retreat and the French advanced their guns, only to be attacked again by the enemy cavalry, which managed to rally. Again it was thrown back with heavy casualties. At 1700 Wrede was in great difficulties; his cavalry had been shattered and both they and the infantry were running short of ammunition. His only chance to prevent absolute disaster was to retire beyond the Kinzig and hope that he would hold Hanau itself. Before he had any hope of extricating his troops, however, Napoleon had to be stopped. Wrede ordered a counterattack on his right (Becker and Bach) against Victor and MacDonald. Initially, it went well and the French gave ground. Napoleon stopped the assault with two battalions of Old Guard and the advance was halted at Neuhof. By 1800, Wrede's troops had crossed the Kinzig; it had been a costly withdrawal, but at 1900 Wrede's troops had rallied around Lehrof and were still in possession of Hanau.

At 0200 on 31 October, Marmont began to bombard Hanau. An assault by Charriere failed, but during the night Wrede ordered the evacuation of the town and by 0900 the following day the French had occupied it. Marmont pushed over the Lamboi Bridge and Wrede fell back to the River Main, then launched a counterattack which sent Marmont back towards the bridge and Hanau. Shortly after, at 0800, Napoleon took Victor, Sébastiani and MacDonald along with the Guard towards Frankfurt; only Marmont and Bertrand remained. By 1200 Bertrand had covered the Lamboi Bridge, the town of Hanau and the road to Frankfurt. At 1300 Marmont retired from the field and Bertrand's 2,500 men now faced Wrede's 20,000 alone.

At 1400 Wrede launched a two-pronged attack, with his left aimed at Hanau and the Lamboi Bridge and the right at the Frankfurt Road. Wrede launched a secondary attack at 1500. Three attempts were made to take the bridge but they were all repulsed at great loss. At 1600, Wrede managed to penetrate the town on the left, the objective being the bridge over the Kinzig. The leading elements managed to get as far as the bridge itself before French artillery shattered the columns at point-blank range. Wrede was wounded and his replacement, Fresnel, ordered a withdrawal.

At 1900 Bertrand ordered his exhausted men to head towards Frankfurt. The Kinzig Bridge had been destroyed and the battlefield casualties had slowly disappeared under the snow.

Napoleon lost 6,000 men at Hanau, and a further 10,000 in the crippling retreat from Leipzig. Of the 170,000 men at Leipzig, 100,000 had been lost; more perilous still, the allies were now advancing unchecked towards France; Germany had been lost for ever.

French infantry. Mario Tomasone

The Battle of Nivelle (1813)

Battle Name	Dates	Campaign
Nivelle	10 November 1813	Peninsular War
Troops Involved		
France	63,000	
	4,351 losses	Commanded by Soult
Britain	80,000	
	2,450 losses	Commanded by Wellington
Outcome:		
British victory		

British infantry. Llynn Holmes

On the day San Sebastian fell, Soult made a last – and unsuccessful – attempt to relieve the garrison. The 10,000 troops under Vandermaesen were ordered back and headed for the fords over the River Bidassoa at Vera. The water level was too high, however, so he made for the bridge. This, however, was held by a detachment of the 95th Rifles, under Cadoux. He held it for two hours before he was killed, along with some sixteen of his men. His force, however, had inflicted 231 casualties on the French and killed Vandermaesen.

All this was a prelude to a major allied offensive. On 7 October Wellington crossed the Bidassoa himself and inflicted 1,700 casualties for the loss of 1,200. Wellington now headed for the main French positions before the River Nivelle.

The French line stretched from the Atlantic to the pass at Roncesvalles, some 16 miles (26 km) in total. They had constructed strong redoubts along the hills and the main strength of the army was around Bayonne. Wellington realised that Soult's troops were thinly spread and that a concentrated attack could break through and hopefully cut the French off. Of particular interest was Soult's left which, if breached, could mean disaster for him.

Wellington detailed Beresford to attack the French centre. Hope's 1st and 5th Divisions, supported by Spaniards under Freire, made up the allied left and the right would be commanded by Hill. Hill's 2nd and 6th Divisions would be supported by Portuguese (under Hamilton) and Spaniards (under Morillo). Beresford had the largest force, consisting of the Light Division and the 3rd, 4th and 7th Divisions.

As far as Wellington was concerned, the major target was the La Rhune area, consisting of two main obstacles: the Greater Rhune (2,800 ft/850 m) and the Lesser Rhune (2,100 ft/640 m). He was fortunate; when his men crossed the Bidassoa and cleared the ridge above Vera, the French evacuated the Greater Rhune and from here an offensive could be launched.

At dawn on 10 November, the Light Division crept down towards the Lower Rhune. Following an artillery barrage, the troops stormed the French positions. Meanwhile, Colbourne's troops attacked the French-held fort on the Mouiz Plateau and carried the position.

Wellington could now launch a full offensive on a 5-mile (8-km) front. Amotz fell, cutting the French in half and by 1400 the French were in full retreat; darkness saved them from an even greater disaster.

The Battle of Nive (1813)

Battle Name	Dates	Campaign
Nive	9–13 December 1813	Peninsular War
Troops Involved		
France	50,000	
	3,500 losses	Commanded by Soult
British	63,500	
	1,500 losses	Commanded by Wellington
Outcome:		
British victory		

After the loss of his defensive positions at the Nivelle, Soult retreated towards Bayonne, a major supply centre. Wellington had considerably fewer men to crack this tough town, which was protected by fortresses, the River Adour and numerous streams and boggy ground. Soult's defences stretched to Cambo on the River Nive, and in order to deal with this situation Wellington would have to split his forces. One part of the army would head out along the Atlantic coast from the south, whilst the rest, having crossed the River Nive, would strike from the east.

Poor weather slowed down preparations, but on 9 December Hill's British and Le Cor's Portuguese crossed the Nive at Cambo and Beresford's troops crossed at Ustaritz. On the evening of 9 December Soult realised he had a chance to turn the tables on Wellington and despatched 50,000 men, under D'Erlon, out of Bayonne to attack at first light. Initially the attack was successful and Hope's troops at Anglet were driven back, with D'Erlon advancing to Arcangues. Here the British dug in and refused to be budged. For the next two days the French threw everything at those of them on the left bank of the Nive.

Determined to keep the initiative, Soult now threw his troops at Hill, who was on the right bank. Attempts to reinforce Hill's 14,000 men failed when the pontoon bridge that was to be used by Beresford was swept away. Hill's troops would have to face 35,000 men alone.

They were thrown back initially and by midday Hill had committed the last of his reserves, retaking ground lost to the French with the bayonet. Just as time seemed to be running out, engineers managed to rebuild the pontoons at Ville Franque and two divisions joined the fray. A third division, the 6th, came up from Ustaritz, closely followed by additional troops with Wellington.

The arrival of the fresh reserves tipped the balance and a general British advance forced Soult to retire towards Bayonne. His opportunity to crush Wellington had failed, despite the fact that he had deployed all of his troops against separate and isolated parts of Wellington's army. Concerned that he would be cut off in Bayonne, he posted 10,000 men, under Thouvenot, in the town whilst he retreated east along the River Adour.

This is considered to have been the most desperate battle of the Peninsular War; it was Soult's last chance and Wellington was now very much on the offensive.

The Battle of Brienne (1814)

Battle Name	Dates	Campaign
Brienne	29 January 1814	Campaign in France
Troops Involved		
France	30,000	
	3,000 losses	Commanded by Napoleon
Prussia	20,000–25,000	
	4,000 losses	Commanded by Blücher
Outcome:		
French victory		

Napoleon had decided to try to deal with the Prussians before the other Allied armies at large in France. The most promising target was Blücher's Army of Silesia as it was closer and it was scattered.

French cavalry being reviewed by an officer. *Mario Tomasone*

Napoleon knew that Blücher was at St Dizier, Yorck was far behind and Marmont was already between them. He ordered Marmont to Bar-le-Duc to ensure that no link could be made between Blücher and Yorck. Mortier and Gérard were assigned to delaying Schwarzenberg, who was south-east of Paris, along the Seine and its junction with the Yonne River. Blücher's troops, comprised of Yorck and Sacken, were near the Aisne River; Kleist and Kapzevitsch were further south, beyond the Marne River.

Victor had been trying to hold Blücher at St Dizier, but he was gradually being forced back towards Vitry. Napoleon hoped to catch the Prussian with his troops separated by the River Marne. But by the time that he moved up, Blücher had already passed through St Dizier and was heading for Brienne, leaving a rearguard at the town. The French retook St Dizier, but it was too late; if there was to be a battle, it would be at Brienne.

Napoleon marched towards Brienne in three columns, knowing that Blücher could now link up with Schwarzenberg any day; he needed to destroy him before he could be reinforced. Napoleon sent a despatch to Mortier, telling him to move to Arcis-sur-Aube but unfortunately for him this instruction was captured by the Cossacks and by early on 29 January, Blücher was aware of his intentions.

Brienne was held by Olssufiev's Russians and Blücher now ordered Sacken to march there from Lesmont and Pahlen's Austrian cavalry (3,000) also to head there. He reversed his march to Arcis-sur-Aube just in time; he would be at Brienne to meet Napoleon.

Grouchy's cavalry and artillery began the engagement in the late morning of 29 January and by 1500 Ney and Victor had arrived and were thrown straight into the battle. Ney advanced with two divisions against Brienne whilst Victor tried to storm the château to the west of the town.

With the rest of the French II Corps heading towards Bar-sur-Abe in an attempt to cut Blücher off, the French fortunes on the field were mixed. Throughout the afternoon, Pahlen was held off successfully, but Victor was forced to give ground. Even Napoleon narrowly missed falling into Cossack hands at one point.

The fighting continued during the evening. By then Victor had succeeded in taking the château, almost capturing Blücher and Gneisenau. The last shots were fired at around 2200, with an abortive allied attempt to seize the château back.

By 2300, Blücher was retiring towards the south; his army was intact and if anything the French had only succeeded in making his meeting with Schwarzenberg more certain.

The Battle of La Rothière (1814)

Battle Name	Dates	Campaign
La Rothière	1 February 1814	Campaign in France
Troops Involved		
France	30,000–40,000	
	6,000 losses	Commanded by Napoleon
Prussia	53,000–110,000	
	6,000 losses	Commanded by Blücher
Outcome:		
Prussian (Allied) victory		

Following his defeat at Brienne, Blücher managed to link up with Schwarzenberg and determined to launch another attack on Napoleon. He had a formidable force at his disposal: his own two corps and two of Schwarzenberg's gave him 53,000 men. The 25,000 Bavarians, under Wrede, would tackle the French left and he had been promised the immediate support of Barclay de Tolly's Russian reserve of 33,000 men.

On the morning of 1 February, the vast allied armies marched north from Trannes to engage. At 1000, Napoleon ordered Marmont to occupy Lesmont and Ney to move up through Brienne. At around 1200 Victor reported large-scale enemy troop movements between Trannes and Éclance. Napoleon had assumed that the main target was Troyes, but he had been mistaken – although he was still unconvinced that this was Blücher's main attack.

Marmont took up position near Morvilliers, Victor held the centre between Chaumesnil and Le Petit Mesnil (with his right at La Rothière), whilst Gérard occupied the area around Dienville. Nansouty and Grouchy were held in reserve behind the centre and further back (to the south-east of Brienne) was the Young Guard.

At 1300, Blücher launched a major assault on La Rothière. The French cavalry beat it off and Guyot's horsemen even managed to overrun a Russian artillery battery. The Russians themselves, however, succeeded in capturing twenty-four French guns in the struggle around La Rothière, as the pendulum swung this way and that as fresh troops poured in.

In the midst of a blizzard, the battle raged on, but the allies could make no headway against

Dienville and Duhesme, and still clung on to the northern end of La Rothière. At 1600, Wrede's Bavarians struck at Chaumesnil and Barclay de Tolly's Russians started driving the French out of La Rothière. Ney counterattacked there whilst the Young Guard bolstered Marmont's flagging efforts against Wrede.

By now, with the snow deep and exhaustion setting in, the odds were simply too high even for Napoleon. It took all of his skills to extricate his men, and the retreat was a disaster in terms of both morale and material. For two days, thousands of French fell from exhaustion, so intent was Napoleon to link up with Mortier.

La Rothière was a catastrophe; honours were even on the battlefield, but Napoleon had allowed himself to face a foe nearly three times his strength and ultimately his men had paid the price.

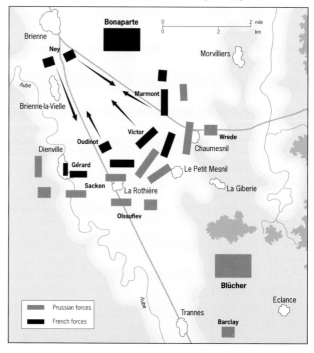

The Battle of Montmirail (1814)

Battle Name	Dates	Campaign
Montmirail	11 February 1814	Campaign in France
Troops Involved		
France	10,000–20,000	
	2,000 losses	Commanded by Napoleon
Prussia/Russia	36,000	
	4,000 losses	Commanded by Sacken/Yorck
Outcome:		
French victory		

French infantry bivouacs. *Mario Tomasone*

After decisively defeating the Russians under Olssufiev at Champaubert on 10 February, Napoleon now turned his attention to destroying the Prussian threat. His troops were at the centre of Blücher's scattered corps and Blücher now ordered Yorck and Sacken to concentrate at Montmirail. Sacken was at Trilport when he received the orders to head east, but Yorck's orders arrived too late for him to move with any speed.

Napoleon, meanwhile, left Marmont and his 4,000 men to shadow Blücher whilst he marched for Montmirail. He sent Oudinot from Provins to co-ordinate with Mortier on the southern flank, whilst MacDonald was given the task of taking Château-Thierry and capturing the vital bridge over the River Marne.

Sacken was following Blücher's orders to the letter and instead of heading for Château-Thierry, where he would more easily make contact with Yorck, he marched straight for Montmirail. By 1030 on 11 February, his 18,000 men were some 6 miles (9.5 km) to the west of the town, at Viels-Maisons. Already, he had collided with advance French units and knew that Montmirail was probably in French hands, as Cossacks had been driven out of the town.

He ran into determined French opposition at Marchais and formed his lines to the south of the road running from Montmirail to La Ferté-sous-Jouarre. Throughout the morning, the battle escalated as Sacken and Napoleon threw in additional troops. Sacken was desperate to beat a way through to Montmirail. Napoleon had set Michel and part of Nansouty's cavalry the task of dealing with Yorck when, and if, he arrived.

At around 1400 Ricard's troops had been pushed out of Marchais and Yorck had arrived at Fontenelles, but he was approaching very cautiously and there was still time for the French to grasp a victory. At 1500, Mortier arrived and Napoleon immediately launched Ney at the head of six battalions of the Old Guard at Sacken's left flank. It crumbled. When Napoleon threw Lefebvre and Ricard against Marchais, Sacken's Russians fled and were pursued to Viels-Maison by nightfall.

Mortier was deployed to deal with Yorck, cutting down his leading elements and finally forcing him to withdraw. Although Yorck had contributed little to the battle, as only 3,000 of his 18,000 were engaged, his arrival had in some ways saved Sacken from complete destruction. Blücher now ordered a general retreat towards Rheims.

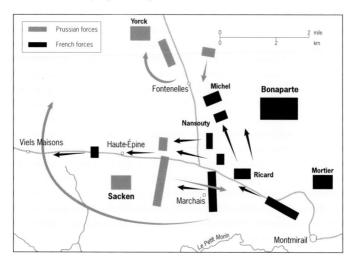

The Battle of Orthes (1814)

Battle Name	Dates	Campaign
Orthes	27 February 1814	Peninsular War
Troops Involved		
France	34,000	
	4,000 losses (1,350 prisoners)	Commanded by Soult
Britain	41,000	
	2,164 losses	Commanded by Wellington
Outcome: British victory		

On the afternoon of 26 February, Hope, who was commanding the left of Wellington's army, crossed the River Ardour with 8,000 men and began to blockade Bayonne.

On the same day, Beresford crossed the Gave de Pau at Peyrehorade and pushed Soult back to Orthes. The British 3rd Division crossed at Berenx and Wellington did so at the same point later in the day. Meanwhile, other British troops had marched to the south of Orthes.

Soult's army occupied a strong ridge running north from Orthes for 1 mile (1.5 km) and then for 3 more miles (5 km) west, to the village of St Boes. Wellington closed with him and opened the engagement at 0830 by driving the French out of the church area of St Boes. Ross's brigade (4th Division) led the attack and continued along the ridge, temporarily taking the village. The French counterattacked under Taupin, supported by artillery, and for some time the village saw vicious hand-to-hand fighting.

Meanwhile, Picton moved up to attack the French centre, but immediately ran into heavy artillery fire and was forced to pull back after suffering high casualties. Wellington had intended this to be a feint to draw off French reserves, as he was still manoeuvring for a major assault.

The British attack was called at 1130, hitting the whole of the French line. Wellington was gambling nearly all of his troops and had only held the Light Division in reserve.

The 3rd Division made progress up the eastern spur of the ridge lines, followed by the 6th Division. The 7th Division took over from the 4th, which had been engaged at St Boes, with more troops moving up to protect the 7th's flank.

The French resisted along the whole of the line and the ridges were not firmly in British hands until nearly 1400, by which time both sides had inflicted considerable casualties.

The 1/52nd, under Colburn, had been assigned the task of covering Walker's 7th Division flank and it was to be this battalion that would turn the tide and win the victory. They had reached the crest and engaged Taupin's division on their left flank and driven them towards St Boes, just as the 7th and the 4th were storming the village. This caused chaos and panic in the French ranks and they fled. By 1430, the ridge and the battle were won.

Soult withdrew to the north-east, towards Toulouse. Wellington had been wounded (his third injury), which would put him out of action for a few days.

French cannon at the ready. Courtesy of Ondrej Tupy, The Club of Military History, Novy Jicin, Czech Republic

The Battle of Craonne (1814)

Battle Name	Dates	Campaign
Craonne	7 March 1814	Campaign in France
Troops Involved		
France	37,000–40,000	
	5,400 losses	Commanded by Napoleon
Prussia	85,000–90,000	
	5,000 losses	Commanded by Blücher
Outcome:		
French victory		

By 5 March, the French line had retreated to the west bank of the River Seine and Schwarzenberg was in control of Troyes and all of the crossings on the Upper Seine. Paris was under immediate threat and Napoleon surged forward to engage Blücher at the earliest opportunity.

On 6 March, his troops advanced from Berry, having captured the bridge there with a dashing charge by his Polish lancers. He then received the news that the Plateau of Craonne was teeming with Prussians; he wrongly assumed that this was Blücher's rearguard. Consequently, Ney was ordered to engage, in doing so postponing his attack on Lâon. Napoleon hoped that this would give Marmont and Mortier time to overcome the Prussian garrison at Soissons and join him on his offensive.

Blücher was, in fact, calling Napoleon's bluff and wanted him to engage at Craonne. He proposed an elaborate trap to lure the Frenchmen holding the heights, with Woronzw and Sacken and using 11,000 cavalry and Kleist's corps (under Winzingerode) to take Napoleon's right flank.

Before Sacken could get into position, Ney had established a presence on the plateau late on 6 March. Temporarily, at least, the initiative fell once again to Napoleon. His plans were well advanced and in the morning he proposed to launch Ney to the north of the enemy, supported by cavalry units from Grouchy and Victor, whilst Nansouty swung around to the south. Napoleon would hold the centre ground and pin down Sacken and Woronzw by attacking the village of Heurtebise.

The engagement opened at 0900, with an artillery bombardment on Blücher's centre. Ney mistook this for the signal to launch his attack; he did so prematurely and it began to falter by 1100. Ney led more attacks from the front and gradually he gained ground. By now, Nansouty had struck and the enemy were beginning to fall back.

The battle swung back and forth and still Kleist had not appeared. Napoleon determined to destroy Blücher's centre and ordered the artillery and the Imperial Guard forward. Now Blücher began to withdraw, the pursuit ending at 2000; Kleist had got lost and never appeared. Sacken's 9,000 troops were never engaged throughout.

Blücher was furious; Winzingerode's attempted counterstroke had been an utter failure and with that he retreated towards Lâon. Napoleon had been fortunate. He had not been facing the rearguard at all, it was only luck which had saved him from disaster.

The Battle of Bergen-op-Zoom (1814)

Battle Name	Dates	Campaign
Bergen-op-Zoom	8 March 1814	
Troops Involved		
France	Unknown	
	Losses unknown	Commanded by Bizonet
Britain	4,000	
	2,100 losses	Commanded by Graham
Outcome:		
French victory		

In order to support the Prince of Orange, who had firmly declared himself to be anti-French, a British expeditionary force was sent to Holland under Graham. It would be reinforced by the 4th Battalion of the Royal Scots, marching into Holland from northern Germany.

The target was the vast fortress of Bergen-op-Zoom and to take it Graham had just 4,000 men. The Royal Scots set out from Lübeck on 17 January and by 2 March, after a hideously difficult march in snow storms, had reached Rozendath.

When Graham approached the fortress, he divided his force into four separate columns. Amazingly, he was intending to storm the fortress with little preparation. Cooke led the left column and started out at 2200 on 8 March and under a hail of fire forced a passage to the ramparts. The right column, under Skerret, fought its way into the town, but his attack petered out when he was wounded.

Graham, leading the centre columns, managed to fight his way through to Cooke's men, but found himself under intense fire from the fortress. The fourth column of the Royal Scots crossed the Zoom and forced their way into the port. As daylight came the French shelled them with howitzers, then sent a detachment of marines to force them out.

Just before dawn, Graham's and Cooke's men withdrew, leaving the Royal Scots to their fate. The four companies had been in action since 2300 the previous day, taking it in turns to hold off the gradually strengthening French attacks. Just after daylight, a large concentration of French infantry and marines closed on their prey. The Royal Scots were holding the arsenal, but grapeshot from French guns drove them out and they retired back towards the port. With French troops moving up rapidly, what remained of the unit was forced to surrender.

The failure to take Bergen-op-Zoom had been something of a foregone conclusion. The British had sealed the walls and had, at one time, taken the gate and drawbridge, and they had even gained part of the ramparts. Graham reluctantly agreed with Bizonet to suspend hostilities; the captured Royal Scots, in accordance with their promise not to bear arms against the French again, sailed for Britain and then America.

The Battle of Bergen-op-Zoom at its height.

The Battle of Lâon (1814)

Battle Name	Dates	Campaign
Lâon	9–10 March 1814	Peninsular War
		Campaign in France
Troops Involved		
France	Day 1: 37,000–47,600	
	Day 2: 47,500	
	6,000 losses	Commanded by Napoleon
Allies	Day 1: 85,000	
	Day 2: 85,000	
	4,000 losses	Commanded by Blücher/Winzingerode/Gneisenau
Outcome:		
Allied victory		

In the early hours of 9 March, Ney advanced along the Soisson–Lâon road, intent on taking Lâon by surprise. The allies anticipated attack, however, and it took a second attempt (with the aid of Mortier) to even gain a foothold in the suburbs of Semilly, which they only held until 1200.

This action was part of Napoleon's attempts to deal with an enemy some 100,000 strong, with two armies, under Ney and Marmont, which in total did not quite make 40,000. Bülow held Semilly and Ardon with 17,000 men, Winzingerode with 25,000, was to the west of Lâon, Yorck and Kleist held Athies, with 25,000, whilst Blücher himself had the 36,000 reserves north of Lâon at Langeron and Sacken.

The Semilly suburbs changed hands several times in the next few hours. The last French attack went in at 1800, but by nightfall Ney had been thrown out again and Napoleon retreated up the Paris road towards Chavignon. Marmont, meanwhile, had pushed up the Rheims road with some 10,000 men and by 1200 he had taken the outskirts of Athies and the whole town by 1700. He settled down to hold his positions during the night, unaware that Napoleon had fallen back.

At 1930, Yorck mounted a counter-attack which

99

Allied firing line. *Mario Tomasone*

cost Marmont 3,500 men and forty-five of his fifty-five guns. Blücher himself had now moved his reserve east to cover the Rheims road.

Fortune favoured the French now, as Blücher's ill-health finally laid him low. His orders to advance in the morning were countermanded by Gneisenau at 0800 on 10 March. The initiative, for what it was worth, lay with Napoleon, who renewed his attacks in the morning. He called off the offensive at 1600 and retreated to Soissons with some 30,000 men. Gneisenau lacked the will and nerve to mount a pursuit, despite the fact that his corps commanders were baying for French blood.

The allies had therefore lost an ideal opportunity to crush the smaller French force. Sacken and Langeron strongly held Bruyères and Yorck and Kleist had moved to Festieux. When the pursuit finally came on 11 March, it was half-hearted and Ney managed to deal with it comfortably.

Blücher had at least had the stomach to stand and fight. He was tired of running from Napoleon and eagerly awaited the opportunity for a much-belated revenge. It was significant that his subordinate did not feel the same.

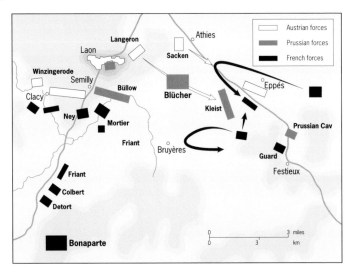

The Battle of Arcis-sur-Aube (1814)

Battle Name	Dates	Campaign
Arcis-sur-Aube	20–21 March 1814	Campaign in France
Troops Involved		
France	Day 1: 18,000–23,000	
	Day 2: 28,000	
	3,000 losses	Commanded by Napoleon
Allies	Day 1: 20,000	
	Day 2: 80,000	
	4,000 losses	Commanded by Schwarzenberg
Outcome:		
Allied victory		

The action at Arcis-sur-Aube was Napoleon's last throw of the dice. He believed that he could still dispute the allied offensive against France and determined to strike at Schwarzenberg's army, which was covering a front of nearly 80 miles (128 km). At a stroke, Napoleon could cut Blücher off from Strasbourg and Schwarzenberg from Basle and also link up with the large French garrisons in Veroun and Metz.

Early on 20 March, he set off for Arcis-sur-Aube, his intelligence suggesting that it was only held by a weak force of Bavarians, under Wrede, who formed the allied rearguard. Schwarzenberg was not to be fooled by such a manoeuvre and was already marching to deal Napoleon a fatal blow. He knew that Sébastiani had crossed the Aube at Planey the day before (19 March) and assumed that Napoleon was heading for Troyes. He therefore decided to concentrate his troops in the Troyes–Arcis area.

Napoleon ordered Marmont and Mortier to march first for Châlons and then for Épernay, so confident was he that Blücher would not dare to continue his advance to Paris. Again, he was mistaken. Confident of his plans, however, he sent Ney and Sébastiani to the south of the Aube to force Wrede to withdraw from Arcis-sur-Aube. He would continue on the north bank and rendezvous with them later for the march to Vitry and ultimately the Seine.

Remarkably, neither Ney nor Sébastiani ran into any opposition and they marched into Arcis-sur-Aube at 1100; even the bridge had not been completely destroyed. Napoleon joined them at 1300, having crossed the Aube at Torcy-le-Grand.

Suddenly, as it began to appear that there would be no engagement, a large force of cavalry was seen coming from the area of Vanpoisson. Ney and Sébastiani could not halt them and it was only the timely arrival of Friant and his Old Guard division, holding the ridge, that stemmed the tide.

At about the same time, Napoleon openly courted death by deliberately riding over an unexploded howitzer shell. His horse was killed, but the Emperor simply mounted another horse and started directing the troops.

The fighting became intense around Torcy-le-Petit and Torcy-le-Grand during the remaining hours of light and by nightfall it appeared that the French had the upper hand. Later that night, Lefebvre-Desnoyëttes arrived with 2,000 cavalry and Sébastiani managed to rout two enemy cavalry divisions, but he was forced back by Russian guns.

Little did Napoleon know that Schwarzenberg was massing some 80,000 men beyond the ridge to the south, stretching all the way from Voué in the south-west to Chaudrey, near the Aube, in the north-east. None the less, he felt uneasy and summoned MacDonald, who was advancing from Bray, to join him as soon as possible.

Schwarzenberg, in turn, could not be sure of Napoleon's strength and he was under pressure from the Tsar not to take unnecessary risks in his renewed offensive. In the end, Napoleon moved first, sending Sébastiani south to the plateau, followed by Ney. It was then that they saw the vast army Schwarzenberg had gathered. Now that Napoleon knew, he could not risk an attack without Gérard or MacDonald; the only option was to retire beyond the Aube. This manoeuvre required more than the bridge at Arcis-sur-Aube and a pontoon bridge was hastily created at Vilette. By 1330, the French were in full retreat, with Oudinot and Sébastiani covering the rear.

Finally, at 1500, Schwarzenberg shook off his lethargy and attacked. Oudinot and Sébastiani faced him with great solidity. The fighting lasted until around 1800, when Oudinot's final rearguard fought their way to the bridge, destroying it as they reached the north bank of the river. Schwarzenberg did not attempt to pursue; he simply shadowed the French as they marched for Sompuis and joined up with MacDonald and Kellerman, who were near Ormes. Napoleon now switched his march to Sézanne and Frignicourt, still intent on reaching St Dizier and the

A detail from a painting by Peter Hess showing the grim reality of war, on the battlefield of Arcis-sur-Aube (March 20 1814).

garrison there waiting for him.

He arrived on 23 March, the worse for wear but still able to summon up the fire to sweep aside some 8,000 cavalry which had ridden on an interception course from Vitry.

Although he did not know it then, he had fought his last engagement of the campaign. On 28 March the allies marched into Paris. Marmont and Mortier failed to regain the capital and at 0200 on the 31st they signed an armistice. On 1 April Napoleon had just 36,000 men at Fontainbleau; by the 6th he had 60,000. But all of this was to no avail, with 145,000 allies in his capital. He had no option but to abdicate and finally did so on 4 April 1814.

The Battle of Toulouse (1814)

Battle Name	Dates	Campaign
Toulouse	10 April 1814	Peninsular War
Troops Involved		
France	42,000	
	3,236 losses	Commanded by Soult
Britain	50,000	
	4,558 losses	Commanded by Wellington
Outcome:		
British victory		

Following the French defeat at Orthes, Wellington's troops caught up with Soult at Aire on 2 March. Here, the pursuit stopped, with Beresford heading for Bordeaux, which he captured on 12 March.

Soult marched into Toulouse on 24 March, his men in a pitiable state, lacking even the most basic of equipment. Here, he licked his wounds, resupplied and gained reinforcements.

The major obstacle facing Wellington was the River Garonne to the west of the city. On 4 April, Beresford crossed with 19,000 men, followed on 8 April by the rest of Wellington's army. The main objective was the dominating Calvinet ridge, but the battle opened with a diversionary attack on the suburbs of Toulouse (St Cyprien). Soult realised that this was a feint and moved troops to support Calvinet (which was actually two ridges, the second of which was Mont Rave).

In the north, Picton's troops stormed the canal, but he was driven back. Spanish troops, under Freire, were only to attack the northern end of the Calvinet ridge once Beresford had opened his attack against Mont Rave. As they wheeled into position, still 1 mile (1.5 km) from their start positions, they came under fire. Despite the heavy barrage, the Spaniards came on, closing to within 60 yards of the French.

Here they were stopped dead and in a sunken road were slaughtered.

Wellington ordered Beresford to attack immediately, and as they approached to within 1_ miles (2.5 km) of Mont Rave, two French brigades, under Taupin, advanced at them in column from the west. They were massacred and the two British divisions swept on towards Mont Rave. By 1600, the French were consigned to the south of the Calvinet ridge and Mont Rave had been taken; at 1630 Soult ordered that the ridge be abandoned.

Meanwhile, Picton had been beaten back again to the north of the city. Elsewhere, Soult was under intense pressure, but luckily for him, by around 1700, the light was fading, which abruptly ended the fighting. The following morning, he began preparations to abandon the city and as night fell, his troops headed south towards Carcassone.

Tragically, the battle need never have been fought. Napoleon had abdicated four days earlier (4 April), but neither Soult nor Wellington had received word. Soult signed the armistice on 17 April. It was the end of the war for now. Wellington's polyglot army of British, Dutch and Germans had marched 6,000 miles since their creation.

The Battle of Tolentino (1815)

Battle Name	Dates	Campaign
Tolentino	2–4 May 1815	Murat's Italian Campaign
Troops Involved		
French Neapolitans	36,000	
	1,700 losses (+ 2,400 captured)	Commanded by Murat
Austria	10,000	
	800 losses	Commanded by Bianchi
Outcome:		
Austrian victory		

On 26 February 1815, Napoleon had left Elba with just 1,100 soldiers. He managed to make landfall in France at Cannes on 1 March and begin his last struggle, which was to culminate in defeat at

Waterloo. He was backed by Murat, the King of Naples, who moved his 36,000-strong army north into central Italy. The Neapolitan troops were, however, of dubious quality and were no match for the smaller but disciplined and experienced Austrian force, under Baron Vincenz Bianchi, he was to meet at Tolentino.

Murat had been recognised as King of Naples by the Austrians, but notably not by the British. The restored Louis XVIII had demanded that he be removed in favour of Bourbon Neopolitans. Murat had turned to Napoleon who had warned him to mobilise, but not to launch an offensive as yet. With Napoleon at loose on the continent, the allies offered to recognise him provided he remained neutral. Murat, ever impulsive and often without reason, crossed the border into Italy on 15 March.

On 13 March the allies had declared Napoleon an outlaw, but by the 20th he was regaining control in Paris. On the 25th the 7th Coalition was formed and just six days later Murat declared war on Austria.

Murat's total available forces in 1815 amounted to around 46,829 infantry, 7,224 cavalry and 78 guns. With this force he hoped to unite Italy and proclaim himself king. He managed to push the Austrians back as far as the River Po and Ferrara, but his troops were decisively defeated at Tolentino. He had tried to use the cause of Italian reunification as a means to support Napoleon and occupy the Austrians, but at Tolentino the brittle nature of the Neapolitan army was revealed. Very few of his men managed to extricate themselves from the disaster. Murat fled to Corsica after the battle and returned to Naples with just six ships and a handful of troops. He was finally captured at Pizzo and executed by firing squad on 13 October 1815.

Tolentino is also known as the Battle of La Rancia and is considered to be the first battle for Italian independence. It was also the site of the signing of the treaty between the representatives of the Pope and Napoleon on 17 February 1797, which signalled the end of Pope Pius VI's powers, the payment of subsidies to the French and the surrender of works of art.

The Battle of Ligny (1815)

Battle Name	Dates	Campaign
Ligny	16 June 1815	Waterloo Campaign
Troops Involved		
France	80,000	
	11,500 losses	Commanded by Napoleon
Prussia	84,000	
	25,000 losses	Commanded by Blücher
Outcome:		
French victory		

On Napoleon's escape from Elba, the allies reacted quickly, promising to restore Louis XVIII, but they were faced with coping with Napoleon with the troops already deployed. Inevitably, the initial responsibilities would fall on the 124,000 Prussians in Belgium and the 95,000 Anglo-Dutch.

Napoleon planned to deal with the allies one at a time, now with no other support. He marched his troops from Charleroi, hoping to drive a wedge between Blücher and Wellington. He would hold one of them with a smaller force and crush the other with his main army.

The choice of where the first blow should fall was made for him as Blücher's Prussians were ahead of Wellington's army. He sent Ney with two corps to Quatre Bras to hold Wellington and sent Grouchy to attack Blücher at Ligny. His reserve and the Imperial Guard would move to assist Grouchy and overwhelm the Prussians. It was then planned to force the Prussian survivors towards Namur and turn their attention to Wellington.

At 1430 on 16 June Napoleon launched his attack on the Prussian positions at Ligny. They were holding a series of ridges and the town and whilst Napoleon struck at the front of the enemy line, Vandamme hit their right. Napoleon had ordered d'Erlon to launch an enveloping attack, but the French commander was unsure whether this meant that he should be supporting Ney at Quatre Bras or Napoleon at Ligny.

Initially, this confusion gave Blücher a chance; but gradually he was forced back. Napoleon was about to launch the Imperial Guard at the Prussians when he saw new troops arriving on the battlefield. Again, there was confusion; Napoleon believed that they were Prussian reinforcements, but they were, in fact, d'Erlon's men. By the time the confusion was allayed, Napoleon had precious little time to launch his planned attack.

The delay meant that the Prussians were beaten, but not annihilated as Napoleon had planned. In the dying moments of the battle Blücher was left for dead after taking part in a cavalry charge, but he and his men would still return to haunt Napoleon. Ligny was the Frenchman's last victory and an indecisive one at that.

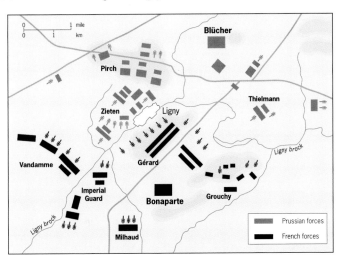

The Battle of Quatre Bras (1815)

Battle Name	Dates	Campaign
Quatre Bras	16 June 1815	Waterloo Campaign
Troops Involved		
France	24,000	
	4,000 losses	Commanded by Ney
Britain/Holland/Brunswick	8,000–36,000	
	4,800 losses	Commanded by Wellington
Outcome:		
British/Dutch/Brunswick victory		

Whilst Napoleon was dealing with Blücher's Prussians at Ligny, Ney's troops were despatched to capture the crossroads at Quatre Bras on the Charleroi–Brussels road. Wellington's Anglo-Dutch army was moving south from Brussels with Prince Bertrand's Dutch in the lead. The Dutch had already reached Quatre Bras on the evening of 15 June when they encountered Ney's forward troops.

Ney did not strike that night and was curiously slow in developing his attacks the following morning. He was faced with around 8,000 Dutch and could have easily swept them aside. He finally deployed for a determined assault at 1400, led by Reille's corps of some 20,000 men. Despite strong Dutch resistance, he began to make headway.

By mid-afternoon, Wellington himself had arrived on the battlefield, immediately sending his Brunswick corps in to support the Dutch. Ney had been relying on d'Erlon to help deliver the knock-out blow, but his corps was marching towards Ligny as a result of a confusion in the orders.

Ney still pressed the enemy, sending in Kellerman's cavalry to capture the crossroads, but British infantry stiffened the centre of Wellington's line. They were under severe pressure from the French cavalry; some of the regiments did not even have the opportunity to form up their squares to counter the attack. As the fighting intensified, time was running out for the French. Each passing minute saw more Anglo-Dutch troops arrive, notably in the form of Picton and his command. These were still difficult times for Wellington; the Prince of Orange's troops were badly mauled by the French cavalry and on several occasions it looked as if Wellington's own line would crack.

By the late afternoon, Wellington had some 36,000 men available to him, supported by seventy artillery pieces. At 1830 he was able to launch a full-scale counterattack on the faltering and exhausted French. The engagement was terminated at around 2100, by which time Ney had been driven from the crossroads and the Anglo-Dutch were firmly in control of the battlefield.

Ney could so easily have won the battle if he had been more proactive when he first encountered the Dutch at the crossroads. None the less, the opportunities still remained until at least midday but, even when d'Erlon was available to him, Ney made little immediate use of the reinforcements.

Wellington retired further up the Brussels road, covering his withdrawal as Napoleon's main army arrived. His chosen position was the village of Waterloo.

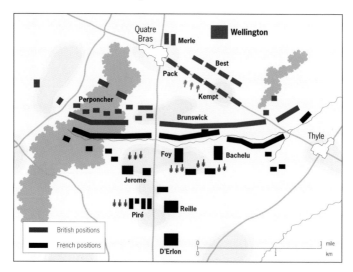

The Battle of Waterloo (1815)

Battle Name	Dates	Campaign
Waterloo	18 June 1815	Waterloo Campaign
Troops Involved		
France	72,000	
	41,000 losses	Commanded by Napoleon
Britain/Holland/Brunswick/Prussia	68,000–140,000	
	22,000 losses	Commanded by Wellington/Blücher

Outcome:
British/Dutch/Brunswick/Prussian victory

Hard on the heels of Ligny and Quatre Bras, Napoleon continued to press Wellington's army and that of Blücher's Prussians. At all costs, he needed to keep them apart and deal with them whilst they were isolated.

After Quatre Bras, Wellington retired towards Brussels and on 17 June set up his troops along a ridge south of Mont St Jean. His left flank rested on two farms, La Haye and Papelotte, and the village of Frischermont. The right was protected by Château Hougoumont and the centre by the farm of La Haye Sainte. The latter two defensive positions were ahead of his main line and he was determined to stand and fight. His two main corps, led by Picton and the Prince of Orange, were positioned behind the ridge, with his main cavalry force led by Uxbridge. Prudently, he had placed a strong force on his right

to prevent Napoleon from outflanking him. He proposed to fight a defensive action, taking advantage of the terrain and hoping to strike against isolated or over-exposed French units. Here he would wait for Blücher, secure in the knowledge that the Prussian would march to the sound of the guns.

Napoleon had detailed 33,000 men under Grouchy to keep the Prussians at bay whilst he dealt with Wellington. Blücher planned to form his army up around Wavre and support Wellington.

Napoleon's battle plan was none too subtle: whilst he held the village of Plancenoit on his right flank to protect against Prussian interference, he would launch a massive frontal assault on Wellington. His troops began to deploy during the early morning of 18 June with some 72,000 men and 246 artillery pieces, many of the latter deployed in a mass battery with which he intended to shatter Wellington's line. Wellington, aware that this was Napoleon's preferred tactic, deployed the bulk of his 68,000 men and 156 guns on the reverse of the slope.

The engagement got under way at around 1130, with Jérôme's division of Reille's corps attacking Hougoumont. This was intended as a feint, as Napoleon hoped to draw off Wellington's reserves in an attempt to hold the position. He could not have accounted for the tenacity of the British Guards holding the châteaux; they were to hold on to the location for the whole day. Gradually more and more French troops were thrown into attempts to take Hougoumont; it became something of an obsession and the attacks continued even after the strategic and tactical value of Hougoumont had ceased to be important.

French batteries, then Napoleon's cavalry struck and by the time the remnants of Uxbridge's command returned to the line, half his men were gone.

At 1530 Wellington appeared to be withdrawing from the battlefield, which convinced Ney to launch an all-out charge with his cavalry. It was unsupported by either artillery or infantry, however, and was ultimately doomed. It appears that Ney took it upon himself to launch the attack; Napoleon was preoccupied by the arrival of Blücher's troops at Plancenoit.

Ney's cavalry, numbering some 10,000 attacked on a front just over 700 yards wide. As the cavalry came on, the British infantry formed up in squares and shattered its cohesion with volley after volley. As the flower of the French martial élite was slaughtered, they had made an impact on Wellington's troops and in many places regiments

Adolf Northern's depiction of French infantry struggling through the village of Plancenoit during the Battle of Waterloo.

At around 1330, Napoleon launched d'Erlon's corps at the ridge. He had already been informed that Blücher was coming up on his right and had formed up a defensive line near Plancenoit. Blücher took some time, as he was still being harried by Grouchy, but only the Prussian rearguard at Wavre was actually being checked. The bulk of the army was heading for the battlefield, slogging along the muddy roads in the rain.

Although Grouchy was performing a useful function against the Prussians, he was increasingly needed on the battlefield at Waterloo. By the time he did turn and head for the main engagement, however, it was too late.

Meanwhile, on the battlefield, d'Erlon's columns were being cut to pieces by the British artillery, but they still came on and engaged Picton's infantry. Picton died in the midst of the battle, then Wellington ordered Uxbridge to launch a counterattack with his cavalry. Initially, at least, the charge was devastating; the French infantry were overwhelmed and were teeming back in disorder. The impetuous cavalry charge tore into the massed

were wavering. It was left eventually to Napoleon to order the withdrawal of Ney's cavalry at 1730.

With several Dutch and Hanoverian units deciding that enough was enough, Wellington was forced to commit the last of his reserves and hold the line. As never before, the battle had been reduced to a war of attrition, but despite his perilous state, the pendulum was swinging Wellington's way.

On the French right, from around 1630, the Prussians began to arrive in ever-increasing numbers. Blücher himself, was personally directing the corps of Bülow and Pirch against Plancenoit. They took the village, but under the command of Napoleon the Young and Middle Guard retook it by bayonet. By now, Napoleon had committed his whole reserves, barring the Old Guard.

In the centre Ney was co-ordinating another attack; this time it would fall on the hard-pressed German Legion holding La Haye Sainte. French infantry gained a foothold in the farm and the Prince of Orange saw two of his battalions sent up to support it slaughtered by French cavalry. The capture of the farm allowed Ney to bring up his artillery to

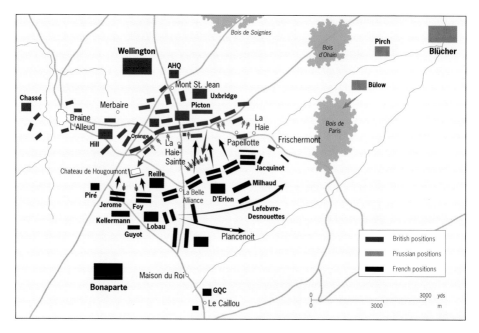

closer range in order to rake the Allied line. As the French artillery opened up, the British regiments began to waver under the incessant bombardment. Only the positioning of Vandeleur's light cavalry prevented the infantry from routing.

Had Napoleon had his reserves available at this moment, the outcome of the battle would have been very different. As it was, they were engaged against the Prussians and gradually cohesion and morale was restored in Wellington's exhausted and shattered regiments.

The only uncommitted French troops were the Old Guard, but these were not thrown against the weakest position of Wellington's line. They headed west of La Haye Sainte and encountered the British guards led by Wellington himself. The leads of the French columns were cut down barely 40 yards from the British positions, and as more British units lapped around the French columns the slaughter was immense. Another Old Guard attack failed similarly against the Dutch. For the first time in their history the Old Guard had been defeated and with it Napoleon's hopes of victory had been lost.

Wellington now seized the initiative and ordered a general advance as Blücher's men overwhelmed Plancenoit. What remained of the Imperial Guard solidly formed a square to cover the retreat and was cut down. By nightfall, the age of Napoleon was over and the two victorious generals, Wellington and Blücher, met at his former headquarters in the battlefield, La Belle Alliance. Napoleon was to die, a broken and embittered man, in exile on St Helena on 5 May 1821.

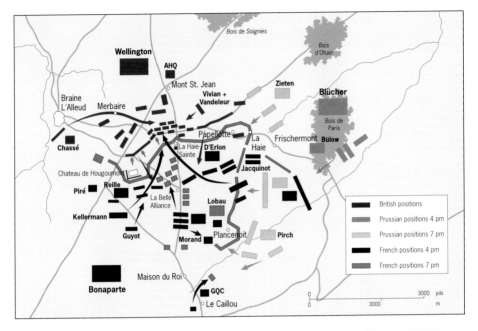

The British counterattack, note Wellington in his blue coat to the left of the picture.

The Battle of Wavre (1815)

Battle Name	Dates	Campaign
Wavre	18–19 June 1815	Waterloo Campaign
Troops Involved		
France	33,000	
	2,500 losses	Commanded by Grouchy
Prussia	17,000	
	2,500 losses	Commanded by Thielmann
Outcome:		
French victory		

After the battle of Ligny, Napoleon had ordered Grouchy to pursue the retreating Prussians. Above all, he was to prevent the Prussians linking up with the Anglo-Dutch army of Wellington, and in addition he was to cover Napoleon's right flank.

Around 1200 on 17 June, Grouchy started off towards Gembloux, his progress impeded by poor weather and an imprecise knowledge of exactly where the Prussians were heading. At 1900, he reached Gembloux, where he decided to halt for the night. An hour later, he sent despatches to Napoleon, telling him he believed that the Prussians had split into two columns. One, he understood, was heading for Wavre and the other for Liège. Grouchy considered the Wavre column to be the greatest threat and he intended to intercept it or force it away from Wellington.

Blücher had different plans and at 0400, he despatched Bülow to assist Wellington. Bülow's orders were explicit: he was immediately to attack Napoleon's right flank if he found him to be engaged with Wellington, otherwise he was to hold in cover in the St Lambert area until matters developed. He would then be supported by Pirch, who was to march next, and subsequently by Zieten and Thielmann.

Grouchy got underway again on the morning of 18 June. Later he heard the battle at Waterloo in the distance, but determined to continue to Wavre and fulfil his orders. He received a despatch from Soult at 1530, reiterating those orders. Only Thielmann's troops still remained at Wavre and it was these that Grouchy engaged at 1400 on the eastern suburbs.

Vandamme's corps struck the Prussian pickets and outlying posts very hard, but he could not dislodge them from the two stone bridges over the River Dyle. Gérard arrived on the battlefield and Grouchy sent him toward Bierge to seize the bridge there, but his attack at 1700 failed. Grouchy now sent troops up-river to Limale and the small Prussian force there was overwhelmed by 1900; the French pressed on and captured Limelette. Around 1700, Grouchy received orders from Napoleon to cover his flank, but as he was engaged he could do little.

He resumed the attack just after dawn and this time the Prussians were forced to retreat; he had his victory at 1000. Just half an hour later, he received word that Napoleon had been beaten at Waterloo. Thielmann already knew and it had seemed pointless to waste more lives.

La vieille garde à Austerlitz – a Czech re-enactment group depicting the French Old Guard. Mario Tomasone

Further Reading

Adkin, Mark (2001) *The Waterloo Companion*. Aurum Press.

Bowden, Scott (1997) *Napoleon and Austerlitz: An Unprecedentedly Detailed Combat Study of Napoleon's Epic Ulm-Austerlitz Campaigns of 1805* (Armies of the Napoleonic Wars). Emperor's Press.

Cate, Curtis (1985) *The War of the Two Emperors: The Duel Between Napoleon and Alexander, Russia 1812*. Random House.

Chandler, David (1973) *Campaigns of Napoleon: The Mind and Method of History's Greatest Soldier*. Macmillan/Scribner.

Connelly, Owen (1999) *Blundering to Glory: Napoleon's Military Campaigns*. SR Books.

Delderfield, R. F. (2002) *Napoleon's Marshals*. Cooper Square Publishers.

Duffy, Christopher (1972) *Borodino: Napoleon Against Russia 1812*. Sphere.

Fletcher, Ian (2001) *Galloping at Everything: The British Cavalry in the Peninsular War and at Waterloo, 1808–15*. Stackpole Books.

Fregosi, Paul (1990) *Dreams of Empire: Napoleon and the First World War, 1792–1814*. Carol Publishing Group.

Grant, James (1897) *British Battles On Land and Sea. Volume 2*. Cassell.

Loraine Petre F. (1993) *Napoleon's Conquest of Prussia 1806*. (Napoleonic Library) Greenhill Books.

Luvaas, Jay (Editor) (1999) *Emperor of the French Napoleon I: Napoleon on the Art of War*. Free Press.

Moiret, Joseph-Marie and Rosemary Brindle (2001) *Memoirs of Napoleon's Egyptian Expedition 1798–1801*. Greenhill Books.

Muir, Rory (2000) *Tactics and the Experience of Battle in the Age of Napoleon*. Yale University Press.

Myatt, Frederick (1996) *British Sieges of the Peninsular War*. Howell Press.

Rothenberg, Gunther (1999) *The Napoleonic Wars*. Cassell.

Smith, Digby George (2000) *Napoleon's Regiments: Battle Histories of the Regiments of the French Army, 1792–1815*. Greenhill Books.

Von Clausewitz, Carl (1995) *The Campaign of 1812 in Russia*. Da Capo Press.

Woodman, Richard (1998) *The Victory of Seapower: Winning the Napoleonic War 1806–1814*. (Chatham Pictorial Histories) Chatham Publishing.

Index

DISEASES AND DISORDERS

PTSD
CAUSES AND CARE

By Simon Pierce

Portions of this book originally appeared in *Post Traumatic Stress Disorder* by Peggy Thomas.

LUCENT
PRESS

Published in 2019 by
Lucent Press, an Imprint of Greenhaven Publishing, LLC
353 3rd Avenue
Suite 255
New York, NY 10010

Designer: Deanna Paternostro
Editor: Jennifer Lombardo

Library of Congress Cataloging-in-Publication Data

Names: Pierce, Simon, author.
Title: PTSD : causes and care / Simon Pierce.
Other titles: Post-traumatic stress disorder
Description: New York : Lucent Press, [2019] | Series: Diseases and disorders
    | Includes bibliographical references and index.
Identifiers: LCCN 2018000571 (print) | LCCN 2017061665 (ebook) | ISBN
    9781534563667 (eBook) | ISBN 9781534563650 (library bound book) | ISBN
    9781534563674 (paperback book)
Subjects: LCSH: Post-traumatic stress disorder. | Post-traumatic stress
    disorder–Treatment.
Classification: LCC RC552.P67 (print) | LCC RC552.P67 P56 2019 (ebook) | DDC
    616.85/21–dc23
LC record available at https://lccn.loc.gov/2018000571

Printed in the United States of America

CPSIA compliance information: Batch #BS18KL: For further information contact Greenhaven Publishing LLC, New York, New York at 1-844-317-7404.

Please visit our website, www.greenhavenpublishing.com. For a free color catalog of all our high-quality books, call toll free 1-844-317-7404 or fax 1-844-317-7405.

CONTENTS

Illness is an unfortunate part of life, and it is one that is often misunderstood. Thanks to advances in science and technology, people have been aware for many years that diseases such as the flu, pneumonia, and chicken pox are caused by viruses and bacteria. These diseases all cause physical symptoms that people can see and understand, and many people have dealt with these diseases themselves. However, sometimes diseases that were previously unknown in most of the world turn into epidemics and spread across the globe. Without an awareness of the method by which these diseases are spread—through the air, through human waste or fluids, through sexual contact, or by some other method—people cannot take the proper precautions to prevent further contamination. Panic often accompanies epidemics as a result of this lack of knowledge.

Knowledge is power in the case of mental disorders, as well. Mental disorders are just as common as physical disorders, but due to a lack of awareness among the general public, they are often stigmatized. Scientists have studied them for years and have found that they are generally caused by hormonal imbalances in the brain, but they have not yet determined with certainty what causes those imbalances or how to fix them. Because even mild mental illness is stigmatized in Western society, many people prefer not to talk about it.

Chronic pain disorders are also not well understood—even by researchers—and do not yet have foolproof treatments. People who have a mental disorder or a disease or disorder that causes them to feel chronic pain can be the target of uninformed

opinions. People who do not have these disorders sometimes struggle to understand how difficult it can be to deal with the symptoms. These disorders are often termed "invisible illnesses" because no one can see the symptoms; this leads many people to doubt that they exist or are serious problems. Additionally, people who have an undiagnosed disorder may understand that they are experiencing the world in a different way than their peers, but they have no one to turn to for answers.

Misinformation about all kinds of ailments is often spread through personal anecdotes, social media, and even news sources. This series aims to present accurate information about both physical and mental conditions so young adults will have a better understanding of them. Each volume discusses the symptoms of a particular disease or disorder, ways it is currently being treated, and the research that is being done to understand it further. Advice for people who may be suffering from a disorder is included, as well as information for their loved ones about how best to support them.

With fully cited quotes, a list of recommended books and websites for further research, and informational charts, this series provides young adults with a factual introduction to common illnesses. By learning more about these ailments, they will be better able to prevent the spread of contagious diseases, show compassion to people who are dealing with invisible illnesses, and take charge of their own health.

WHAT IS PTSD?

Although most people have heard of post-traumatic stress disorder (PTSD), many people do not have an accurate understanding of what it is. Some think it is something only soldiers can experience. Others believe people who have PTSD are dangerous and out of control. Still others think it is not a serious condition or that it is an overreaction to normal stress.

Everyone gets stressed. Students may feel stress when they have many homework assignments, when they feel pressure about their grades, or when they argue with friends, parents, or siblings. The list of stressful situations is endless. What might be stressful for one person may not affect another. Stress is part of everyday life, and the human body has ways of coping with it.

However, the mind-body system that deals with everyday stressful situations becomes overloaded during extraordinary events such as war, sexual assault, a natural disaster, or a car accident. The brain is not able to turn off the stress response. Horrifying memories and experiences are involuntarily relived. Sounds, sights, and smells can trigger extreme reactions. These symptoms can persist for years after the danger has passed, and their effects can interfere with the way someone lives their life. Additionally, since PTSD is not well understood, there is a stigma, or negative view, surrounding it. People may think those who have PTSD are weak, seeking attention, or not trying hard

Everyone deals with stress sometimes, but PTSD is more than just normal stress.

enough to "get over" their trauma. Understanding the symptoms and causes of PTSD is one way to break the stigma that surrounds this disorder.

DEALING WITH TRAUMA

People have been experiencing PTSD for centuries. As early as 1300 BC, symptoms of PTSD were recorded in soldiers who returned from battle in the Assyrian kingdom in Mesopotamia. However, at the time, psychological conditions were not understood, and PTSD was thought to be caused by the ghosts of people the soldier had killed in battle. In reality, it was likely caused by the threat of extreme injury or death as well as witnessing their friends being killed. According to *Archaeology* magazine, "the chance of death from injuries, which can nowadays be surgically treated, must have been much greater in those days."[1] However, all of these factors still contribute to PTSD for today's soldiers as well.

PTSD is most frequently associated with soldiers. In fact, until recently, it was commonly believed even

There is evidence to suggest that even in ancient times, soldiers around the world suffered from PTSD.

by medical professionals that soldiers were the only ones capable of experiencing PTSD, and this myth still persists today. In reality, there are many different types of trauma that can cause PTSD.

However, early studies of PTSD focused only on soldiers. In one example, Dr. Jacob Mendez Da Costa, a physician during the American Civil War, recorded the number of wounded Union soldiers who had rapid heart rates and high blood pressure combined with severe exhaustion and the ability to be easily startled.

It was clear that many men who fought in the war suffered from their experiences. One study that looked at medical and pension records from the Civil War confirmed this and suggested that the soldiers who witnessed the most death and destruction were more likely to suffer from anxiety, depression, and other illnesses later in life. The youngest soldiers, ages 9 to 17, were almost twice as likely as soldiers over 30 years of age to show signs of mental illness after the war.

Unsuitable Names

PTSD has been called by many different names over the decades. For instance, during the Civil War, doctors called it "soldier's heart" or "irritable heart." They did not yet understand the workings of the brain and were just beginning to study mental illnesses. They noticed that people with PTSD had symptoms that affected their cardiovascular system, such as high blood pressure and an increased heart rate, so they assumed it was a physical rather than mental problem. Another name for it, coined by Swiss doctor Johannes Hofer in the late 1600s, was "nostalgia." Today, the term is used to refer to feelings of happy remembrance or longing; for instance, an adult might feel nostalgic for their childhood whenever they eat a piece of their mother's apple pie. When the term was used to identify PTSD, however, it referred to symptoms such as

homesickness, insomnia (sleeplessness), and anxiety.

The same symptoms were seen in soldiers who fought in World War I. This time it was called "shell shock" or "combat fatigue." According to Dr. Matthew Friedman, senior advisor at the U.S. Department of Veterans Affairs National Center for PTSD, the term "shell shock" was used because of "the notion … that being close to the big guns pounding out the artillery on both sides of the barbed wire in the trench warfare was somehow disrupting neuronal connections, so the nerves were actually affected."[2] Charles Myers, a psychologist serving at the front, wrote that shell shock occurred "where the tolerable or controllable limits of horror, fear, anxiety etc. are overstepped."[3]

The term "shell shock" comes from the mistaken belief that PTSD was caused by nerve damage from being too close to artillery guns similar to these.

This limited understanding of the disorder affected the treatment doctors provided. Some therapies were useless, while others were actively harmful. Soldiers with PTSD were often evacuated, hospitalized, and treated with electric shock therapy. Men who wandered away from the front on their own were labeled deserters and set before a firing squad, even if they were not trying to desert. During the Civil War, "some military doctors viewed the illness as a sign of

weakness and one that only affected men with a 'feeble will'—and public ridicule was sometimes the recommended 'cure' for nostalgia."[4]

Even after wars ended, physicians were dealing with veterans who still suffered. Observing World War I veterans at a Red Cross medical hospital near Liverpool, England, Major R.G. Rows, a physician with the Royal Army Medical Corps, noted,

> In some cases the physical expression of a special emotion, such as fear or terror, persists for a long time without much change. This condition is usually associated with an emotional state produced by the constant intrusion of the memory of some past incident.[5]

Dr. Millais Culpin, a psychologist with the Royal Army Medical Corps, witnessed one of his patients experiencing a flashback and wrote, "He seemed to be living his experience over again with more than hallucinatory vividness, ducking as shells came over or trembling as he took refuge from them."[6]

Few doctors wrote about what these veterans experienced, and friends and family of the soldiers rarely spoke of it. It was seen as an embarrassment to a military that needed strong, fearless soldiers. After World War II, for instance, veterans raised their families and built careers without mentioning the horrors that they saw. "Society didn't want to hear it," said Andrew Pomerantz, the chief of mental health services for the Veterans Administration in Vermont. "You don't want to hear that your hero who has just come back from winning the war is troubled by what he did over there and the people he bombed, the people he shot. People didn't want to hear that kind of thing."[7] This emphasis on downplaying the horrors of war may have made civilians feel better, but it took a huge psychological toll on veterans.

Changing the Culture of Silence

The expectation for soldiers to remain strong and silent did not start to change until after the Vietnam War. The 1960s and 1970s were a time of social change in many areas of society, and many of the veterans of the Vietnam War were activists. Even though soldiers had been tormented for centuries, the medical community still had not adequately recognized their symptoms as a defined and treatable illness. There was no medical name for the set of symptoms that plagued so many veterans and no organization to help them. Some veterans repressed the bad memories deep inside to lead what they thought were normal lives, while others acted out, abusing alcohol and drugs.

In the early 1970s, a small group of veterans in New York City got together to talk about their feelings. They had never heard that intense stress could cause lasting effects, but they did know that something was wrong. "We were talking a mile a minute and jumping on each other's stories, and we suddenly realized we all had similar kinds of experiences and we were having the same kinds of problems,"[8] Vietnam veteran Jack Smith said in an interview on National Public Radio (NPR). The group decided to meet again and invited two psychiatrists to participate.

Many Vietnam veterans protested the war once they came home and also began to speak out about how combat affects soldiers.

Dr. Robert Jay Lifton and Dr. Chaim Shatan had read about "war neurosis," but when they met with the group of Vietnam War veterans, they witnessed it in more than one person. In 1972, Shatan wrote an article about this phenomenon in the *New York Times* and called it Post-Vietnam Syndrome. It was the first time this disorder had been so publicly acknowledged and examined. The article attracted the attention of hundreds of veterans who were relieved to know that they were not alone, as well as the attention of the Veterans Administration (VA), which was uneasy about this new diagnosis of an old problem. The government was afraid it would go bankrupt paying for treatment and benefits. However, Shatan, Lifton, and Smith did not let that concern them. Their only priority was to get help for soldiers. One way to do that was to get Post-Vietnam Syndrome recognized officially by the American Psychiatric Association (APA).

Defining PTSD

A mental disorder becomes an official part of the medical vocabulary after much debate by members of the APA when it is defined and listed in the APA's *Diagnostic and Statistical Manual of Mental Disorders* (*DSM*), a book defining all recognized mental illnesses.

The first edition (*DSM-I*) was written in 1952 and included the first attempt to define this disorder that so many men from World War II and wars past had suffered from. It was called Gross Stress Reaction. However, the name and definition of this disorder seemed to be reinvented each time a new generation of doctors tried to treat a new generation of soldiers. It even disappeared from the second edition of the manual.

In the late 1970s, a committee of psychiatrists examined the research provided by Lifton and Shatan

supporting the existence of Post-Vietnam Syndrome. They also studied data from other trauma research that included rape victims, Holocaust survivors, and people who had survived natural disasters. The evidence clearly showed that traumas other than war could cause similar severe symptoms. Post-Vietnam Syndrome was renamed post-traumatic stress disorder (PTSD) to account for these other influences, and it was added to the third edition (*DSM-III*) in 1980.

Defining and identifying the condition was important for several reasons. First, it allowed veterans to get the help they needed. In 1989, Congress mandated the Department of Veteran Affairs to establish the National Center for PTSD. Second, it crushed the notion held for decades that the symptoms of PTSD were caused by natural weakness or character flaws. Third, it made clear that people other than soldiers can and do suffer from PTSD, which helped them recognize that they needed to seek treatment and that their symptoms were not simply a normal reaction to stress.

PTSD was previously defined as an anxiety disorder, but in the *DSM-5*, it has been moved to the category of Trauma- and Stressor-Related Disorders. It can occur after experiencing or witnessing a traumatic or life-threatening event that causes intense feelings of fear or helplessness. Although many situations can be traumatic, the disorder primarily arises from life-threatening situations such as war, terrorism, rape, abuse, a severe accident, or natural disasters such as hurricanes and tornadoes.

According to the National Center for PTSD, about 60 percent of men and 50 percent of women will experience a traumatic event in their lifetime. However, because not everyone who experiences trauma develops PTSD, only about 7 to 8 percent of the population—about 8 million people—will experience the

disorder. Additionally, although men are more likely to experience trauma, women are more likely to develop PTSD—about 10 percent of women compared to about 4 percent of men, although some experts place these rates slightly higher.

Myths versus Reality

Despite research into PTSD, many myths about the disorder persist, including:

- **Only combat veterans get PTSD.** In reality, soldiers who have not seen combat as well as people who have experienced other types of traumatic events are at risk for developing the disorder.

- **Everyone who experiences trauma gets PTSD.** People have different ways of coping with trauma, and reactions vary from person to person. There are several factors that can place someone at a higher risk of developing the disorder after trauma, including whether someone felt helpless during the event, whether they had a good emotional support system afterward, and whether they have a history of another mental illness, such as depression.

- **PTSD is a sign of weakness.** Mental illnesses such as PTSD are not a sign of weakness. Like physical illnesses, they are problems with the body that someone does not choose to have.

- **PTSD is not serious.** This disorder can make it difficult for someone to carry out their normal activities, and the mental strain places people at increased risk of committing suicide.

- **PTSD cannot be treated.** While there is no cure-all medication for PTSD, a combination of therapy and various medications, such as antidepressants and sleep aids, can greatly reduce the symptoms of PTSD.

- **Only men experience PTSD.** Men and women both experience PTSD; in fact, the rate of PTSD is higher in women than in men.

Combating these myths is essential to help people with PTSD find the treatment and emotional support they need to overcome the worst of their disorder.

Diagnosing PTSD

According to the *DSM-5*, eight criteria must be present for someone to be diagnosed with PTSD. The

U.S. Department of Veterans Affairs summarized them as follows:

Criterion A (one required): The person was exposed to: death, threatened death, actual or threatened serious injury, or actual or threatened sexual violence, in the following way(s):

- *Direct exposure*
- *Witnessing the trauma*
- *Learning that a relative or close friend was exposed to a trauma*
- *Indirect exposure to aversive details of the trauma, usually in the course of professional duties (e.g., first responders, medics)*

Criterion B (one required): The traumatic event is persistently re-experienced, in the following way(s):

- *Intrusive thoughts*
- *Nightmares*
- *Flashbacks*
- *Emotional distress after exposure to traumatic reminders*
- *Physical reactivity after exposure to traumatic reminders*

Criterion C (one required): Avoidance of trauma-related stimuli after the trauma, in the following way(s):

- *Trauma-related thoughts or feelings*
- *Trauma-related reminders*

Criterion D (two required): Negative thoughts or feelings that began or worsened after the trauma, in the following way(s):

- *Inability to recall key features of the trauma*
- *Overly negative thoughts and assumptions about oneself or the world*

- *Exaggerated blame of self or others for causing the trauma*
- *Negative affect [negative emotions such as anger, guilt, etc.]*
- *Decreased interest in activities*
- *Feeling isolated*
- *Difficulty experiencing positive affect [positive emotions such as happiness, excitement, etc.]*

Criterion E (two required): *Trauma-related arousal and reactivity that began or worsened after the trauma, in the following way(s):*

- *Irritability or aggression*
- *Risky or destructive behavior*
- *Hypervigilance*
- *Heightened startle reaction*
- *Difficulty concentrating*
- *Difficulty sleeping*

Criterion F (required): *Symptoms last for more than 1 month.*

Criterion G (required): *Symptoms create distress or functional impairment (e.g., social, occupational).*

Criterion H (required): *Symptoms are not due to medication, substance use, or other illness.*[9]

In addition to these symptoms, if someone experiences high levels of depersonalization—feelings of "being an outside observer of or detached from oneself … [as if] one were in a dream"[10]—or derealization—feelings of "unreality, distance, or distortion (e.g., 'things are not real')"[11]—they may be diagnosed with PTSD with dissociative specification. If not all of the symptoms listed above are present until at least six months after the trauma, they may be diagnosed with PTSD with delayed specification.

Complex PTSD

Complex PTSD, or C-PTSD, is PTSD that develops as a result of repeated or prolonged trauma. This may include things such as being a prisoner of war, long-term physical or sexual abuse, or being kidnapped or exploited—for instance, C-PTSD is commonly seen in people who have been the victims of sex trafficking. In addition to the symptoms of PTSD, people with C-PTSD may experience the following:

- *Emotional Regulation. May include persistent sadness, suicidal thoughts, explosive anger, or inhibited [suppressed] anger.*

- *Consciousness. Includes forgetting traumatic events, reliving traumatic events, or having episodes in which one feels detached from one's mental processes or body (dissociation).*

- *Self-Perception. May include helplessness, shame, guilt, stigma, and a sense of being completely different from other human beings.*

- *Distorted Perceptions of the Perpetrator. Examples include attributing total power to the perpetrator, or becoming preoccupied with the relationship to the perpetrator or preoccupied with revenge.*

- *Relations with Others. Examples include isolation, distrust, or a repeated search for a rescuer.*

- *One's System of Meanings. May include a loss*

Many people who survived the Nazi concentration camps during the Holocaust developed C-PTSD.

*of sustaining faith or a sense of hopelessness
and despair.*[12]

Although many people today have heard of
PTSD, few have heard of C-PTSD, which may
lead some to believe the person is making up their
diagnosis. However, C-PTSD is real and can be just
as difficult to deal with as PTSD that results from
short-term trauma.

Risk Factors

As previously mentioned, not everyone who experiences trauma develops PTSD. Researchers have iden-
tified several factors that increase a person's risk of
getting the disorder. According to Dr. Rachel Yehuda,
a PTSD specialist, "You're considered at risk if you
have a family history of PTSD or other mood and
anxiety disorders, if you've had adverse childhood
experiences, or if you have a tendency to dissociate
or panic."[13] Other factors, according to the National
Institute of Mental Health (NIMH), include:

- *Getting hurt*

- *Seeing another person hurt, or seeing a
  dead body …*

- *Feeling horror, helplessness, or extreme fear*

- *Having little or no social support after the event*

- *Dealing with extra stress after the event, such as
  the loss of a loved one, pain or injury, or the loss
  of a job or home*[14]

Fortunately, there are also factors that can protect
someone against developing this disorder. Seeking
help and emotional support immediately after the
event, having a healthy coping strategy such as jour-
naling, finding something good—no matter how

small—that occurred as a result of the event, and being able to act effectively even in the face of fear can all help people avoid developing PTSD after a traumatic event.

PTSD and Young People

When thinking about mental illness and trauma, many people forget about or ignore children and teenagers. Some believe young people are not capable of experiencing PTSD; they may think childhood is a carefree and easy time and that children have nothing to worry about. Others may simply assume PTSD shows up the same way in young people as it does in adults. However, neither of these assumptions are entirely true. While some people do have enjoyable childhoods, others experience short-term trauma—such as natural disasters, car accidents, or the suicide of a close friend—or long-term trauma—such as repeated physical or sexual abuse.

According to the National Center for PTSD, anywhere from 15 to 43 percent of girls and 14 to 43 percent of boys experience at least one trauma in their lifetime. Of those, 3 to 15 percent of girls and 1 to 6 percent of boys develop PTSD. As with adults, there are certain factors that increase a person's risk of developing the disorder, including how severe the trauma was, how their parents or other trusted adults reacted to it, and how close the child was to the trauma. For instance, if a child is sexually abused by one parent and both parents deny or dismiss it, the child is likely to have a very high level of PTSD symptoms. In contrast, a child whose friend suffered a trauma and whose parents encouraged them to talk about their feelings is likely to suffer little or no PTSD.

The symptoms of PTSD vary depending on age. In children under age six, who are not yet able to communicate well, symptoms may include bed-wetting,

PTSD can cause very young children to fear being separated from adults they trust.

forgetting how to talk, using playtime to act out the trauma, or being unusually clingy with trusted adults. Children between the ages of 6 and 12 are less likely to have flashbacks or memory problems, but they may associate events that happened before the trauma with the trauma itself and become certain that if they pay attention to those signs, they can prevent future trauma from happening. For instance, if there was a thunderstorm the day before the child was in a car crash, they may believe the thunderstorm was a bad omen and that bad things will always follow thunderstorms in the future. Teenagers' PTSD symptoms are closer to those of adults, but they are more likely than either children or adults to act aggressively or impulsively. Like adults, they are more likely to abuse drugs and alcohol or engage in self-harm to try to escape their problems than people who do not have PTSD. Children and teens who experience repeated trauma are also at risk for C-PTSD.

MORE THAN JUST STRESS

Everyone experiences stress at some point in their life; it is a normal part of being human. When someone has an important test to take; a difficult situation to deal with, such as an argument with a friend or a sick family member; or is in a dangerous situation, such as encountering a wild animal, they often feel stressed. In some cases, stress can even be useful; for instance, someone who is stressed about a test may feel more motivated to study, which can help them get a better grade.

However, PTSD is more than just normal stress. In people who have this disorder, their stress reaction is heightened, lasts longer, and often has nothing to do with the circumstances happening around them. For instance, while it is normal for someone who has been through a natural disaster to feel upset and have nightmares about it for several days afterward, these symptoms generally go away after some time has passed. For people with PTSD, the symptoms persist for longer than one month—sometimes for years. They can be triggered by seemingly innocent things, such as loud noises, a particular smell or taste, or a situation that reminds them of something related to their trauma. When this happens, the person's stress response goes into overdrive.

The Structures of the Brain

The brain is not one single mass. It is made up of

What Is a Neuron?

The building blocks of the brain are cells called neurons. A neuron is made up of three parts: a cell body, a long section called the axon, and many shorter branches called dendrites. All communication happens through complex networks of neurons.

The space between neighboring neurons is called the synapse. Neurons communicate with each other using chemicals called neurotransmitters that are released from the ends of the axons and travel into the synapse. Then, the neurotransmitters attach to special receptor sites on the neighboring cell, and the message is transmitted. There are also special sites at the end of the axon that pull back excess chemicals. They are called reuptake sites and effectively stop a message once it has been received by the other neuron.

several different structures that interact with each other and have distinct functions. The area that deals with stress, called the limbic system, is found deep inside the brain; it is essentially the same in all mammals, and it controls the most basic survival behaviors, producing responses that a person does not consciously control.

Within this part of the brain are the thalamus, hippocampus, amygdala, and hypothalamus. These structures work together to determine which emotions are attached to the things the ears, eyes, and other sensory organs perceive; for instance, does the person at the door seem dangerous or friendly?

The thalamus lies in the center of the limbic system and serves as the gateway between the outside world and the inner brain. It is the central relay point where information from the senses comes in and is distributed to the appropriate parts of the brain. It screens information and determines what is and what is not important to react to.

The hippocampus is a sausage-shaped organ that puts data into context. It connects the information the senses perceive with other information already in the brain. It organizes memories, retrieves them when necessary, and sends memories out to the appropriate

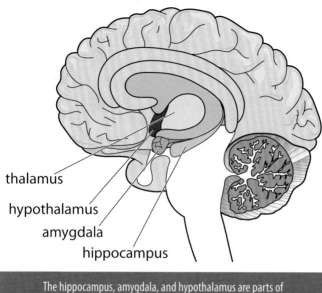

thalamus

hypothalamus

amygdala

hippocampus

The hippocampus, amygdala, and hypothalamus are parts of the brain's limbic system, which lies on both sides of the thalamus. The limbic system controls emotions, memories, and instincts.

places in the cerebrum for long-term storage. It helps people have a sense of place and time—letting them know what is the past, present, and future and how to relate new information to past information.

The amygdala is an almond-shaped structure about an inch long that is involved in learning and memory. It regulates emotions and connects them—especially fear and aggression—to a stimulus. For example, rats that have had their amygdala removed show no fear and calmly approach cats, unaware of their danger.

The hypothalamus is small, but it directs a lot of important functions. It controls the neurotransmitters that control the endocrine system—the glands that make hormones. The pituitary gland, which is located within the hypothalamus, is the most important of these glands. Because it controls the activity of all the other glands, it can make a person feel anger, sadness, or happiness. It triggers the adrenaline rush one might experience during an accident or a roller coaster ride. It also controls the fight-or-flight response—

the split-second reaction that happens when a person must decide whether to fight or run from danger.

All these structures are connected through a complex system of nerve cells. These communicate with each other and the rest of the body through chemical messengers called neurotransmitters and hormones. Neurotransmitters are chemicals released by nerve cells, or neurons, to pass information from cell to cell. There are many neurotransmitters, and they act within the synapses, or spaces, between nerve cells. Hormones are chemicals released by glands; for instance, the adrenal gland releases adrenaline—also called epinephrine—which heightens awareness when someone is nervous or excited. Neurotransmitters travel a relatively small distance from one neighboring neuron to another, while hormones travel through the bloodstream throughout the body to reach the cells they target.

Neurotransmitters and PTSD

Neurotransmitters are chemical messengers; they act as keys that fit into a target cell's lock. They may tell a cell to activate or to stop working. For example, the neurotransmitter acetylcholine makes a cell more excitable, increasing its activity. Gamma-aminobutyric acid (GABA), on the other hand, calms or inhibits a target cell. An imbalance in this delicate system can result in many of the symptoms seen in patients with PTSD. Too much of the excitatory chemical norepinephrine results in a keen startle response, hypervigilance, flashbacks, and nightmares. Too little of the inhibitory chemical serotonin causes depression, aggressive behavior, suicidal thoughts, and anxiousness. A healthy brain has a balance of inhibitory and excitatory chemicals.

How Stress Affects the Brain

The brain is always taking in stimuli from what the eyes see, what the ears hear, what the nose smells, and any other sensory information. The data from the senses are sent to the thalamus, which screens out unimportant information.

The important data is sent to the hippocampus, which determines what the information means. It could be the sound of a gunshot, movement in a dark alley, or the feeling of a snake slithering against the skin. The hippocampus asks, "Have I experienced this sensation before? What did it mean in the past? What other sensory details are there?" If the hippocampus perceives a threat to survival, then the amygdala switches on the fear response and tells the hypothalamus to sound the alarm.

When activated, the hypothalamus releases corticotropin-releasing factor (CRF), which switches on the sympathetic nervous system and the hypothalamic-pituitary-adrenocortical axis, which prepare the body to respond to the threat.

The sympathetic nervous system works on nerve pathways throughout the body to send messages. It sends out impulses to glands and muscles and tells the adrenal glands, located just above the kidneys, to pump epinephrine, norepinephrine, and other hormones into the bloodstream. Instantly, the heart beats faster and the bronchial tubes in the lungs open wider for easier breathing. Blood pressure rises to pump more oxygen-rich blood to the brain and to the muscles in the arms and legs.

Participating in extreme sports such as skydiving or white water rafting releases chemicals such as epinephrine because they involve risk, which the body interprets as danger.

The pupils of the eyes dilate to let in as much light as possible and take in every visual detail. The other

senses become sharper, and stress hormones enhance memory formation. This is why a person sometimes remembers even the tiniest details about a horrible event, as if it happened in slow motion.

At the same time, the CRF switches on the pituitary gland, which pumps adrenocorticotropic hormone (ACTH) into the bloodstream. It travels through the blood to activate the adrenal glands so they release cortisol and other hormones. Cortisol keeps the initial burst of energy high and keeps the blood pressure elevated for a longer period of time. Certain body functions that are not necessary during an emergency, such as digestion, are temporarily shut down to conserve energy for running or fighting. Once the threat is gone, the brain releases a different set of chemical messengers to halt the stress response, bringing the body back to a normal resting state.

When Stress Becomes a Problem

Although the stress response is lifesaving in the short term, it can be damaging to the body if activated for too long. Those who suffer from PTSD have lived through an event so powerful that it actually changes the chemistry of the brain, causing symptoms such as constant alertness, nightmares, sleeplessness, depression, or flashbacks. These symptoms occur when the normal, healthy balance of brain chemicals tips out of balance. During a PTSD-influencing event, the amygdala goes into hyperdrive and the hippocampus is unable to rein it in. Too much CRF floods the system, and the body cannot shut off the fight-or-flight response. Patients with PTSD have elevated levels of norepinephrine coursing through their system, which can give them a sense of hypervigilance (searching for danger where there is none), a hair-trigger startle response, intrusive memories, and flashbacks. They also exhibit abnormally low levels of serotonin.

Serotonin is a neurotransmitter that influences mood and may fuel the fear response. Low levels of serotonin can make people feel depressed and emotionally numb, and may cause them to have a poor memory.

Scientists are still figuring out how each chemical imbalance affects the brain, but they do know that even though PTSD is invisible to others, it is a physical injury as real as a cut on the skin. For example, research has shown that the hippocampus, which is vital for memory and learning, shrinks in size. Scientists experimenting with rats showed that daily injections of cortisol for several weeks killed brain cells in the hippocampus. The same results occurred without the injections when rats were put under stress for a specified amount of time each day.

Dr. J. Douglas Bremner, the director of Mental Health Research at the Atlanta Veterans Administration Medical Center, studied the brain scans of Vietnam veterans. He said, "What we found is that the hippocampus was smaller in the PTSD patients than the comparison group, 8% smaller for the right hippocampus. We also found that the more problems the veterans had with memory, the smaller the hippocampus."[15] The toxic level of cortisol caused the neurons to become overstimulated to the point that they died. This cell death correlated with the veterans' symptoms of not being able to remember new information and not being able to control the fear response that went along with the old memories. Other PTSD patients, including victims of child abuse and women who suffered non-combat trauma such as rape, also have a hippocampus that is smaller than normal.

Additionally, some researchers have proposed that being born with a naturally smaller hippocampus could be a risk factor for developing PTSD. To test this theory, one study examined identical twins—one had been exposed to trauma while the other had not.

According to the website VeryWell, in the twin study:

> *People with severe PTSD had a smaller hippo-campus, and they also had a non-trauma exposed twin with a smaller hippocampus. Consequently, a smaller hippocampus may be a sign that a person is vulnerable or more likely to develop PTSD after a traumatic experience.*
>
> *Of course, it is important to remember that twins often share the same environment growing up, so it is difficult to tease apart the role nature versus nurture plays in the size of a person's hippocampus. So, the verdict is still out on the true relationship between the hippocampus and PTSD.*[16]

How Memories Are Made

The same parts of the brain that help a person escape from danger also play important roles in creating memories. When a person is almost hit by a car, it makes sense to remember the connection between a car and danger so the next time the person encounters a busy road, they can act appropriately.

There are several theories about how memories are created. There are basically three types of memory: short-term memory, long-term memory, and procedural memory.

Procedural memory is used for skills that have been learned by repetition. For example, riding a bike, brushing teeth, getting dressed, and playing the piano all use this type of memory.

Like the RAM of a computer, short-term memory is used for recalling things such as a phone number that has just been recited. The information is stored for a short time and then recycled. It does not become a permanent memory.

Long-term memory is the hard drive of the brain. In it is stored all the facts, names, and information

a person has ever learned. All this information has to be processed through the hippocampus before it is consolidated and filed away in another part of the brain.

Every time a person remembers something, the memory is brought out of long-term memory into short-term memory for temporary use. In short-term memory, the memory can be altered, so each time a memory is remembered and restored, it is subtly altered and goes back into the brain like a new version of a text document, rewritten and saved over an old one. When a person recalls a memory, they are not only recalling the original memory, they are also recalling the last time they remembered it as well as all the times before.

Memories are not like photographs; they change each time they are recalled.

The center of memory organization is the hippocampus, and many studies have shown a correlation between the size of the hippocampus and the ability to remember well. For example, one study conducted among London taxi drivers showed that they had a larger than normal hippocampus. This stands to reason, since taxi drivers must remember how to navigate through hundreds of busy city streets.

Memory and PTSD

The strongest memories generally have a strong emotional component. People tend to remember their proudest and happiest moments as vividly as their most frightening or embarrassing experiences. The brain's chemistry is what links emotions to memories.

Researcher Christa McIntyre said,

> Emotionally neutral events generally are not stored as long-term memories. On the other hand, emotionally grounding events, such as those on September 11, [2001,] tend to be well-remembered after a single experience because they activate the amygdala.[17]

During a stress response, the stress hormones tell the amygdala and hippocampus that any memories recorded in the next few minutes need to be strong and vivid. The hippocampus generally acts to counterbalance the amygdala and the emotion associated with the memory, keeping it in context. For instance, if someone gets stressed by pop quizzes, they should only feel that stress response under certain circumstances. The memory of a pop quiz should make them feel less stress than they would while actually taking the quiz or when their teacher starts acting in a way that reminds them of the last time a pop quiz was announced.

In PTSD, however, the stress is so severe or continual that the flood of chemicals sears the memory into the brain, and the hippocampus is unable to rein in the fear response associated with it. The memory is stored without context, so the brain is unable to determine whether a real danger is present. In the above example, someone will likely not feel stress when recalling the memory of a pop quiz if they are not in school at the time because their brain understands that it is not an immediate threat. In someone with PTSD, this context is absent; for instance, if someone associates the smell of freshly cut grass with the memory of abuse they endured as a child, they may panic every time they smell it even if their abuser is nowhere nearby.

Every time a person recalls the trauma, the exceptionally vivid memory transfers back to the hippocampus, where it triggers the release of more hormones.

The person may experience a flashback, where they recall the trauma as if it was happening all over again. People experiencing a flashback have generally temporarily lost touch with reality, either partially or fully; they are unable to tell that what they are experiencing is not actually happening at that moment. There are three main types of flashbacks: visual, in which the person seems to experience the sights and sometimes sounds or smells of a trauma; somatic, in which a person whose trauma comes from physical harm feels pain in the part of the body that was originally affected, even if the injury is healed; and emotional, in which the person feels the emotions they felt during the trauma even if these emotions are not related to what is currently happening. Because they are not seeing the event the way they would with a visual flashback, these are sometimes not understood as being flashbacks.

During a somatic flashback, someone may experience pain even though their physical injuries healed long ago.

Sometimes memories surface for seemingly no reason; these are called intrusive memories. They are different than flashbacks because while they are still distressing, the person remains aware that the event is in the past and is not currently happening. The person may also have frequent nightmares about the event that cause them to wake up scared and disoriented. Other times, memories or flashbacks are triggered by a scent, noise, or other stimulus that reminds them of the trauma. Additionally, sometimes the fear is

triggered without any memory attached. According to *Medical Daily*,

> If you nearly drowned during your childhood, you may have a fear of water as an adult—the near death experience was so traumatic it still impacts your life ... but new research shows that you don't have to have a vivid memory of your trauma to develop PTSD. Your mind may subconsciously remember the fear that you experienced many years ago, even if you don't recall any or very few of the details.[18]

Some PTSD patients often find it hard to remember other things. In this case, there may have been too much cortisol, which prevents the brain from laying down a new memory or from accessing an existing one. A 1999 study showed that four days of high levels of cortisol impaired patients' ability to perform in a memory test. The test subjects felt they could not think straight.

However, an animal study showed that cortisol affects memory in very specific ways. Rats were stressed using an electric shock and then made to go through a familiar maze. The rats had no problem when the shock was given two minutes before going through the maze or when it was given four hours afterward. However, when the shock was given 30 minutes before, the rats were unable to remember their way through the maze. Memory was not lost, but it was made temporarily inaccessible. This was backed up by more recent research showing that increased cortisol makes it easier to form memories but harder to retrieve them later. According to the Cognitive Neuroscience Society,

> In the brain, cortisol binds to receptors that are found in the hippocampus and amygdala, which are important brain regions for learning and memory.

Past work has found that inducing stress, thereby increasing cortisol, during or after learning benefits memory consolidation, while increasing cortisol during retrieval hinders recall. Furthermore, chronically elevated cortisol levels seem to impair memory.[19]

For example, a student who feels stressed while studying for an important test is more likely to remember the information they study afterward, but if they feel stressed while taking the test, they will likely find it harder to recall what they studied. Long-term stress,

Related Health Problems

Many studies have found that people with PTSD are at increased risk for other physical and mental health problems. Health problems that appear together are called comorbid conditions. According to VeryWell, "it has been found that people with PTSD are about six times as likely as someone without PTSD to develop depression and about five times as likely to develop another anxiety disorder."[1] They are also much more likely to attempt suicide or engage in self-harm behaviors, such as cutting. Therapy can help with these problems as well as the underlying PTSD, although these conditions are harder to treat when they occur with PTSD as opposed to occurring alone.

For reasons that are not yet fully understood, people with PTSD are also at increased risk for physical problems such as pain, diabetes, obesity, and heart problems. Some experts believe this "may be due to the fact that the symptoms of PTSD result in the release of stress hormones that may contribute to inflammation and eventual damage to a person's body."[2] They are also more likely to smoke, drink, and use illegal drugs to try to cope with their problems, which can create further physical damage. Finding healthy coping mechanisms may be one way to reduce this risk.

An addiction to alcohol or drugs does not solve problems—it creates them.

1. Matthew Tull, "The Effects of PTSD on a Person's Everyday Life," VeryWell, last updated November 8, 2017. www.verywell.com/how-does-ptsd-affect-daily-life-2797536.

2. Tull, "The Effects of PTSD."

such as the kind associated with PTSD, makes remembering things harder in general.

Avoidance and Triggers

Avoidance behaviors appear as the person consciously or unconsciously tries to avoid experiencing any situation that reminds them of a traumatic event. For example, people who have narrowly survived fatal car crashes may refuse to drive or get into a car. A woman who has been raped in an alley may avoid dark, narrow places.

Avoiding things that create stress is natural to a certain extent. Most people do not like to do things that upset them, and many doctors advise avoiding unnecessary stressors to minimize the negative effects on the body. However, avoidance becomes a problem when it interferes with a person's daily life. For instance, Michael Risenhoover, a police captain who responded to the 1995 Oklahoma City bombing domestic terror attack and experienced PTSD afterward, stayed in his house for weeks after the bombing. Everyone around him had been affected by the disaster, and he could not bear to see his neighbors. Eventually, he moved to California to distance himself from the scene of the crime.

Avoidance can also extend to emotions, which is why some people with PTSD feel emotionally numb. The feelings people experience during a traumatic event are often overwhelming, so people with PTSD may be scared to experience even mild emotions later for fear that they will grow too intense.

Avoiding things that remind people of trauma can be helpful in the short term as a way to continue engaging in everyday life. According to the National Center for PTSD,

Distraction is a useful skill that can help you to get on with your daily life after a trauma. It can allow you to go to school or work, or buy groceries, even in the face of difficult life events. Although distraction and avoidance can be helpful in the short-term, they should not be your primary way of coping.[20]

To help those with PTSD, some people have begun using trigger warnings. This practice has been highly controversial. Some people do not fully understand what being triggered means and use it in a mocking way; they believe it simply means feeling uncomfortable, and since feeling uncomfortable sometimes is part of life, they think an attempt to avoid it is a sign of immaturity. People who believe this may use the phrase "triggered" as a joke and complain about people who they believe expect special treatment.

In reality, being triggered is a response that occurs when people who have PTSD encounter something that sets off the feelings associated with past trauma. People who support trigger warnings on things such as blog posts, books, and TV shows believe someone who has PTSD should be able to know if they are about to encounter something that will lead to an emotional response much stronger than discomfort.

Fireworks are a commonly reported trigger for people who have experienced gun violence, due to the loud noises, flashes of light, and smell of gunpowder. However, triggers can take any form—even ones that may not seem directly connected to the trauma—and are often highly personalized.

Trigger warnings, like the act of being triggered, are also not currently well understood. Some organizations have been outspoken in opposing them

because they believe they limit freedom of speech. For instance, John Ellison, the University of Chicago's dean of students, wrote a letter in 2016 to incoming freshman letting them know that the school does not support trigger warnings. In part, the letter said,

> Our commitment to academic freedom means that we do not support so-called "trigger warnings" … We do not cancel invited speakers because their topics might prove controversial, and we do not condone [support] the creation of intellectual "safe spaces" where individuals can retreat from ideas and perspectives at odds with their own.[21]

According to some mental health experts, this statement shows a lack of understanding about how people expect trigger warnings to be used. Rather than expecting information to be avoided completely, many people with PTSD hope a trigger warning will give them enough time to mentally prepare themselves for whatever is about to come their way. For instance, if a college professor notes on a class syllabus that one of the lectures will deal with rape, a person who is recovering from trauma associated with being raped can take steps to deal with that; many people feel better prepared to deal with a trigger when they know it is coming rather than being taken by surprise. Some people may prefer to skip the lecture entirely. Although avoidance, as previously mentioned, is not recommended by professionals as a long-term coping strategy, it can be useful when someone has just started the recovery process. According to psychologist Andrea Bonior, "While there's an active wound you're working on healing, it makes sense not to aggravate it … You can use trigger warnings to avoid making the wound deeper in the interim."[22]

However, even people who understand the point of trigger warnings may find them controversial. In an

article for the *Huffington Post*, Joni Edelman—who has triggers relating to her recovery from an eating disorder as well as several other mental illnesses—questioned the practice of providing trigger warnings. Her reasons included things such as "Trigger warnings don't exist in temporal ['real'] life. There is no trigger warning at the grocery store line for the cover of *Vogue* or *Star*," and "Trigger warnings victimize … If you have come out the other side [of] rape or bulimia, and you've recovered, what does a trigger warning imply? That you are still triggered and have not yet recovered? … Can you still call yourself recovered if someone is constantly reminding you that you should be triggered?"[23] Some agree with her views, while others disagree, stating that requesting a trigger warning is an act of self-preservation and a sign of strength. Additionally, they point out that trigger warnings need to be observed only by people who need them and can be ignored by others, the way someone who is not in a wheelchair can choose to take the stairs instead of walking up a wheelchair ramp. The debate over where trigger warnings are appropriate—and whether they are appropriate at all—is likely to continue for the foreseeable future.

Hypervigilance and Negative Thinking

Hypervigilance, also known as hyperarousal, is another part of PTSD. This involves feeling constantly alert and on edge, always looking for threats. In a dangerous situation, hypervigilance assures a person's survival; for example, if a soldier is not keeping watch, the enemy might be able to sneak up on them. However, at home, this feeling of constant alertness may create symptoms of insomnia, irritability, anger, trouble concentrating, and a sharp startle reflex. People who have been in battle may insist on always keeping their back to a wall even

though there is no danger of someone sneaking up on them from behind, while people who have experienced a natural disaster may constantly be checking to see if the sky is showing signs of a storm. Instead of keeping them safe, these hypervigilance symptoms interfere with their day-to-day activities and cause interpersonal problems; for instance, they may yell at a friend who accidentally startles them. They may also make it difficult for someone to focus at work or school; people with PTSD tend to have higher rates of unemployment and lower rates of high school and college graduation than the general population.

Someone who is hypervigilant is constantly looking for danger. This means they can never feel relaxed.

Another symptom that can create interpersonal problems is called negative affect, which means negative thoughts and feelings. People who have experienced a trauma may start feeling distrustful of the world around them, even their friends and family. They may also have difficulty feeling loving toward the people closest to them. This can be difficult for their loved ones to deal with, especially if they are unaware that this is a symptom of PTSD. In extreme cases, PTSD may cause someone to become violent to those around them; for instance, if they are triggered, they may accidentally hurt someone who is standing close to them. While this does not happen to everyone with PTSD, stories of this happening tend to get told

more often, leading to the false idea that everyone with PTSD is dangerous.

Friends and family members of those with PTSD can also be affected. Loved ones often feel sympathetic toward people with PTSD, but the difference in their loved one's behavior may also make them feel angry, depressed, and guilty—either because they cannot do much to help the person overcome their PTSD or because they feel bad for feeling angry. These negative feelings may cause the loved one to avoid the person with PTSD in an attempt to ignore the issue; they may also cause them to turn to negative coping behaviors, such as smoking, drinking, or drug use. For these reasons, education about the causes and symptoms of PTSD is important, and loved ones may benefit from therapy as well. According to the National Center for PTSD,

> Family members may feel hurt, alienated, or discouraged because your loved one has not been able to overcome the effects of the trauma. Family members frequently devote themselves totally to those they care for and, in the process, neglect their own needs.
>
> Social support is extremely important for preventing and helping with PTSD. It is important for family members to take care of themselves; both for their own good and to help the person dealing with PTSD.[24]

The center recommends that loved ones remember PTSD symptoms are something it takes time and treatment to overcome, but it also cautions against treating a person with PTSD as someone who is permanently disabled, as PTSD can be overcome with support and treatment. Additionally, it is important for everyone involved not to excuse bad behavior. For instance, if someone with PTSD is physically harming those around them when they have flashbacks, this is not something that should be excused and endured;

it is something that should be addressed immediately. The person with PTSD may not always be able to help what they do in the moment, but if they are aware of the effects their PTSD has on them and those around them, they can take precautions and address their own behavior, which may take away some of the powerlessness the disorder can make them feel. If they do accidentally do something to harm someone else, whether physically or emotionally, they can apologize and take steps to make sure it does not happen again.

It can be difficult for loved ones to understand what someone who experiences visual flashbacks is going through because although the flashback seems very real to them, no one else can see it. This disconnect may make loved ones feel angry or guilty.

People with C-PTSD may have additional negative views because it develops after repeated trauma. For instance, someone who has been raped repeatedly may begin to see their rapist as someone who has total power over them and may become obsessed with getting revenge. They may also have difficulty trusting others, even people who have not harmed them in the past. If they are religious, they may lose their faith due to a belief that if God was real, God would have saved them from the situation. They may also have negative feelings about themselves; for instance, they may falsely believe that they caused the situation to happen or let it continue, or that they deserved what happened to them. This emotional state is called "toxic shame," and it is often encouraged by the perpetrator

because it allows the perpetrator to continue their abuse and makes the victim less likely to fight back. Toxic shame can keep someone with C-PTSD from seeking the help they need, which also contributes to their constant search for someone to rescue them; their sense of shame and guilt often makes them feel unable to take action for themselves, so they look for someone who can do it for them. This often leads them to people who treat them in abusive ways to keep them dependent.

Lingering Effects

Nightmares, feeling on edge, and avoidance are natural coping mechanisms and occur in many survivors of trauma. Anyone who has experienced a tragedy might take time off from work or want to be alone for a while. However, most people return to normal activities and behavior within a short time. People who suffer from PTSD experience these symptoms for a much longer period. They find it difficult to function normally at work and in social situations for many months, or even years. "What we know about trauma and PTSD is that it runs a natural course," said Dr. John Bradley, chief of outpatient psychiatry at Walter Reed Army Medical Center. "Most of its symptoms gradually resolve. A person who still has symptoms after 30 days needs to seek help."[25]

How does an outside event cause such havoc in a person's life? In the same way that a body is injured in a car crash, the brain can be physically changed by a traumatic experience. Although scientists are just beginning to understand how the brain works, they already have evidence that many different types of traumatic events can cause this kind of change.

CAUSES OF PTSD

PTSD is unfortunately far more common than many people think. Because it is traditionally associated with soldiers, people who have undergone a different kind of trauma may not even recognize the symptoms in themselves. They may believe they are experiencing a normal level of stress or that the symptoms they are experiencing are coming from some other source, such as a different mental illness. Alternatively, they may realize something is wrong but be too scared to tell anyone for fear that people will think they are overreacting.

The Effects of Gender, Age, and Race

Studies conducted around the world point to a strong gender difference in who is vulnerable to PTSD, with women experiencing it at much higher rates than men. It is unknown why this difference exists, but the National Center for PTSD suggests several reasons:

- *Women are more likely to experience sexual assault.*

- *Sexual assault is more likely to cause PTSD than many other events.*

- *Women may be more likely to blame themselves for trauma experiences than men.*[26]

Additionally, recent research has suggested there may be a genetic component to this gender

difference. In 2011, *TIME* magazine reported on a study led by Dr. Kerry Ressler from Emory University that studied 64 nonveteran PTSD patients, focusing on their bodies' levels of a hormone-like chemical called pituitary adenylate cyclase-activating polypeptide (PACAP), which the researchers already knew plays a role in the way stress affects the body. *TIME* reported,

> *They found that patients who suffered from PTSD had higher levels of PACAP than patients without the psychiatric disorder. What's more, the higher the patients' blood levels of PACAP, the more severe their PTSD symptoms.*
>
> *But when researchers split the data by gender, they found that the association between PACAP and PTSD was significant only in women.*[27]

A follow-up study of 74 women with PTSD confirmed these results and also found that some of the genes involved in stress respond to the hormone estrogen, which women have higher levels of. The women in the study had variations of these genes that increased their sensitivity to estrogen and stress; these variations "are acquired over time, through environmental influences—suggesting that people who are not genetically hardwired to be vulnerable to PTSD may become vulnerable through experience."[28] A second follow-up study confirmed that these differences were found only in women.

Although the symptoms of PTSD are similar in men and women, there are some differences. Women are more likely to develop a quicker startle response and feel more emotionally numb than men; men are more likely to have difficulty controlling their anger and are more likely to abuse alcohol and drugs.

A person's age affects their susceptibility also. Children and teens are more likely than adults to

Men with PTSD are more likely than women to display anger problems. This may be because of societal expectations that women should keep anger hidden.

develop PTSD, but research has focused less on these age groups because for a long time, it was believed only adults got PTSD. Again, this was mainly because people believed only soldiers got PTSD, and since people have to be over 18 to sign up or be drafted into the army, no one thought to study young people who had experienced trauma. Additionally, many researchers previously believed that children—especially those too young to fully understand what is happening around them—handle trauma better than adults and therefore could not be impacted by PTSD. However, a study reported by *TIME* in 2010 found that not only do children and teens sometimes experience PTSD, they may be impacted more strongly when adults they trust are suffering similar symptoms. According to child psychologist Claude Chemtob, "There is increasing evidence that kids know what is going on if they are directly exposed and see something like planes crashing into the [World Trade Center] towers [on September 11, 2001],"[29] even if they are not fully aware of why it is happening. In fact, young children are more likely to develop PTSD than older ones. Scientists suggest that a very young child may not have the capacity to deal with the high levels of stress because their brain is not yet fully formed. They also have not developed behavioral coping skills to handle a life-threatening trauma. Those skills are learned

through the process of dealing with age-appropriate stresses and from watching parents and other adults.

Additionally, a person's race may play a role in the development of PTSD. According to *Bustle,*

> *A survey found that 9.1 percent of African-Americans had PTSD, compared to 6.8 percent of white Americans ... and it's been suggested that the many micro-aggressions and overt acts of racist discrimination that POC [people of color] deal with on a daily basis create such an environment of stress that PTSD occurrence becomes more likely.*[30]

Other researchers, such as trauma expert Kali Tal, have noted that Native Americans, especially women, are also more likely to suffer from PTSD than the general population. Race and poverty may be interconnected in regard to PTSD; since many black and Native American people live in poverty and impoverished neighborhoods tend to be less safe than wealthier neighborhoods, it is possible that these factors play a larger role in the development of PTSD than exposure to racist comments. More research is needed to determine whether race and PTSD are connected, and if so, how much one influences the other.

Because of the correlations between race, gender, and PTSD, black women have a higher risk of developing PTSD.

Elevating the Risk

There are several other factors that appear to elevate a person's risk for PTSD. Previous psychological problems such as depression or phobias—intense fears of specific things, such as spiders or flying—make it more likely that a person will develop PTSD if they were to encounter a triggering event. Trauma early in life may also increase the risk. A child who is traumatized may not develop the normal ability to cope with stress, leaving them more vulnerable. According to Chris R. Brewin, a professor of clinical psychology at the University of London, "This may produce an adult whose responses to new traumas are more extreme, are possibly more alarming in their own right and may take longer to extinguish themselves."[31]

Additional life stress—such as marital problems, an illness, or a death in the family—just before or just after the triggering event adds to the equation. It may act as the last straw that pushes a person over the edge.

People who lack a strong social network are also at risk. Talking to others and being supported by family and friends are important elements in coping with any trauma. Without that social support, recovery is less likely.

These risk factors are simply indicators or red flags that can identify who may need help after a traumatic event. However, the key ingredient in developing PTSD is a triggering event that sets off the debilitating cluster of symptoms.

Understanding Trauma

News coverage often gives the impression that PTSD only develops after a massive event involving dozens of victims. War, terrorism, and natural disasters are powerful and PTSD-provoking traumas, but the triggering event can also be individual and personal.

The Struggle of First Responders

Police officers, firefighters, and emergency medical technicians see, hear, and experience life-threatening traumas every day they go to work. They run into fires, haul bleeding bodies out of crushed cars, and try to bring the dying back to life. Most can handle these difficult and emotional tasks because they rely on their professional training and skill to keep them focused. However, suppressing or compartmentalizing one's emotions can be costly. Studies suggest that firefighters suffer from PTSD at a rate of 7 to 37 percent. According to VeryWell, this range is so large for several reasons, "including how PTSD was assessed (through a questionnaire or interview), whether other emergency responders were also surveyed along with the firefighters, whether the firefighters were volunteer or not, and where the firefighters worked."[1]

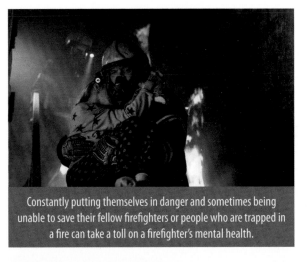

Constantly putting themselves in danger and sometimes being unable to save their fellow firefighters or people who are trapped in a fire can take a toll on a firefighter's mental health.

1. Matthew Tull, "Rates of PTSD in Firefighters," Very Well, last updated February 15, 2017. www.verywell.com/rates-of-ptsd-in-firefighters-2797428.

The physical and emotional wounds of child abuse are deep and often life-threatening. The feelings of fear and helplessness are intense and can last into adulthood. Many adults who have suffered abuse struggle to maintain an outwardly ordinary life and try to avoid reminders of the past. They generally feel worthless, fearful, guilty, abandoned, isolated, and terrorized all at the same time. These are the same emotions that plague the young abused child.

Unfortunately, it is difficult to identify children who have been abused when there are no outward physical signs. A child's behavior is key to uncovering abuse. If a child shows signs of suffering PTSD and has not

experienced an obvious triggering event, child abuse may be the cause. Children suffering from PTSD due to child abuse often act agitated or withdrawn; they have frequent nightmares and play in a repetitive manner, often reenacting aspects of the abuse.

Rape is another frequent cause of PTSD. According to the Rape Trauma Services, people who have experienced sexual assault are six times more likely to suffer from PTSD than those who have not. Rape is not only an attack on the body, it is also an assault on a person's mind. Long after the body heals, a rape victim is left feeling betrayed, guilty, and shamed. Victims of rape are more likely to experience PTSD if they know their attacker, have a low sense of self worth, experience a negative response from family, or dissociate during the attack, which means they mentally distance themselves from what is happening to them physically.

Rape victims with PTSD symptoms commonly suffer from uncontrollable thoughts about the attack, nightmares, and flashbacks. They tend to withdraw from social situations, and they become numb and uninterested in living. Survivors also often become hypervigilant and have difficulty sleeping. Although women are more likely to experience rape and other forms of sexual assault, PTSD can affect all sexual assault survivors, regardless of gender.

Car accidents are a common occurrence, so people may not realize they can be a cause of PTSD. "Serious car accidents are perhaps the most commonly experienced traumatic events in the United States," said Gayle Beck, a professor of psychology at the University at Buffalo. "The lives of accident survivors can be totally derailed by PTSD."[32] It is not uncommon for a survivor to avoid driving, be obsessed with thoughts of the accident, and become estranged from family and friends because they will no longer drive.

Some people find it difficult to concentrate; they may become irritable and develop insomnia.

PTSD is often overlooked in these situations because the emotional impact of car accidents is frequently underplayed by society, but nearly 9 percent of the 3.5 million people injured in accidents will develop the disorder.

Bad car accidents can cause PTSD, especially if someone in the car was injured.

Acts of Terrorism

Before September 11, 2001, very few Americans worried about a terrorist attack affecting their lives. Over time, however, these fears have grown; in 2016, the Pew Research Center noted that 40 percent of all U.S. citizens believe the United States has become more vulnerable to terrorism. Organized terrorist attacks and brutal acts of mass violence such as school shootings have become part of everyone's lives; they have become communal experiences shared through television, the internet, and print coverage.

However, those most affected are the people closest to the center of the action. For instance, eight months after the attack on the World Trade Center on September 11, 2001, more than 7 percent of the high school students living in the Bronx—an area of New York City—met the criteria for PTSD. This number may not seem significant, but compared with only

2 percent of students living in other areas who showed symptoms of PTSD, it is a high rate. Proximity to the event also had an effect among workers at the Pentagon on September 11. Of those who worked on the day of the attack, 22 percent suffered PTSD symptoms, compared to only 6 percent of those who were not working that day. Those who were injured exhibited symptoms at a rate of 47 percent versus only 10 percent of those who were unharmed.

Post-Traumatic Growth

Although PTSD often has debilitating effects, a small percentage of people view a traumatic event as something that ended up helping them. For instance, after Hurricane Katrina, about 5 percent of participants in a study conducted by Sarah Lowe, an assistant psychology professor at Montclair State University in New Jersey, displayed a phenomenon Lowe called "post-traumatic growth." She explained, "their mental health actually improved … They had severe distress prior to the storm and then afterward were indistinguishable from people we would call resilient—who maintain low levels of distress."[1]

The reasons why this growth occurs are unclear; one theory is that some people who had been suffering from undiagnosed or untreated PTSD before the storm, due to something such as childhood trauma, may have only been able to take advantage of mental health services after the storm. Another is that for some people, moving to a new area or finding that they have come through a traumatic event physically unharmed gives them new opportunities and makes them feel stronger. Like developing PTSD, not everyone who experiences trauma will also experience growth.

1. Quoted in Susan Scutti, "Resilience, Suffering and Silver Linings After a Disaster," CNN, last updated September 20, 2017. www.cnn.com/2017/09/19/health/psychological-aftermath-hurricanes-harvey-irma/index.html.

Acts of Nature

Natural disasters such as tornadoes, earthquakes, tsunamis, floods, or hurricanes have a devastating effect on entire communities. The devastation of Hurricane Katrina that hit the Gulf Coast in 2005 covered 90,000 square miles (233,099 sq km) of territory and destroyed social networks throughout the area that were designed to help people—churches,

synagogues, mosques, schools, hospitals, and community centers were wiped out. People were forced to move to new towns, where isolation from friends, family, and hometowns made PTSD symptoms worse.

Even those who did not move out of the area were constantly reminded of the disaster. Gina Barbe, a New Orleans resident, told a *New York Times* reporter, "I thought I could weather the storm, and I did—it's the aftermath that's killing me. When I'm driving through the city, I have to pull to the side of the street and sob."[33] Because Hurricane Katrina was such a major natural disaster and happened a relatively long time ago—compared with more recent disasters such as Hurricane Harvey in 2017—it is often used by experts to illustrate the effects this kind of disaster can have. According to CNN, "Some mental health conditions become more prevalent over time for survivors of the hurricane that struck the Gulf Coast in 2005."[34] These conditions may not yet have had time to appear in victims of more recent disasters. Studies have found that in areas affected by Hurricane Katrina, PTSD rose from 15 percent a few months after the storm hit to 21 percent one year later, showing that the effects of the disorder can be delayed or undiagnosed for some time. Additionally, the number of people who reported having suicidal thoughts increased from 2.8 percent to 6.4 percent. Children

In addition to being life-threatening, natural disasters such as tornadoes can cause PTSD when someone loses their home and possessions.

who endured recent hurricanes such as Harvey and Irma should be aware that PTSD can increase their risk for physical and mental health problems later in life, making it crucial for them to seek care as soon as possible if they believe they have PTSD.

According to Matthew Friedman of the National Center for PTSD, "Social support is the best way to prevent trauma after a disaster."[35] However, he cautioned that a full recovery takes time. In a comparison of two communities, one affected by flood and one untouched, the flood-damaged community had significantly higher rates of mental illness even 14 years later.

The Effects of Violence

Being in a war zone has intense effects on many soldiers. No amount of training can fully prepare a new soldier for the real experience of combat in a foreign land. In Iraq or Afghanistan, for example, the front line is not clearly defined. There are no safe zones. The threat is often invisible and unpredictable, and it surrounds soldiers on all sides 24 hours a day, 7 days a week. It is difficult to identify the enemy. They do not dress in combat fatigues but may appear as civilians driving a taxi or walking down the street pulling a wagon. Every object is suspect: a baby carriage, a suitcase, or a lunch bag could be a potential bomb.

Not being able to tell the difference between civilians and enemy combatants is one of the most difficult situations a soldier faces. Civilian casualties are especially difficult for a soldier to cope with. Children get caught in the crossfire, and apartment buildings get bombed. These accidents are often difficult to reconcile. It is also troubling for soldiers to see their friends get hurt or have to carry a wounded soldier to safety. Soldiers often have feelings of guilt for surviving when others have not. Additionally, soldiers are often

exposed to sexual assault in the military. It can affect both men and women, but women experience it at much higher rates. No matter their sex, victims of sexual assault in the military generally feel pressured not to talk about it to protect their attacker's military career. This forced silence, as well as the fact that the victim must often continue living and working near their attacker, can increase PTSD symptoms.

It has been known for years that experiencing battle often causes PTSD, but there are other parts of military life that can contribute as well.

The same long-term effect of PTSD occurs in people, especially children, who live in a war zone. Growing up with a battle raging around them is a chronic stress that desensitizes the person. They become numb to death and loss, and they suffer nightmares. Without treatment, they may carry symptoms of PTSD for the rest of their life. Additionally, people who do noncombatant work in war zones often experience PTSD. These people, who can include federal workers, journalists, and aid workers, often call themselves "frontline civilians" because they are not in the military, but they work in war zones. In an article for the *Los Angeles Times*, social science researcher Rebecca Zimmerman—a frontline civilian working in Afghanistan—described feeling discouraged because no one in charge wanted to hear about her research. While she was finding that the military presence in Afghanistan was doing more harm than good, military officials did not want to hear it because they wanted to project an image of success. However, the main factor involved in her development of PTSD was the

death of an eight-year-old Afghan girl Zimmerman had befriended. She described how the military culture contributed:

Even among civilians, war encourages a cowboy culture in which the biggest risks, the toughest tours, earn respect—and can lead to post-trau-matic stress disorder. Yet there are powerful taboos against frontline civilians seeking help, mirroring what it was like for the military in the early days of the wars in Iraq and Afghanistan.

Many frontline civilians feel that to admit trau-ma is to inappropriately equate our experiences with those of veterans who've known combat. I used to feel that way too, until a Marine friend sat me down ... and assured me that it was OK to seek help.[36]

According to Zimmerman, it was difficult for her to find a therapist who was comfortable talking to her about her experiences. Just as some civilians dis-miss PTSD because they are uncomfortable with it, many mental health experts find the stories of veter-ans and frontline civilians too disturbing. It can take time and effort to find a therapist who is willing and able to help someone with PTSD, but it is important for people to find the therapist who works best with them personally, otherwise progress will not be made.

Another often-overlooked category of people who are at high risk for developing PTSD is people who live in violent neighborhoods in the United States. There are areas of the country that are torn apart by violence, often between opposing gangs. For instance, "Chicago's Cook County Hospital has one of the busiest trauma centers in the nation, treating about 2,000 patients a year for gunshots, stabbings and other violent injuries."[37] In 2011, when researchers began screening patients at that hospital for PTSD, they

found that 43 percent of the patients they talked to showed signs of the disorder. This rate was especially high in people who had been shot—more than half of the gunshot victims the researchers examined had PTSD. This study and others like it have shown that people who live in violent neighborhoods experience rates of PTSD that are similar to combat veterans'. In Atlanta, Georgia, researchers "interviewed more than 8,000 inner-city residents and found that about two-thirds said they had been violently attacked and that half knew someone who had been murdered. At least 1 in 3 of those interviewed experienced symptoms consistent with PTSD at some point in their lives."[38] This problem often goes untreated because hospitals either cannot or do not want to spend the money required to hire staff who would screen patients for PTSD. People who live in violent neighborhoods are generally poor and cannot afford their own health insurance:

> *Many public hospitals rely on state Medicaid programs to cover treatment of low-income patients. But several surgeons across the country said they did not know of any way they could bill Medicaid for screenings ... Hospitals are often unwilling to foot the bill themselves.*
>
> *Trauma surgeons and their staffs expressed frustration that they know PTSD is having a serious impact on their patients, but they can't find a way to pay for the help they need ... John Porter, a trauma surgeon in Jackson, Miss., [said] "When you think about it, if someone gets shot, and I save their life, and they can't go out and function, did I technically save their life? Probably not."[39]*

Like soldiers, many young men in gangs feel they are expected to keep quiet about PTSD symptoms as a sign of mental strength, which prevents them

Research has shown that people who live in violent neighborhoods in the United States are just as much at risk for PTSD as people in war zones.

from seeking help. Hospital screenings would minimize this problem, but many doctors believe "hospitals are unlikely to make significant progress until the American College of Surgeons makes systematic PTSD screening a requirement for all top-level trauma centers."[40]

Secondhand Trauma

Sometimes witnessing another person's trauma, especially if the person is a loved one or the trauma is severe, can be enough to give people PTSD. For instance, in 2010, award-winning journalist Mac McClelland was in Haiti, driving in a car with a Haitian woman who had been gang-raped and severely injured. On the way back from the hospital, the woman saw one of her attackers on the street and began screaming. According to the British newspaper the *Guardian*,

> *It was over in moments, but this glimpse of someone else's pain, compounded by other dangers and perhaps long-buried memories, was enough to set McClelland on a path of unmooring mental and physical illness and a healing process that took years … But her experience was also, in the eyes of the world and often of McClelland herself, not enough to warrant the label of "trauma" or a diagnosis of post-traumatic stress disorder.*[41]

McClelland explained that people's tendency to downplay their own trauma and feel guilty for having PTSD when, in their eyes, they have not suffered as badly as others have—as well as society's tendency to reinforce this view—makes PTSD symptoms worse and prevents people from seeking treatment. She said, "I talked to a lot of people who had PTSD and they all have similar experiences … They feel like they didn't deserve to be traumatised, and they feel like other people don't feel like they deserve to be traumatised."[42] The article noted that families who live with a veteran who has PTSD may develop symptoms of PTSD themselves simply by witnessing their loved one's suffering and hearing about the things that caused it. Although not officially recognized by the *DSM*, this has been called secondary traumatic stress disorder (STSD). Although it can be just as difficult to deal with as PTSD, people feel too embarrassed or guilty to admit to it, believing that whatever they are feeling could not possibly be as bad as seeing combat.

This stigma surrounding PTSD and STSD stops many people from seeking the care they need, which is why many people have become committed to speaking out and letting the general public know that it is not just soldiers who suffer from this disorder. As McClelland noted, "This is insane, that we can only conceive of PTSD in terms of combat, when that's not even where most of it comes from in our own country."[43] Although it is important not to downplay the suffering of veterans who have seen combat, it is equally important to recognize that PTSD can come from other sources.

PTSD and Crime

PTSD also has an effect on crime. There is a perception, partially because of the way PTSD is portrayed in the media, that people who have PTSD

are dangerous and violent. For instance, in a 2009 episode of the TV show *Grey's Anatomy*, the characters Owen Hunt—a veteran with undiagnosed PTSD—and Cristina Yang are taking a nap when Yang suddenly wakes up to Hunt strangling her; the ceiling fan above the bed, which resembled helicopter blades, had triggered a flashback and made him believe he was back in combat, strangling an enemy. This portrayal of a person with PTSD as violent is not a reflection of the typical PTSD sufferer; according to the National Center for PTSD, "Individuals with PTSD are not dangerous. Although PTSD is associated with an increased risk of violence, the majority of Veterans and non-Veterans with PTSD have never engaged in violence."[44] *Grey's Anatomy* does go on to show Hunt getting the therapy he needs after he first downplays his problems—at one point, he tells a fellow doctor that because he was not physically injured like some other soldiers, his problems are not important. Eventually, his coworkers and friends convince him that PTSD is just as important to treat as a physical injury. Because it addressed these important issues, many people applauded the show's storyline overall.

In its fifth season, *Grey's Anatomy* introduced Dr. Owen Hunt, a character who had PTSD.

Although most people with PTSD do not engage in violence, "there's a subgroup of people who are at risk, in the wrong place, at the wrong time, of reacting in a violent way or an aggressive way, that they might not have if they had had their PTSD treated,"[45] according to

researcher Dr. Kerry Ressler. Studies have found that people with untreated PTSD have an increased risk of abusing drugs and alcohol as well as having related mental illnesses—all of which may increase the risk of engaging in violent behavior, such as hurting a spouse or child. According to the National Center for PTSD, it is these related behaviors—not the PTSD itself—that make someone more likely to be violent. These findings highlight the importance of getting proper treatment.

PTSD may be a psychiatric disorder, but its effects reach beyond the mind and emotions of sufferers. It is important to treat the disorder effectively, not only for the good of the individual, but also to benefit families and society.

TREATMENT FOR PTSD

Because everyone experiences PTSD differently, treatment plans tend to be individualized. What works for one person may not work for another. However, over the last several decades, some therapies have proven effective for a majority of people. These include cognitive behavioral therapy (CBT), exposure therapy, and eye movement desensitization and reprocessing (EMDR). Some form of therapy or potentially a combination of therapies is recommended for most people with PTSD. Additionally, some people may benefit from medication or alternative therapies such as meditation and yoga. Some people find that the first thing they try works well, while for others, it is a process of trial and error until they find the combination that works for them.

Some therapy treatments for PTSD can last from three months to two years or more, depending on the severity of patients' symptoms and how much it adversely affects their work and social life. Long-term treatment might be required for patients who are suffering from additional problems, such as depression or alcohol or substance abuse. However, the key to effectively shortening the treatment time is to begin shortly after the trauma. Researchers know that memories are flexible or modifiable for only a short period of time, generally a month or less. After that, the memory becomes part of the long-term storage in the cerebral cortex, where it is more difficult to change.

Self-Help

It can be hard for people with PTSD to start therapy. In addition to the stigma that causes people to convince themselves they do not need help, it is often difficult and overwhelming for them to start looking for a therapist who specializes in PTSD. NIMH recommends that patients ask their regular doctor for suggestions in addition to searching online. While this search is happening or while treatment is in the early stages, there are several things patients can do to help themselves:

- *Talk with your doctor about treatment options.*

- *Engage in mild physical activity or exercise to help reduce stress.*

- *Set realistic goals for yourself.*

- *Break up large tasks into small ones, set some priorities, and do what you can as you can.*

- *Try to spend time with other people, and confide in a trusted friend or relative. Tell others about things that may trigger symptoms.*

- *Expect your symptoms to improve gradually, not immediately.*

- *Identify and seek out comforting situations, places, and people.*[1]

1. "Post-Traumatic Stress Disorder," National Institute of Mental Health, last updated February 2016. www.nimh.nih.gov/health/topics/post-traumatic-stress-disorder-ptsd/index.shtml.

Changing Thoughts

Talk therapy is based on the principle that thoughts and feelings are connected and that it is beneficial to get them out into the open. It looks at the way a person processed the event in their mind at the time it occurred and how they understand it afterward. Talk therapy helps a person identify any troublesome thinking patterns.

Cognitive behavioral therapy (CBT) goes one step further. It identifies negative thoughts and emotions, teaches survivors a different way to think about the events, and helps them react in a more positive manner. Psychologists call this restructuring or reframing.

For example, a survivor of a natural disaster may

CBT helps people identify and change their negative thought processes.

feel guilty for having survived when others died. They may feel as if they could have done something more to help others. After talking the event over in CBT sessions, they would learn how to challenge their feelings and restructure the guilt into more healthy feelings of gratitude and pride for doing what they needed to do to survive. By changing the way they thought about the event, they could change the way they felt about it.

Therapy gives patients much-needed support and encouragement, and according to Lisa Najavits of the National Center for PTSD, "It helps to know you're not crazy. People need to be told not to lie in bed all day and not to drink or use drugs to escape the emotional pain."[46] The best therapy gives the patient confidence in their ability to cope.

Sometimes meeting with others who have experienced the same type of trauma helps patients share their feelings. Group therapy offers a safe atmosphere for survivors to tell their stories, which psychologists call "trauma narratives." Rape victims in particular recover faster with help from a support group, where they learn to come to terms with the past and alleviate stress in the present.

Gayle Beck at the Center for Anxiety Research at the University at Buffalo works with PTSD survivors of traumatic car accidents. "Our recent work has shown that you can treat PTSD within a group therapy setting and obtain results that are just as effective as individual format CBT,"[47] Beck said. This is

especially important given the rising cost of mental health services.

What Not to Say

Sometimes people try to help someone with PTSD but are unaware that their comments or questions are actually hurtful. Other times, people simply do not think about the effect their words may have on someone; they may ask a stranger a question that is insensitive without realizing how upsetting it is to the person with PTSD. Some of these insensitive comments or questions include:

- "Just get over it/Shouldn't you be over it by now?"
- "Your situation isn't as bad as some other people's."
- "You volunteered for the military; you should have expected this."
- "How many people did you kill?"
- "How can you have PTSD if you weren't a soldier?"
- "I had a traumatic experience, and I'm fine."
- "I know how you feel. My mom got mad at me today, and I think I have PTSD now."
- "Ha, looks like someone's been triggered [to someone who is just angry or upset]."

Instead of joking about or downplaying PTSD and triggers, someone who wants to help a loved one with PTSD should be compassionate and supportive. They should let the person know that although they cannot fully understand what the person is going through, they support their loved one and are there for them. They can offer to help the person find a therapist, ask kindly what the person's triggers are so they can be avoided, let the person know they are willing to listen if they want to talk, leave them alone if they request space, and be encouraging throughout the difficult process of overcoming PTSD.

Facing the Trauma

Prolonged exposure (PE) therapy literally exposes a survivor to aspects of the trauma so they can reexperience the feelings and fears that have overwhelmed them. In the safe surroundings of a therapist's office, patients can face their fears and gain control of their emotions so that with time, the trauma is no longer so stressful.

In PE, patients are carefully and repeatedly exposed to their triggers and trauma. In the first few sessions, they will get to know their therapist, talk a little bit about past experiences, and learn some breathing exercises to calm anxiety. After that, the patient will provide a list of triggers, and the therapist will help them confront those triggers in reality, which is called "in vivo exposure." For instance, someone who nearly drowned as a child and is afraid of water may go to a beach or pool. After the triggers have been overcome, the patient talks with their therapist in detail about the trauma. This is called "imaginal exposure" because the person is experiencing it only in their mind. This helps the person deal with the emotions the trauma made them feel. According to the National Center for PTSD, treatment generally lasts about 3 months and involves 8 to 15 weekly sessions that last between 60 and 90 minutes, although the patient also listens to recordings of their imaginal exposure between sessions.

Although many patients find it difficult at first to face their triggers and discuss their trauma, studies have shown that PE can be effective. According to psychological scientist Richard J. McNally, "One recent study of over 300 female assault survivors revealed that 8.1% of patients on a wait list experienced reliable worsening of their symptoms, whereas none of the patients receiving PE did so."[48] McNally explained that this shows PE often does not cause a patient's PTSD symptoms to get worse, although waiting to get treatment does. However, he also noted that PE may not help some people, since there is no one cure-all treatment for PTSD.

When triggers cannot be faced directly, some therapists have found that using technology can help. For example, at New York Presbyterian Hospital's Weill Cornell Medical Center, patients put on

headgear so they could hear sound recordings from the September 11 attack on the World Trade Center and watch images of buildings collapsing. Patients had the ability to shut off the simulation any time, but with each viewing, their anxiety decreased as they became desensitized to images and sounds that once triggered flashbacks or nightmares. These simulators are designed with the same technology as the latest computer games.

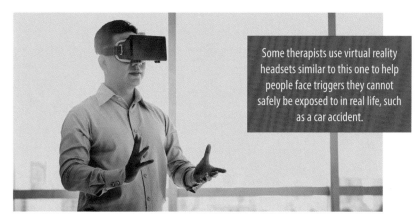

Some therapists use virtual reality headsets similar to this one to help people face triggers they cannot safely be exposed to in real life, such as a car accident.

EMDR Therapy

People who do not benefit from PE may find success with a treatment called eye movement desensitization and reprocessing (EMDR), which was developed in the 1980s by Francine Shapiro, a psychologist in private practice. She discovered that her anxious thoughts disappeared when she went for a walk in the woods, and she attributed it to her rapid eye movements as she scanned her surroundings.

During an EMDR therapy session, patients are told to think of their anxiety-provoking memories, such as the moment they saw their attacker or the sound of a bomb blast. As they recall this memory, patients watch the therapist's finger as the therapist moves it from left to right and back again. It is similar to a scene of a patient being hypnotized with a swinging

pocket watch. However, during this procedure, patients are told to replace the negative thoughts about the remembered events with positive ones. In addition to finger movement, some therapists use a pen or other object, alternately tap the left and right hands of the patient, or alternate sounds in the patient's ears.

EMDR involves following an object with the eyes while talking about trauma.

No one is sure why this technique works. It may be that the lateral eye motion back and forth stimulates both hemispheres of the brain, or it may be the exposure of repeated imagining of the real experience that brings about relief. According to *The Atlantic*, "Some experts think the eye movements help re-shuffle the memories so that when they are stored again, they lose some of their traumatic power."[49] Whatever the reason, while some studies have found the eye movements to be unnecessary, others have found EMDR to be effective. For instance, one 2011 study found that patients who moved their eyes during EMDR "had a more significant reduction in distress and had less sweat on their skin—a symptom of unease"[50]—than patients who kept their eyes closed. Some believe that EMDR is fundamentally the same as CBT but gives faster results. It is recommended by numerous organizations, including the APA and U.S. Department

of Veterans Affairs, but like other types of therapy, it may not work for everyone.

Other Types of Therapy

Some types of therapy are less common or are complementary therapies that are meant to be performed along with more traditional therapies. One type of CBT that may provide benefits involves training the patient to manage the anxiety they encounter. Stress inoculation training (SIT) teaches patients how to relax their muscles and control their breathing during times of stress. This helps diminish the symptoms of hypervigilance and the startle response. Practicing thought stopping or cognitive restructuring allows the patient to block those intrusive thoughts and nagging anxieties. It works by exposing patients to milder forms of stress so they can learn healthy coping skills that can be put into practice when they encounter a PTSD trigger. Rather than addressing the triggers or the trauma directly, the person learns how to handle the anxiety they provoke.

Another type of therapy that is similar to CBT is called cognitive processing therapy (CPT). It is often described as a combination of CBT and PE; in the process of discussing their trauma, the patient learns to identify and change negative thought patterns—for instance, the idea that they deserved what happened to them.

For some people, talking about the event or their feelings can be difficult. They struggle to find the words to express themselves. Psychoanalyst Belleruth Naparastek explained that trauma often produces changes in the brain that impede a person's ability to think and talk about the event because the trauma was experienced both visually and through the other senses. If the verbal side of the brain is hindered, she suggested that it is more effective to use the visual

side as a basis for treatment: "Imagery-based solutions use the right hemisphere of the brain—perception, sensation, emotion and movement—rather than the left side's standard cognitive functions of thinking, analyzing, verbalizing and synthesizing."[51]

Based on the principle that people can imagine themselves anywhere—under a cozy blanket, on top of a peaceful mountain, or on a quiet beach—guided imagery or guided meditation lets the imagination provide relief. Some patients are directed to visualize themselves in a calming place so that each time an intrusive flashback occurs, they can call up this vision. Adults who have suffered abuse may be guided back to the past where they can imagine themselves as an adult confronting the abuser or rescuing themselves as a child. Studies have shown that this technique does have an effect on the body. It can lower blood pressure, decrease the length of hospital stays, and reduce pain in those who practice it. For PTSD patients, it can relieve fears and increase coping skills, especially when combined with a practice called healing touch. According to the *Huffington Post*,

> *Researchers at the Scripps Center for Integrative Medicine found that healing touch with guided imagery ... helped to decrease symptoms of PTSD and depression and increase quality of life for returning active-duty soldiers, when used in tandem with the usual PTSD treatment.*[52]

Healing touch is a treatment that has not been studied much; it "is an 'energy therapy' that uses gentle hand techniques purported [claimed] to help re-pattern the patient's energy field and accelerate healing of the body and mind."[53] While some people may not see a benefit from this type of therapy, it is not harmful. Like guided imagery, it is considered a complementary therapy, meaning one that can add to the

effectiveness of more traditional treatment methods.

Somatic therapy is another less commonly used therapy that some people have had positive experiences with. It involves the view that the body and brain are connected and that treatment should address both, even for a disorder that is primarily mental. Practitioners of somatic therapy believe "the sensations associated with past trauma may become trapped within the body and reflected in facial expressions, posture, muscular pain, or other forms of body language."[54] By focusing on the body, they believe, the mind will naturally feel less stress.

Healing touch therapy (shown here) involves using hand motions to redistribute a person's energy in ways that are meant to be relaxing. Not everyone experiences results from this type of therapy.

Other complementary treatments include yoga, acupuncture, aromatherapy, and meditation. These are generally recognized as ways to reduce stress rather than treat a disorder, but in the case of someone with PTSD, that stress reduction can make a big difference in their day-to-day life.

Medication for PTSD

For some people, therapy may be all they need to recover from the worst symptoms of PTSD, but other patients may need additional help through medication. A physician might prescribe medication when a patient is not eating or sleeping properly or is struggling to get through the day. If patients are putting too much energy into balancing their lives with

therapy, exercise, and stress relief, then medication is the next step.

Currently there are four medications commonly prescribed for the treatment of PTSD, which are all also commonly prescribed to treat anxiety and depression: sertraline (Zoloft), paroxetine (Paxil), fluoxetine (Prozac), and venlafaxine (Effexor). The first three are selective serotonin reuptake inhibitors (SSRIs), and the last one is a serotonin-norepinephrine reuptake inhibitor (SNRI). SSRIs work by blocking the site on neurons that remove serotonin from the synapses, a process called reuptake. This allows the body access to more serotonin. It has a calming effect on the body and relieves the PTSD symptoms of hypervigilance and intrusive thoughts as well as countering depression and panic attacks. SNRIs work similarly, but they also prevent the reuptake of norepinephrine, another calming neurotransmitter.

Although these four medications have been found to improve PTSD symptoms, every drug has its side effects, and patients should discuss these with their doctor before trying them. SSRIs and SNRIs may cause sleeplessness, nausea, anxiety, and restlessness in some patients; some experts have also expressed concern over the fact that some patients show an increase, rather than a decrease, in suicidal thoughts.

Another type of medication that can be prescribed for PTSD is benzodiazepines, a class of antianxiety medications such as alprazolam (Xanax) and clonazepam (Klonopin). These work by improving the action of the calming neurotransmitter GABA. However, benzodiazepines have a high potential for addiction, so they are generally not approved for long-term use.

Physicians are continuously searching for alternative medications to help their patients, and, although they are not approved to treat PTSD, many other drugs are used to treat similar conditions or

specific symptoms. For example, a drug called prazosin (Minipress) was created to treat high blood pressure, but it has also been prescribed to treat PTSD because it stops some of the effects adrenaline has on the body. This is especially helpful for reducing nightmares and insomnia, which can help someone handle stress better overall. Side effects include sleepiness, headache, and lack of energy. Because Minipress is a newer medication and not approved by the U.S. Food and Drug Administration (FDA) for PTSD, more research is needed to see how effectively it works for PTSD symptoms.

LOOKING AHEAD

There are no reliable numbers to tell whether PTSD has been increasing or decreasing in recent years, especially since many people never admit they even have the disorder. Additionally, PTSD has only been a recognized medical condition for about 50 years, which is a relatively short time; the long-term effects of many treatments are still not completely apparent. However, it is certain that cases of PTSD will continue to be reported in the future because people will still encounter situations such as rape, violence, war, and natural disasters. With that in mind, combined with the fact that as many as 50 percent of patients do not respond to current treatment methods, experts are continually researching new and better methods of treating PTSD.

Looking at the Brain

Scientists used to believe that the brain was like a computer—hardwired and fixed. Once a person reached adulthood, experts thought, they did not grow any more new brain cells. However, thanks to new brain research, neurologists now know that the brain is adaptable and changing. Adults can grow new neurons, and damage to the brain due to stress can be reversed.

These discoveries have been made because of technology that lets researchers see the brain at work. Functional magnetic resonance imaging (fMRI) uses radio waves and a strong magnetic field to measure

tiny changes that occur in active parts of the brain. It identifies which blood vessels are expanding, where extra oxygen is being delivered from the blood, and where chemical exchange is taking place—all signs that that particular area of the brain is at work.

A patient is placed on a table and slid into the MRI machine. The patient is given specific mental tasks to perform, such as solving a math problem in their head, thinking up a shopping list, or recalling a frightening event while the machine scans their brain. In this manner, scientists

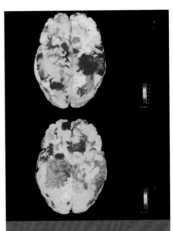

An fMRI (shown here) shows which parts of the brain are most active at certain times, such as when recalling a traumatic memory.

can see the functional difference between a brain that is suffering from PTSD and one that is not. The areas of particular interest are the amygdala, the hippocampus, and the cerebral cortex located in the front of the brain. Patients who have PTSD do not show activity in a certain area of the cerebral cortex. This correlates with not being able to turn on the part of the brain that controls and balances the amygdala, the part of the brain that deals with memory and helps control emotions.

Brain imaging can also reveal the link between trauma and memories. A brain scan study took fMRI images of people who had experienced the terrorist attacks of September 11, 2011, firsthand and those who were 2 miles (3.2 km) or more away. The brain scans were taken while the participants recalled the event. A significantly different pattern emerged between the two groups. In the close proximity group, there was greater activity in the amygdala and less in the hippocampus, the part of the brain that generally restrains the amygdala. Their memories were

stronger because the amygdala kicked into high gear as the tragedy unfolded. The hippocampus's ability to evaluate and tone down the fright response was impaired. "Individuals that were closest to the event had multi-sensory stimulation. They experienced the event, they could feel it, see it, smell it, hear it. That's another factor involved in producing especially vivid memories,"[55] said Dr. Grant Mitchell, director of psychiatry at Northern Westchester Hospital Center.

Another study shows that PTSD responds to mindfulness training, which is a technique that is often taught in CBT and other kinds of therapy. It involves paying attention to things such as the sensations of the body and its surroundings rather than internal thoughts. When a group of veterans with PTSD were examined with fMRI after learning how to manage their anxious, repetitive thoughts, the results showed visible changes in the brain:

> *Before the mindfulness training, when the veterans were resting quietly, their brains had extra activity in regions involved in responding to threats or other outside problems. This is a sign of that endless loop of hypervigilance often seen in PTSD.*

> *But after learning mindfulness, they developed stronger connections between two other brain networks: the one involved in our inner, sometimes meandering, thoughts, and the one involved in shifting and directing attention.*[56]

These results were not seen in the group that had not learned mindfulness techniques, which suggests that mindfulness training was the key to helping these veterans break their cycle of hypervigilance and negative thoughts. Additionally, fewer veterans involved in the study dropped out of therapy

that included mindfulness than dropped out of therapy that did not include it, suggesting that they saw more improvement in their condition.

In time, brain imaging may provide a way to diagnose psychological disorders by looking at the brain pattern revealed on an fMRI. Using fMRIs to look for the biological markers or specific patterns that occur only

Meditation is one form of mindfulness.

during PTSD would be a visible means of diagnosing a patient. Finding that physical test could change the stigma of mental health problems in the military. For the first time, invisible processes such as making a memory, feeling fear, or hallucinating can be seen as clearly as a fractured bone on an X-ray. Knowing which circuits or neurotransmitters are involved in these processes could pave the way for pharmaceutical companies to develop better drugs that can target these areas.

Looking for New Medications

Although certain drugs, especially antidepressants such as sertraline and paroxetine, have been widely prescribed to treat PTSD, they do not work for everyone, and in some cases, they may actually make the condition worse. Pharmaceutical companies are continuously testing other medications that are FDA-approved for other disorders to see if they would be appropriate to relieve PTSD symptoms. One such medication is called propranolol.

Propranolol is a blood pressure medication doctors have been prescribing to patients for more than 25 years.

It is also a prospective PTSD treatment. Research has shown that propranolol may tone down the harmful memories that a PTSD patient experiences.

Propranolol is a beta-blocker; it blocks the stress hormones from acting on the amygdala so the event becomes just a regular memory, not one that causes a panic attack. Although beta-blockers will not get rid of thoughts, they may block the stress reaction that accompanies them. Studies in mice showed that propranolol increased the effectiveness of PE training; they were given a shock every time they heard a particular noise, then were exposed to the noise without the shock. The mice that were given propranolol did not feel as afraid when they heard the noise, so they got over their fear faster. Researchers hope the drug will work the same way in humans who are undergoing PE therapy, allowing it to provide long-term results more quickly.

Another drug that is currently being tested on human patients is 3,4-methylenedioxy-methamphetamine (MDMA), more commonly known as ecstasy. For years, MDMA has been illegal; it is generally associated with raves and electronic dance music (EDM) concerts, where people take it to experience increased energy as well as feelings of happiness, relaxation, and increased affection toward others. In the 1980s, before it was banned, MDMA was used in therapy to make people more willing to talk about their feelings. Since then, some mental health experts have urged the FDA to look into this use again, and in August 2017, the FDA did approve MDMA specifically for the treatment of PTSD. MDMA is illegal because it has the potential to be dangerous; drug dealers have been known to add filler drugs such as cocaine and synthetic cathenones (otherwise known as bath salts), which people may not be aware they are taking, thinking they have bought pure MDMA. Additionally,

MDMA causes body temperature to rise, so when people are doing strenuous activity and not drinking enough water, they can get sick from overheating. Some people have died this way. However, under the supervision of a doctor, these risks can be avoided, and MDMA has no other known negative effects on the body. However, since little research has been done on MDMA alone, more is needed before it can be given to patients. Some studies have shown that people experience negative effects after taking MDMA, such as depression, insomnia, and irritability, but since many people take MDMA in combination with other drugs, it is unclear which drug causes these effects.

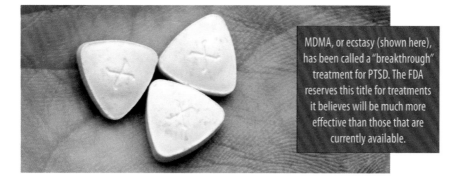

MDMA, or ecstasy (shown here), has been called a "breakthrough" treatment for PTSD. The FDA reserves this title for treatments it believes will be much more effective than those that are currently available.

As long as clinical trials prove it to be safe, there are several benefits to using MDMA to treat PTSD, according to *Popular Science*:

> On MDMA, the user's brain is flooded with all the neurotransmitters that make them feel good, and that can make it a lot easier to recall painful memories ... It becomes much easier for people to deal with those experiences with their therapist when they're not fighting visceral fear. MDMA helps patients have more productive conversations about past trauma with their therapists ...
>
> In one study, 67 percent of PTSD patients had no signs of the disease after three MDMA therapy

sessions. Just 23 percent of non–MDMA-assisted patients had the same results.[57]

Using MDMA this way is controversial; many people believe it is illegal for good reason, and some therapists feel it is unnecessary or a barrier to effective therapy sessions. However, others believe it could help people whose PTSD does not respond to other therapies.

There's an App for That

It is not surprising that with the increasing prevalence of technology, apps have been created to help people deal with PTSD and the conditions that often accompany it. Some of these include:

- Feerless, a free Google Chrome plug-in for Netflix. Users can specify what their triggers are, and when a scene that involves one of them is about to happen onscreen, a small blue and white circle pops up in the corner, warning them to look away if they do not want to see it or allowing them to face their trigger to help overcome it if they feel ready to.

- PE Coach, a mobile app from the National Center for PTSD. It is intended to be used while someone is undergoing prolonged exposure therapy. Using the app, patients can record their sessions to listen to later, track their symptoms over time to evaluate their progress, and do interactive breathing exercises.

- Calm Harm, a mobile app that discourages self-harm—which people with PTSD are at increased risk for—by offering activities to comfort or distract the person until the urge to self-harm passes.

- TalkLife, an app that creates an online community so people can reach out to others. It helps people connect with others who are experiencing similar feelings, get support, and support others.

- Lantern, an app that allows people to connect with a personal coach if they want to talk or browse through CBT practices they can do immediately to feel better.

With so many apps available today, it is unsurprising that some of them help people with their mental health.

Medical and Social Research

One way to develop new treatments is to identify the genes that play a part in PTSD. In the past, genetic research focused on inherited factors that may make a person more likely than others to be negatively affected by trauma. Now, geneticists are looking for the genes that control the creation of the chemicals that may cause the adverse reactions. The study of how genes can be turned on and off through environmental interactions is called epigenetics. Scientists believe there is no one PTSD gene but rather many genes that contribute to the disorder. For example, they have found a gene that controls the level of serotonin, the neurotransmitter in the brain that influences mood and may fuel the fear response. Once they can identify the gene, the next step is finding out what environmental interactions turn it on and off. Other researchers are looking at the ways the body and brain are related; for instance, one study is exploring the possible connection between PTSD and stomach problems.

Other researchers are looking at social factors that may cause PTSD or make it worse. For instance, Dr. Monnica Williams is studying the relationship between racism and PTSD. Her research, which has focused specifically on black people, has found that repeated small racist acts can build up over time to make black people feel anxious every time they interact with others. This is increased by the fact that the incidents are often so small that they can easily be confused with non-racist acts—for instance, a white person may be standing while riding the subway because their stop is coming up or because the only open seat is next to a black person. Trying to figure out which it is or to explain to someone else why they felt upset can lead the black person to feel paranoid, and remaining hypervigilant by

constantly watching out for racist acts can lead someone to experience PTSD or make it worse after a
bigger traumatic incident.

Donating Brain Tissue

To study diseases such as cancer, scientists can take a sample of a diseased lung or
liver and analyze the tissue to determine the extent of the disease. However, they cannot take samples from a living brain. Aside from imaging the brain of living patients
using MRIs or CAT scans, scientists must examine the brains of those who have died
to learn more about how the brain works. Researchers get brain tissue from brain
banks such as the Harvard Brain Tissue Resource Center in Belmont, Massachusetts,
where they have more than 6,000 samples. The U.S. Department of Veterans Affairs
funded a PTSD brain bank so researchers can learn more about the changes PTSD
causes in the brain. Both veterans and nonveterans can enroll to donate their brain
after they die. Because researchers need to be able to compare PTSD brains to non-
PTSD brains, even people who do not have any mental disorders can offer to donate
their brain.

Focusing on Prevention

Experts agree that some kind of treatment for PTSD
is necessary; studies have shown that patients who
receive treatment recover more quickly and effectively
than those who leave their PTSD untreated. However,
there is some disagreement as to which treatment
method works best. Although some experts prefer
one method over another, many agree that there is no
single "best" treatment—it all depends on the individual. However, some believe the currently available
treatments fall short for most people who have PTSD.
Trauma expert Kali Tal wrote in *Scientific American*,
"Trial criteria often exclude those with comorbid disorders, multiple traumas, complex PTSD, and suicidal ideation, among others."[58] This means studies are
generally only representing a small portion of people
who have PTSD, so their results may not be as accurate as many people believe. Since most people with

PTSD have at least one and often multiple comorbid conditions, they may feel discouraged when a treatment that is considered highly effective fails to help them. This problem is made worse by the fact that most trials are done on veterans with PTSD and then recommended for everyone with the disorder, "even though treatments for veterans may not meet the needs of survivors of other traumas."[59] Additionally, some say the criteria by which trials judge the effectiveness of treatment is flawed. Currently, clinical trials of therapy methods generally judge effectiveness by how much PTSD symptoms decrease; however, since symptoms often come back even after treatment, some say clinical trials should actually be measuring how effectively someone can function in their day-to-day life, whether or not they have symptoms.

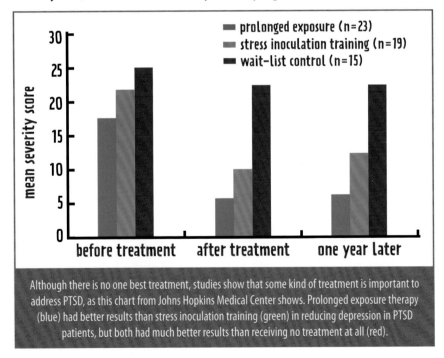

Although there is no one best treatment, studies show that some kind of treatment is important to address PTSD, as this chart from Johns Hopkins Medical Center shows. Prolonged exposure therapy (blue) had better results than stress inoculation training (green) in reducing depression in PTSD patients, but both had much better results than receiving no treatment at all (red).

Some experts, such as Tal, have proposed that to truly decrease the number of people suffering from PTSD, measures need to be put in place to protect

people from developing it in the first place. Since rape is a major cause of PTSD, she cited the Violence Against Women Act (VAWA) Congress passed in 2000 and renewed in 2005 as a good preventative measure:

> *Significantly reducing PTSD in the female pop-*
> *ulation would first require us to name the factors*
> *that cause violence against women, and then to*
> *make rational and radical changes in the legal, so-*
> *cial, and economic systems of the country in which*
> *we live. The majority of U.S. residents would need*
> *to change their beliefs and attitudes, and mod-*
> *ify their actions to significantly reduce violence*
> *against women ... the government has spent be-*
> *tween $500–625 million a year [since 2005] to*
> *support a wide variety of prevention programs. A*
> *November 2012 Department of Justice Report on*
> *intimate partner violence records a steep drop in*
> *1999–2000, when the VAWA was enacted.*[60]

The bill was renewed in 2013, and a section was added that allowed Native American groups to punish people who commit violence against Native American women on reservations, even if the perpetrator is not Native American. Tal also noted other measures that would play a role in decreasing PTSD, including "preventing the gun violence that is pervasive in both urban and rural settings ... and, addressing the inability of the police, the courts, and the prisons to effectively serve victims, ensure their safety, and reha-bilitate perpetrators."[61] Additionally, she stated that ending American involvement in wars on foreign soil would provide more funding to treat existing PTSD cases as well as removing one source of new PTSD cases. In other words, Tal said, "Whatever treatments you advocate and provide, if you aren't working to prevent violence, you aren't working to cure PTSD."[62]

Chapter One:
Dealing with Trauma

1. "PTSD in the Ancient World," *Archaeology*, January 16, 2015. www.archaeology.org/news/2922-150126-ancient-world-ptsd.

2. Quoted in "'Soldier's Heart' and 'Shell Shock:' Past Names for PTSD," *The Soldier's Heart*, PBS *Frontline*, March 1, 2005. www.pbs.org/wgbh/pages/frontline/shows/heart/themes/shellshock.html.

3. Charles S. Myers, *Shell Shock in France, 1914–1918*. Cambridge, MA: The University Press, 1940, pp. 25–26.

4. "PTSD and Shell Shock," History.com, accessed December 15, 2017. www.history.com/topics/history-of-ptsd-and-shell-shock.

5. R. G. Rows, "Mental Conditions Following Strain and Nerve Shock," *British Medical Journal*, vol. I, 1916, p. 441.

6. Millais Culpin, *Recent Advances in the Study of the Psychoneuroses*. London, UK: J.A. Churchill, 1931, p. 28.

7. Quoted in "'Soldier's Heart' and 'Shell Shock,'" *The Soldier's Heart*, PBS *Frontline*.

8. Quoted in "Profile: History of the Creation of the Concept of Post-Traumatic Stress Disorder," *All Things Considered*, NPR, originally aired August 19, 2003.

9. "PTSD and DSM-5," PTSD: National Center for PTSD, U.S. Department of Veterans Affairs, last updated February 21, 2017.

www.ptsd.va.gov/professional/PTSD-over-view/dsm5_criteria_ptsd.asp.

10. "PTSD and DSM-5," PTSD: National Center for PTSD.

11. "PTSD and DSM-5," PTSD: National Center for PTSD.

12. "Complex PTSD," PTSD: National Center for PTSD, U.S. Department of Veterans Affairs, last updated February 23, 2016. www.ptsd.va.gov/professional/ptsd-overview/complex-ptsd.asp.

13. Quoted in Katie Charles, "Post-Traumatic Stress Disorder Affects a Wide Range of People, Not Just Soldiers," *NY Daily News*, July 14, 2013. www.nydailynews.com/lifestyle/health/ptsd-affects-people-military-article-1.1393098.

14. "Post-Traumatic Stress Disorder," National Institute of Mental Health, last updated February 2016. www.nimh.nih.gov/health/topics/post-traumatic-stress-disorder-ptsd/index.shtml.

Chapter Two:
More Than Just Stress

15. J. Douglas Bremner, *Does Stress Damage the Brain? Understanding Trauma-related Disorders from a MindBody Perspective.* New York, NY: W.W. Norton & Company, 2002, p. 116.

16. Matthew Tull, PhD, "What You Should Know About the Effect of PTSD on the Brain," VeryWell, last updated June 25, 2017. www.verywell.com/the-effect-of-ptsd-on-the-brain-2797643.

17. Quoted in "Neuroscientists Identify How Trauma Triggers Long-lasting Memories in

the Brain," Science Daily, August 18, 2005. www.sciencedaily.com.

18. Erica Robinson, "PTSD in Adults May Develop Without Memory of Childhood Trauma," *Medical Daily*, August 17, 2014. www.medicaldaily.com/ptsd-adults-may-develop-without-memory-childhood-trauma-298412.

19. Lisa M. P. Munoz, "Stress Hormone Hinders Memory Recall," Cognitive Neuroscience Society, July 24, 2013. www.cogneurosociety.org/cortisol_memory.

20. "Avoidance," PTSD: National Center for PTSD, U.S. Department of Veterans Affairs, last updated August 13, 2015. www.ptsd.va.gov/public/problems/avoidance.asp.

21. Quoted in Casey Gueren and Anna Borges, "10 Things Psychologists Want You to Know About Trigger Warnings," BuzzFeed News, September 8, 2016. www.buzzfeed.com/caseygueren/trigger-warnings-in-the-classroom?utm_term=.oc3rj9oqv#.iwrg5RyAM.

22. Quoted in Gueren and Borges, "10 Things Psychologists Want You to Know About Trigger Warnings."

23. Joni Edelman, "Trigger Warnings: The Good, the Bad, the Pancakes," *Huffington Post*, October 20, 2016. www.huffingtonpost.com/joni-edelman/trigger-warnings-the-good-the-bad-the-pancakes_b_8332786.html.

24. "Effects of PTSD on Family," PTSD: National Center for PTSD, U.S. Department of Veterans Affairs, last updated August 13, 2015. www.ptsd.va.gov/PTSD/public/family/effects-ptsd-family.asp.

25. Quoted in Beth Reece, "Invisible Wounds," *Soldiers Magazine*, May 2005.

Chapter Three:
Causes of PTSD

26. "Women, Trauma, and PTSD," PTSD: National Center for PTSD, U.S. Department of Veterans Affairs, last updated August 13, 2015. www.ptsd.va.gov/public/PTSD-overview/women/women-trauma-and-ptsd.asp.

27. Meredith Melnick, "Why Are Women More Vulnerable to PTSD than Men?," *TIME*, February 25, 2011. healthland.time.com/2011/02/25/are-women-more-vulnerable-to-ptsd-than-men/.

28. Melnick, "Why Are Women More Vulnerable to PTSD than Men?"

29. Quoted in Anita Hamilton, "After a Disaster, Kids Suffer Posttraumatic Stress Too," *TIME*, July 21, 2010. content.time.com/time/health/article/0,8599,2004902,00.html.

30. JR Thorpe, "Why Do Women Have More PTSD Diagnoses than Men?," *Bustle*, September 16, 2016. www.bustle.com/articles/183864-why-do-women-have-more-ptsd-diagnoses-than-men.

31. Chris R. Brewin, *Posttraumatic Stress Disorder: Malady or Myth?* New Haven, CT: Yale University Press, 2003, p. 60.

32. Quoted in Patricia Donovan, "UB Researchers Use Virtual Reality to Treat Car-accident Survivors Suffering from Posttraumatic Stress," *UB Reporter*, vol. 35, no. 13, November 20, 2003. www.buffalo.edu.

33. Quoted in Susan Saulny, "A Legacy of the Storm: Depression and Suicide," *New York Times*, June 21, 2006. www.nytimes.com/2006/06/21/us/21depress.html.

34. Susan Scutti, "Resilience, Suffering and Silver Linings After a Disaster," CNN, last

updated September 20, 2017. www.cnn.
com/2017/09/19/health/psychological-after-
math-hurricanes-harvey-irma/index.html.

35. Quoted in "Post-Disaster Response: Learning
from Research (Part 2)," *SAMHSA News*, vol.
14, no. 4, July/August 2006. www.samhsa.gov.

36. Rebecca Zimmerman, "The Hidden Casualties of War: Civilian Frontline Workers," *Los
Angeles Times*, July 6, 2015. www.latimes.com/
opinion/op-ed/la-oe-0706-zimmerman-ptsd-
20150706-story.html.

37. Lois Beckett, "The PTSD Crisis That's Being Ignored: Americans Wounded in Their
Own Neighborhoods," ProPublica, February
3, 2014. www.propublica.org/article/the-ptsd-
crisis-thats-being-ignored-americans-wound-
ed-in-their-own-neighbor.

38. Beckett, "The PTSD Crisis That's
Being Ignored."

39. Beckett, "The PTSD Crisis That's
Being Ignored."

40. Beckett, "The PTSD Crisis That's
Being Ignored."

41. Joanna Scutts, "Mac McClelland's Irritable
Hearts: 'It's Insane That We Can Only Conceive of PTSD in Terms of Combat,'" *Guardian*, March 2, 2015. www.theguardian.com/
books/2015/mar/02/mac-mcclelland-irrita-
ble-hearts-ptsd-combat-sexual-assault-abuse.

42. Quoted in Scutts, "Mac McClelland's
Irritable Hearts."

43. Quoted in Scutts, "Mac McClelland's
Irritable Hearts."

44. Sonya Norman, Eric B. Elbogen, and Paula
P. Schnurr, "Research Findings on PTSD and
Violence," PTSD: National Center for PTSD,

U.S. Department of Veterans Affairs, last updated January 10, 2017. www.ptsd.va.gov/professional/co-occurring/research_on_ptsd_and_violence.asp.

45. Quoted in Beckett, "The PTSD Crisis That's Being Ignored."

Chapter Four:
Treatment for PTSD

46. Quoted in Sudip Mazumdar, et al., "Living with Fear," *Newsweek*, vol. 145, no. 3, January 17, 2005, p. 27.

47. Quoted in Chrissy Casilio, "Help Through Research and Therapy," *Spectrum*, February 28, 2007. spectrum.buffalo.edu.

48. "The Facts About Prolonged Exposure Therapy for PTSD," Association for Psychological Science, January 26, 2015. www.psychological-science.org/publications/observer/obsonline/the-facts-about-prolonged-exposure-therapy-for-ptsd.html.

49. Olga Khazan, "Can Eye Movement Work Like Therapy?," *The Atlantic*, July 27, 2015. www.theatlantic.com/health/archive/2015/07/emdr-trauma/399650/.

50. Khazan, "Can Eye Movement Work Like Therapy?"

51. Quoted in Belleruth Naparastek, *Invisible Heroes*. New York, NY: Bantam, 2007, p. 13.

52. "Healing Touch with Guided Imagery Could Help Relieve PTSD Symptoms in Soldiers, Study Suggests," *Huffington Post*, September 30, 2012. www.huffingtonpost.com/2012/09/30/healing-touch-guided-imagery-ptsd-soldiers_n_1910954.html.

53. Quoted in "Healing Touch with Guided Imagery," *Huffington Post*.

54. "Somatic Psychotherapy," Good Therapy, last updated July 21, 2017. www.goodtherapy.org/learn-about-therapy/types/somatic-psychotherapy.

Chapter Five:
Looking Ahead

55. Quoted in "9/11 Study Offers Insight into How Memories Are Formed: The Brain's Fear Center Created Stronger Memories for Those Nearest Ground Zero," Health Day News, December 18, 2006. consumer.healthday.com/cognitive-health-information-26/brain-health-news-80/9-11-study-offers-insight-into-how-memories-are-formed-600227.html.

56. "Brain Changes Seen in Veterans with PTSD After Mindfulness Training," Michigan Medicine, University of Michigan, April 1, 2016. www.uofmhealth.org/news/archive/201604/brain-changes-seen-veterans-ptsd-after-mindfulness-training.

57. Sara Chodosh, "The FDA Says Ecstasy Is a 'Breakthrough' Drug for PTSD Patients," *Popular Science*, August 29, 2017. www.popsci.com/fda-says-mdma-is-breakthrough-drug-for-ptsd-patients.

58. Kali Tal, "PTSD: The Futile Search for the 'Quick Fix,'" *Scientific American*, February 26, 2013. blogs.scientificamerican.com/guest-blog/ptsd-the-futile-search-for-the-quick-fix/.

59. Tal, "PTSD."

60. Tal, "PTSD."

61. Tal, "PTSD."

62. Tal, "PTSD."

amygdala: One of two structures in the brain that deal with memory and emotion.

cognitive behavioral therapy (CBT): A form of mental health treatment that deals with how a person thinks and feels about something. It focuses on changing harmful beliefs and thought patterns into positive ones.

consolidation: The process by which a memory is stored for the long term.

fight-or-flight response: The natural survival mechanism the body has for dealing with the threat of danger.

flashback: A particularly vivid memory that feels as if it is happening in real time. The person is often out of touch with reality during the experience.

genes: Inherited material that controls a person's traits, such as blue eyes or brown hair.

hippocampus: A part of the brain that retrieves and organizes memories.

hormones: Chemical messengers that are released by glands and travel throughout the body.

hypervigilance: The feeling of being on constant alert, watching for danger, and feeling on edge.

neurologist: A scientist who studies the brain and the nervous system.

neurotransmitter: A chemical that is released by neurons in the brain as a means of cellular communication.

prolonged exposure (PE) therapy: A form of treatment that desensitizes a person to a stress by constantly exposing them to that stress.

selective serotonin reuptake inhibitors (SSRIs): A class of drugs that work to increase the level of serotonin in the brain.

trauma: An event or incident that causes severe mental or physical injury.

Mental Health America
500 Montgomery Street, Suite 820
Alexandria, VA 22314
(800) 969-6642
www.mentalhealthamerica.net
This organization's mission is to educate the public
about mental health, fight for equal and appropriate
mental health care for all people, and provide support
to people living with mental health issues or substance
abuse problems.

National Center for Post Traumatic Stress Disorder
810 Vermont Avenue NW
Washington, DC 20420
www.ptsd.va.gov
The National Center for PTSD, which is associated
with the U.S. Department of Veterans Affairs, is the
leading authority for research and treatment of PTSD.
Its website is packed with easy-to-read fact sheets for
researchers as well as the general public.

National Center for Victims of Crime
2000 M Street NW, Suite 480
Washington, DC 20036
(855) 484-2846 (confidential victim referral line)
webmaster@ncvc.org
The NCVC keeps statistics about violent crime and
provides information for research and for those who
need treatment.

National Institute of Mental Health (NIMH)
6001 Executive Boulevard, Room 6200, MSC 9663
Bethesda, MD 20892
(866) 615-6464
nimhinfo@nih.gov
nimh.nih.gov
NIMH provides information on all mental health issues
and lists the most current research projects that are going
on. A live chat can be found on its website.

The National Suicide Prevention Lifeline
(800) 273-8255
suicidepreventionlifeline.org
This service provides free, confidential crisis support for
anyone who is considering suicide for any reason. A live
chat is also available through the website.

Books

Lohmann, Raychelle Cassada, and Sheela Raja. *The Sexual Trauma Workbook for Teen Girls: A Guide to Recovery from Sexual Assault & Abuse*. Oakland, CA: Instant Help Books, 2016.
Women are more likely than men to suffer from PTSD, and much of this comes from their increased risk for domestic and sexual violence. This workbook offers exercises to help victims of these types of abuse deal with their symptoms.

Palmer, Libbi. *The PTSD Workbook for Teens: Simple, Effective Skills for Healing Trauma*. Oakland, CA: Constable & Robinson, 2013.
This workbook provides exercises to help teens deal with their PTSD symptoms.

Parks, Peggy J. *Teens and PTSD*. San Diego, CA: ReferencePoint Press, Inc., 2017.
PTSD often has different symptoms in teens than in either adults or children.

Poole, Hilary W. *PTSD, Post-Traumatic Stress Disorder*. Broomall, PA: Mason Crest, 2015.
Traumatic events can cause distress and anxiety for months or even years after the event happened. Learning about what PTSD is and how to treat it can give hope to young adults who are struggling with this disorder.

Wiener, Gary. *Microaggressions, Safe Spaces, and Trigger Warnings*. New York, NY: Greenhaven Publishing, 2018.
This book discusses what trigger warnings are and the controversy surrounding them.

Websites

Helpguide: Helping Someone with PTSD
www.helpguide.org/articles/ptsd-trauma/helping-
someone-with-ptsd.htm
This part of the Helpguide website gives people
information about how to help a loved one with PTSD,
including how it affects friends and family members and
where caregivers can find support.

PTSD Alliance
www.ptsdalliance.org
This organization offers information about PTSD and
related disorders, such as substance abuse. Its website
includes resources where sufferers can turn for help.

TED Talks: PTSD
www.ted.com/topics/ptsd
This collection of videos on the TED website
features experts in various fields and people with
firsthand experience discussing PTSD causes,
symptoms, and treatment.

The Tribe Wellness Community
support.therapytribe.com/anxiety-support-group/
This online support group for anxiety disorders allows
people to connect with others who are suffering from
the same thing. A link is provided to help people find
therapists near them.

Your Amazing Brain
www.youramazingbrain.org
This website has a section about stress and how it
affects the body and the brain.

INDEX

A

abuse, 14, 28, 48–49
   long-term, 18, 20, 21, 41
African Americans, 46, 80
aggression, 17, 21, 24, 25, 59–60
alcohol abuse, 12, 21, 34, 40, 44, 60, 61
American Civil War, 9, 10–11
American Psychiatric Association (APA), 13, 67
amygdala, 23, 24, 26, 27, 31, 33, 74, 75, 77
anxiety, 9, 10, 14, 19, 25, 34, 68, 71
apps to help with PTSD, 79
avoidance behaviors, 35, 42

B

Beck, Gayle, 49, 63–64
benzodiazepines, 71
beta-blockers, 77
Bradley, John, 42
brain
   how stress affects, 25–27, 68
   new research into, 73–74
   PTSD and the, 27–29, 42, 74–76
   structure of, 22–25
brain tissue, donating, 81
Bremmer, J. Douglas, 28
Brewin, Chris R., 47

C

car accidents, 6, 20, 21, 35, 49–50
Chemtob, Claude, 45
children and PTSD, 20–21, 44–45, 47–49, 54

functional magnetic resonance imaging (fMRI), 73–76

R

S

ABOUT THE AUTHOR

Simon Pierce grew up in Jamestown, New York. He later moved to New York City and completed his education at NYU. He now lives in Brooklyn with his partner and their son. He has written for various health and wellness publications over the past seven years. He and his family enjoy people-watching in the park or reading the names on cemetery headstones and inventing stories about them.